The Maltese Sangweech

and Other Heroes

BILL CARDOSO

The Maltese Sangweech and Other Heroes

New York • ATHENEUM • 1984

To the people who helped
when my lips were chapped

The pieces in this book originally appeared in *City of San Francisco, Harper's Weekly, New Times, Outside, Ramparts, Rolling Stone,* and *San Francisco* magazines.

Library of Congress Cataloging in Publication Data

Cardoso, Bill.
The Maltese sangweech and other heroes.

I. Title.
AC8.C26 1984 081 83-45501
ISBN 0-689-11443-5

Published simultaneously in Canada by McClelland and Stewart Ltd.
Composition by P&M Typesetting, Waterbury, Connecticut
Printed and bound by Fairfield Graphics, Fairfield, Pennsylvania
Designed by Mary Ahern
First Edition

Contents

The Golden Dragon Labor Day Massacre 1
Chowchilla Kidnap 30
Korczak Ziolkowski 63
Oregon: Sometimes a Great Nation 86
The Carnival of Crusader-Quacks 110
The San Francisco Bosox 136
The Maltese Sangweech 191
Singing in the Canaries 203
The Second Coming of Monti Rock, III 213
The Smothers Brothers Get Their Sh–t Together 223
Evel is Dead 240
Zaire 263

The Maltese Sangweech

and Other Heroes

The Golden Dragon

Labor Day Massacre

I was on my way to Oregon to do a piece on former Governor Tom McCall, who was dying of cancer and openly discussing this sad fact on his Portland TV program. What a guy. One in a million. Homespun. Spoke in quotes. Great copy. I remember standing next to him in the state capital a few years before. We were waiting for an elevator, each lost in private thought.

"Hey, governor." He turned to look at me. "You know who would make a great presidential ticket?"

"Who?"

"You and Pearl Bailey."

His blues eyes caught fire and a grin spanked his face. "Ah," he said, "what a gal!"

I never saw Tom McCall again. The Golden Dragon Massacre intervened. I called New York to switch plans. "They shoot tourists," I told them.

The piece is straight-ahead journalism. It was exciting and challenging and dangerous to do. In the end, it practically wrote itself. I had weeks' worth of research and interviews and was struggling to make sense of it and get it down on paper. It was the middle of a Sunday afternoon. Mary Miles Ryan was hiking on Mount Tam with Doc Taylor and I elected to stay home and watch an inept Niners team get clobbered on television by the Rams. Jim Plunkett, at the nadir of his topsy-turvy career, was at the helm. After yet another errant Plunkett pass I flicked off the TV, sat down at the kitchen table and commenced to work. I believe I owe old Plunk a debt of gratitude for getting me going. And I owe one to John Lombardi, who did a sweet job editing the piece. He stayed out of it.

Blood was all over the place. Literally. All day men scrubbed the stains. They did nice work. By late afternoon the only telltales were many bullet holes and some shredded leatherette upholstery. Anyone happening by for the first time would not realize that the worst mass murder in San Francisco's violent history had occurred therein only hours earlier.

And so the Golden Dragon restaurant opened its doors for business as usual.

Business as usual.

The streets of Chinatown, San Francisco, must be made safe . . . not so much for those who dwell there as for Mr. and Mrs. Truly Nebraska. See them over yonder—he with the white plastic belt and white buckled loafers? And she, a little too old and wide for her orange polyester pantsuit, yet still agile enough to click an Instamatic. Let us eavesdrop: "Oh," she is exclaiming to the little almond-eyed urchin, "you're so cute! I wish I could take you home!"

Meanwhile, Truly Nebraska has just spotted a nice plastic pagoda atop a bank on Grant Avenue and wants wifey to snap a picture. "No, not that bank, dear! The one next to it!" *Click*. And they are off again, this time into a curio shop where they lay out ten dollars for a pair of T-shirts bearing the legend "Chinatown—San Francisco" and depicting a red-tile roof pagoda, souvenirs for their twins, Jumbo and Melissa, back home in Honker's Corners.

Tourism is San Francisco's biggest industry. It is San Francisco's *only* remaining major industry, and Chinatown is its main attraction.

In 1976, according to the Visitors and Convention Bureau, 2.9 million people visited the city. This figure represents only people who stayed at intown hotels. It does not include people who stayed at airport hotels or Oakland hotels or with friends. Last year's official 2.9 million visitors left a known minimum of $661 million behind. The local tourism dollar is increasing at the rate of $100 million yearly and soon will surpass $1 billion. Quiz: When the California Street cable car crosses the Powell line, the conductor hollers "Powell Street, transfer for Chinatown." How many people make the switch? To say 2.9 million would not be wrong, merely conservative.

So, business as usual. Sweep it under, wash it away: None of this is new.

Directly across the street from the Golden Dragon, Little Pete Fong, the King of Chinatown, was assassinated in a barber's chair. Frank Norris wrote about the funeral. That was 1897. Half a block away, up at the corner of Waverly Place, known then as the Street of Slaves, hitmen dressed all in black cleaved each other with hatchets in the first pitched battle of the warring tongs—rival gangs of toughs vying for the right to work as enforcers for the various Chinese gambling, dope and prostitution operations already flourishing. That was 102 years ago. In the old days there were many warring tongs; today there are at least two, the Hop Sings and the Suey Sings. The newspapers ran headlines that read like baseball line scores: Hop Sings 3, Suey Sings 2.

The tongs are still around, but their hitman activities have been augmented and/or replaced by younger groups, teen-age hitmen—some as young as eleven or twelve, say the police—because, if caught, they'll get lighter sentences. Guns fall out of their pockets, sometimes in junior high classrooms. These teen-age hitmen have in turn divided into two main groups—the Wah Ching, allied with the Hop Sing Boys in old Chinatown, and the Joe Boys, weird independents who hustle and extort in the Richmond, the new Chinatown, to the west.

Scene from a true nightmare, 2:40 A.M., September 4, 1977, Labor Day weekend: Three masked gunmen enter the Golden Dragon, 816–22 Washington Street, and take up positions. They carry a shotgun, a .38 caliber pistol and a .45 caliber semiautomatic rifle—known in the military as a grease gun. They appear to be young Chinese. Forty or so people are eating late supper. They include gangsters, tourists, locals, an off-duty cop, and an on-duty cop. The young Chinese open fire. Time and again they spray the diners, relentless in their wickedness. The one with the shotgun calmly climbs three stairs and lets go a blast at those in the mezzanine, then returns to the main room for a parting blast. Elapsed time: one minute. Body count: five innocents slaughtered, eleven more wounded, two critically. Not a hoodlum scratched.

Police attributed the massacre to the Joe Boys because the Golden Dragon is a Wah Ching hangout. (The Joe Boys and Wah Ching are always shooting each other up, usually for territorial encroachment purposes, sometimes for the sheer hell of it.)

This time, however, the causes are murkier: Was this teen turf warfare? Renewed tong warfare? Personal revenge? Or the inevitable result of a complex system of overlapping business and criminal corruption that binds Chinatown's major businessmen—family associations (people of the same last name), district associations (a.k.a. the Six Companies) and tongs (some legitimate fraternal/business organizations, some paramilitary enforcement groups)—to the San Francisco establishment?

In any case, about a dozen Wah Ching and allied Hop Sing Boys were seated at three tables when the shooting started. Among them, police identified Michael Louie, a current Wah Ching boss, and Frankie Yee, described as the leader of the Hop Sing Boys. None was hit because someone in their group yelled "man with a rifle!" in Cantonese and they hit the deck. Everybody else became part of the menu: Sitting Duck à la Fromage Suisse.

For Louie, twenty, it was at least his second close call. He was one of four wounded on September 25, 1976, at the Jade Palace restaurant by a Joe Boy who is now serving a two-year Youth Authority sentence for that crime. Louie himself is on probation after doing juvenile time with a half-dozen other Wah Ching for the kidnap and torture murder in 1974 of a fifteen-year-old Joe Boy named Lincoln Louie (no relation).

Youth gangs like the Joe Boys and Wah Ching were always accorded a certain respectability in Chinatown because they are recruited by gambling bosses to provide muscle. "To enforce whatever needs enforcing," in the words of a veteran Chinatown cop, "whether it's a gambling debt or an insult that has to be avenged." The younger gang kids are hired as look-sees by the gambling operators at four or five dollars an hour. This makes it all the easier for the youth gangs themselves to recruit. The look-see system is ancient and simple: kid sits in doorway of gambling house where dice, poker, fan-tan and mahjongg games are trimming the Chinese marks, infamous for their rabidness, of their measly earnings; kid is reading comic book, observed by inside man who peeps through a look-see window in the door. If cops or robbers are coming, kid tips inside man by closing comic book. Presto—the joint converts into some kind of Moose Lodge.

The only problem with the system is that some young kids demanded a bigger share of the action once they realized how much money was changing hands. A large betting establishment could easily handle from twenty to fifty thousand dollars a night.

Enter Joe Fong, the Joey Gallo of oriental organized crime.

Clazy Joey

Joe Fong was eight when he arrived in San Francisco from the slums of Macao in 1963, one of ten children of Jack and Sui Mui Fong. Three years later he was found guilty of burglary. Statistically, he was part of an alarming trend in juvenile delinquency, which rose 600 percent in Chinatown between 1964 and 1969. Mostly, the bad actors were immigrants like Joe Fong, youngsters who found difficulty in adjusting to their new world. The first time he was called upon to read in class, he was laughed at. "The ABCs [American-born Chinese] called us FOBs—Fresh Off the Boat—or China Bugs. Even the American-born Chinese referred to us as 'Chinese'—as though they were not." To be Chinese with an accent, Joe Fong was made to feel, was degrading to other Chinese.

At the time, the baddest gang in Chinatown was the Raiders, who took their name from the football team. It was composed of American-born oriental kids who made life hot for the newcomers. The American-born oriental was becoming absorbed in the mainstream culture and tended to abandon his ethnicity, in the classic immigrant manner.

Eventually, the foreign-born kids banded together in self-defense. By 1965, they had a name: Wah Ching (Chinese youth). There were a series of rumbles, but soon the battle was won; a period of relaxation was ushered in. During this time, there was no further split between FOBs and ABCs. By 1968, the original Wah Ching had dissolved, but since it *was* 1968, and a lot of oriental kids were going to college, left-oriented street gangs on the order of crude SDS units began to replace the Wah Ching. Naturally, the hard-core street kids who weren't going to college weren't interested in the programs being espoused by the political radicals. Like all street kids, they wanted to get down with some money. That's how Joe Fong felt.

The first Chinese-American leftist group was called Le Way (Legitimate Way), but a year later, in 1969, it split in two, forming the Red Guard; these kids were mostly Berkeley-educated American-born radicals. Meanwhile, the street toughs were coming under the influence of two tongs, the Hop Sing and the Suey Sing, ancient rivals. (During the long years of the Chinese Exclusion Acts [1882–1943] when Chinese were forbidden entrance to the United States, the tongs had been losing their potency. But when President Kennedy relaxed the barriers in 1962, a regenerative supply of new tong members became available. Naturally, many of the new arrivals felt decidedly more comfortable with the old ways. Also, there were practical considerations. Joining a tong meant having a place to sleep and money or credit for meals. The money came from gambling and protection-racket profits.)

The Red Guard was viewed as a threat by the Chinatown elders, who steadfastly maintained close personal and business ties with Taiwan. The elders used the fresh Chinese arrivals to break up Red Guard rallies and bust heads. They paid five to ten dollars a beating. At this price, the street kids made short work of the Commies. But those battles were as nothing compared with the war that raged between the youth of the two rival tongs. The Hop Sing had had a slight edge over the Suey Sing in power, and now revived the old Wah Ching label as an attention-getter; they use it as a front name to this day. The new Wah Ching was greatly strengthened when it absorbed a street gang led by Joe Fong, who was then all of fifteen. The Suey Sing, meanwhile, used unaffiliated street kids from wherever they could find them. They had no special name, except Suey Sing tong kids, but they fought often and savagely.

The Dien Bien Phu of the Hop Sing/Suey Sing kid war came in March 1970. Glen Fong, nineteen, Joe's brother, was cut down by bursts from a .30 caliber automatic carbine. His Wah Ching caught up with a fellow named Tom Tom, the Suey Sing youth gang leader, as he was spooning a bowl of rice soup in a Chinatown restaurant. He was beaten badly and hospitalized. A bedside visitor had little trouble negotiating peace. In return for his life, Tom Tom and his boys would move across the bay to Oakland.

Joe Fong, however, still angry, and developing as a leader, continued raiding the enemy. In the spring of 1971, he drew a six-month sentence at Log Cabin Reformatory for his part in continuing the forays across the Bay Bridge to whack out the Suey Sing kids. By then he was a charismatic standout; he'd yanked his boys away from the Hop Sing's Wah Ching and formed his own group, the Yau Lay (Good Fortune). When Fong entered the reformatory he had a handshake agreement with the Hop Sing and Wah Ching boys that his new group would remain independent, but when he got out, he found that the Yau Lay had fallen under the domination of the Wah Ching again. Joe didn't like that. A showdown came on October 1.

Fong and his chief lieutenant, Raymond Leung, nineteen, announced they were pulling out of Yau Lay and taking their trusted boys along. Leung was shot to death the next day.

Joe Fong and friends regrouped in the Richmond district, where there were plenty of oriental businesses to extort and plenty of cars to steal. On the next Chinese New Year they formed Chung Ching Yee (a name derived from the Water Margin Heroes, a band of Robin Hoods in Chinese classical literature).

But 1972 was to be a very bad year for Fong. He'd organized the most serious threat to Chinatown's status quo since the last tong wars of the 1920s. He had shaken the hierarchy from top to bottom, in effect telling the old men to get the hell out of his way, as Joey Gallo had done in New York. And like Joey Gallo, he would be made to pay for it.

A series of complicated troubles befell him. He was arrested for aggravated assault in February, shortly after organizing his new gang, but never prosecuted. In March, he was arrested for the murder of Harry Kwan at the Chinatown Police Athletic League. Despite six prosecution witnesses who said he was on the murder scene, he was acquitted in juvenile court. Luckily, he was able to prove he was visiting a college with a friend at the time Kwan was killed. That spring he was accused in the murder of Harry (the Professor) Ng, sixty, the martial arts mentor of the Wah Ching/Hop Sing youth. However, Joe Fong was in jail on the Kwan murder charge when the Professor opened the door of his Kung Fu studio to receive five bullets. (Police later pinned the Ng murder on a fourteen-year-old.)

Fong again was the prime suspect when Barry Fong-Torres, twenty-nine, the brother of *Rolling Stone* music editor Ben Fong-Torres, was shot three times in the head, once in the abdomen and once in the chest, in the doorway of his home. Fong-Torres, on leave from his job as a probation officer, was executive director of the Chinatown Youth Services and Coordinating Center. A manila envelope with his name and address on it was found under his body. Inside, was the message: "Pig Informers Die Yong [*sic*]."

In September, Fong was rebuffed when he sought a meeting with then-Mayor Joseph Alioto. Fong reportedly offered to name names in Chinese-American criminal activity in the city. That same night his gang's headquarters were raided and Fong and nine others arrested on kidnapping charges that were later dropped. However, two weeks later, on October 2, he was arrested on a murder conspiracy charge that stuck.

At his trial, the prosecution called Joe Fong "Al Capone," picturing him as the "most dangerous criminal" in Chinatown. He was sentenced to life in prison on February 4, 1973; he spent his eighteenth birthday inside Duell Vocational Institute, where he is presently confined.

There remain serious questions as to the guilt of Joe Fong in the murder conspiracy case, which stemmed from a bloody midnight encounter between members of his gang and a carload of Wah Ching. There is evidence that places Fong miles away from the shooting. Three friends took lie detector tests to back up this claim. Polygraph expert George Harmon concluded that the trio "told the truth as to the questions put to them." The district attorney's office, however, has declined to reopen the case, citing the testimony of seven prosecution eyewitnesses, several of whom were Wah Ching members, as proof of Joe Fong's guilt.

Since Joe Fong's conviction, his group's power has grown, and it has changed its name from Chung Ching Yee to Joe Boys. Some never have met their maximum leader. They were too young when he went to jail.

The Joe Boys are now allied with the Cookies in the never-ending battle against the Wah Ching–Hop Sing Boys. The Cookies are about 50 percent Japanese, with the remainder being Korean and Chinese. Until the recent heat, the Joe Boys frequented pool halls and other haunts of the Cookies in Japantown, about three miles west of Chinatown. Mostly, though, the Joe Boys operate out of the new Chinatown, the Richmond and Sunset districts that border Golden Gate Park on the city's western edge, known familiarly as the Avenues, desolate, almost treeless suburban neighborhoods built over sand dunes, mostly after World War II.

If the Joe Boys venture into Chinatown, the Wah Ching and Hop Sing Boys shoot on sight. So when the Joe Boys come, it's usually to shoot first. "The Wah Ching more or less unofficially control Chinatown," a cop on the beat there contends. "Fear is power." Fully half of Chinatown shopkeepers, he estimates, pay some form of protection to the Wah Ching or Hop Sing, directly.

Police intelligence claims it is difficult to determine the total number of gang members on both sides because of "the constant flow in-and-out, with some nonmembers claiming to be members, and with members claiming they are not." Sources closer to the gangs, however, say hard-core members are all four groups—Hop Sing/Wah Ching vs. Joe Boys/the Cookies—probably number no more than two hundred.

The two main sides are in fact loosely-knit groups of autonomous cells. Each cell operates the way it wishes and can initiate whatever activities it desires. These cells operate in areas within the larger geography controlled by the gang. The youngest gang members are about thirteen, though some have been younger. The average age is about eighteen or nineteen.

The Golden Dragon massacre was the third known encounter this year—a quiet year—between the rival gangs.

On the Fourth of July, three Joe Boys were trapped in Chinatown. A seventeen-year-old was shot to death and both his companions were wounded, but so was a Wah Ching.

A month earlier, Kin Chuen Louie, twenty, identified by police as a leader of the Hop Sing Boys, was shot eight times in the face and neck by a Joe Boy and died as he sat in his car on Telegraph Hill. One of the first to pass the scene was the esteemed literary figure Michael McClure, who thought the corpse not grotesque, but strangely beautiful in its angle of repose, with the eight punctures clean and all in a line . . . he went home and wrote a poem about it.

McClure, in his poetic way, registered more concern than San Franciscans usually do. The proceedings of the San Francisco County Grand Jury on December 16, 1976, illustrate the common attitude. What follows is dialogue between an assistant district attorney and witness Paul (Fat Paul) Wong, an admitted Wah Ching, who testified in a murder case under immunity. At the end, the grand jury foreman is briefly heard. Here is the conversation:

"And Kenneth told you he thought he shot Edward? *Uh-huh*. Did he tell you at a later time that he thought Edward was a member of the Joe Fong gang? *Yeah*. And the Joe Fong gang and the Wah Ching don't get along, do they? *No*. How long have they been fighting each other? *About five, six years, really*. Are you familiar that there have been a number of men killed in that fight, correct? *Yes*. Did you know Anton Wong? *Yeah*. He was killed, was he not? *Yeah*. Do you know who killed him? *Well, I heard he's Joe Fong's brother*. Chung Wai? *Yeah*. I have no further questions." Whereupon, the foreman says, "I think we better break for lunch now." Not a follow-up question, mind you, from the foreman or any other grand juror . . . just a tummy growl.

Forty-five persons have died in Chinatown warfare during the last eight years, according to police statistics. Yet justice would rather be out to lunch.

The very traceable history of Chinatown warfare leads to an implication every bit as nightmarish as the Golden Dragon massacre itself: that the gangs are controlled and directed by some of the Chinese community's most respected and influential leaders.

Suddenly, everything is at stake: careers are on the line, lives are on the line, the whole economy of Everybody's Favorite City is on the line. Everyone is pointing the finger at everyone else. The police chief blames it on racketeers and cannon-fodder kids. The Chinatown establishment blames it on young punks from Hong Kong and clown cops. The teeny torpedoes blame corrupt elders in cahoots with crooked cops. And the mayor goes on television wearing the look of a man with a bad pain in his stomach.

In the massacre aftermath, Mayor George Moscone announced that all flags on city buildings would fly at half-staff until the dead were buried. He also announced a twenty-five-thousand-dollar reward for information leading to conviction. But he was swiftly overtaken by events. The next two Saturday nights were filled with guns and death.

Vengeance dealt from ambush claimed a Joe Boy. The next weekend a high roller was slain with his own .357 magnum when he resisted during the holdup of a five-hundred-dollar-a-game mah-jongg parlor, the apparent message from the independent Joe Boys to Chinatown being that protection could no longer be guaranteed by the old Hop Sing Boys or Wah Ching.

After the retaliatory ambush, Moscone added ten thousand more to the reward. In the wake of the gambling den heist, the mayor offered an unprecedented hundred thousand dollars. One Hundred Big Ones! City Hall was taking on the trappings of a TV quiz show.

While this was unfolding, Police Chief Charles Gain was hit with accusations of checkbook detective work. But Gain would be nobody's fall guy. Instead, he named a twenty-one-man task force to get to the bottom of the killings, and picked Lieutenant Dan Murphy, chief of homicide, to head the special squad. And while Moscone was throwing six-figure sums around, Chief Gain decided to throw Chinatown a curve.

"This is a very complex thing that involves adults without question, and involves businessmen who are profiting by the activities of the gangs," Gain let it be known. "And, the gangs, in my judgment . . . are no more than pawns. And they are being used. Now, what we have to do—and we are going to do it to the extent that we possibly can—is to identify who the leaders are, and who in fact is benefiting by way of the big money that is being acquired in Chinatown."

The big money, Gain acknowledged, derives from gambling. "It is blatant, historic and rampant," the chief declared. It is a multimillion-dollar annual business his police are unable to control, he confessed.

But asking Chinese about gambling in Chinatown is like asking Teamsters about their pension fund, admitted J. K. Choy, the eighty-five-year-old president of the Greater

Chinatown Community Service Association, and a retired vice-president of San Francisco Federal Savings and Loan Association: "If you're going to untangle the gambling . . . it's not that simple." One of the few truly refreshing comments in a month that began in tragedy and ended in throat-clearing and obfuscation.

In an earlier, angrier statement regarded as being without precedent for a San Francisco police chief, Gain deplored what he termed "a subculture of fear" in the Chinese community. "Chinese people simply will not talk to police," he flatly insisted. Going one step beyond, Gain condemned Chinatown leaders for an "absolute abdication of responsibility."

He soon learned that he might have been asking about some Teamsters' pension fund or something. Superior Court Judge Harry Low immediately disputed Gain's charge of "abdication" and reminded the chief that the responsibility is a dual one. Postmaster Lim P. Lee acidly suggested that Gain "could do a better job if he would spend less time giving press conferences on television." County Supervisor Gordon Lau, a recent Moscone appointee who stands for election in November, called for more Cantonese-speaking cops, and noted that there are only thirteen Cantonese or Mandarin-speaking cops on a force of 1,688. Chinatown bigwigs called the chief a racist and claimed he was making self-serving statements to cover police incompetence. And Quentin Kopp, president of the board of supervisors, a non-Chinese, demanded an apology from Gain, who refused. No apology is due and none is planned, the chief said. Tom Kotoske, head of the Justice Department's Organized Crime Strike Force in San Francisco agreed: "He's absolutely right. You can quote me."

The furor mounted. A delegation of thirty Chinatown leaders headed by Judge Low and Supervisor Lau demanded a meeting with Gain. Before they met with the chief, however, they released to the press a three-page statement branding as "unforgivable" Gain's "racial slurs." Gain, in turn, branded the statement "a bunch of junk."

The meeting was rancorous. One participant said, "The chief was rude. First, he tried to snow us. Then he talked tough. I think he finally realized that we were unified, and that we were not going to pick up and go away. But even that did not appear to chasten him."

Gain was incensed during the meeting, an aide explained, because a major push against extortion of Chinatown merchants earlier this year failed due to a lack of response from Chinatown's leaders, after initial agreement. "When it got right down to it, the leaders never came back."

As the rhetoric increased, the central facts became obscured: people were being killed because a war over a wide-open gambling racket is out of control; and because of this, the Chinatown economy is being devastated.

The Visitors Bureau reported that tourists wanted names of Chinese restaurants outside Chinatown. Restaurateur Al Chan noted that business was the worst it's been in twenty-six years. Meat and vegetable suppliers suffered. The Gary Kjar street jazz quartet's take was down. The night watchman at the Portsmouth Square underground garage said they'd normally have two hundred cars parked at 1 A.M., but "now at 10 P.M. we have fifty." The operator of J. J. Walking Tours said business was down 100 percent and that worried customers had written him from New Jersey, Ohio, even Taipei. The Golden Dragon itself, almost without customers, was closing at 11:00 P.M.

On a recent night, miles away from Chinatown, a Joe Boy flattened himself against the wall of a hallway as I turned a key in a lock and opened the door to a borrowed apartment. The Joe Boy's reaction had been automatic. A relaxed guard could be fatal. His friend, Mark Chan, eighteen, had been ambushed fewer than forty-eight hours earlier in revenge for the Golden Dragon slayings. The Joe Boy refused a beer and remained taut. Mark Chan, he said, had been "sloppy."

I informed him that business in Chinatown was way off, that walking the streets these nights was like walking through some back lot in Culver City, eerie and forlorn.

His eyes brightened, took on a gleam. "Yeah," he smiled. "The tongs messed up. The people in the shops are gonna wake up that they're paying off to the tongs, and the tongs can't protect them. We're getting tired of being pushed around [by the tongs]. The shopkeepers are gonna figure, 'We might as well pay the kids instead of the tongs.' "

The group—he always seemed to call the Joe Boys "the group"—doesn't see each other all the time. Just two or three guys are operating in a unit. No one else knows. They have no interest in bothering with anybody from the outside, as long as they are not bothered. They decided years ago "to hell with Chinatown" and the old ways and went out to The Avenues (the Richmond). There are plenty of Chinese merchants to extort, cars to steal for resale, homes and stores to burgle, grass to sell.

The Joe Boy is nineteen now, and was born in San Francisco and raised in a neighborhood other than Chinatown. He has been a gang member since he was thirteen—"We give the little kids .25 caliber revolvers to start out." He hasn't regularly set foot in Chinatown in four and a half years, but no matter: "We're all over the place. Seattle, Canada, New York. We *make* it that way." If somebody is out to kill the group, they'll move farther. But they'll still come back.

"Everybody gives a different story by design, to make confusion." And because of this, "the cops are running around crazy." Somewhere, there was a hint that the Golden Dragon gunmen were safely tucked in Canada. No one helped the Joe Boys—not the city, not the mayor, not the tongs. Now, it's too late. "Why is Joe still in? Nobody got killed! They want him in because they know how big he is.

"We killed all their leaders [Wah Ching's]. The youth of Chinatown know this. They know that we are the strength. The Wah Ching have no leaders left." The Wah Ching "were going to start messing around" with the Joe Boys again, so they headed them off.

"Most of our people go to college. The Wah Ching drop out of high school. At City College, and State, I see maybe one Wah Ching or Hop Sing out of a hundred."

It was very late and he wanted to go. He predicted in parting that more, much more, would come down. I reassured him that his anonymity would be guaranteed. I said, "I think I never even saw you."

"You don't *think*," the Joe Boy corrected, "you *know!*"

In the following days, the Chinatown economy did not rebound. A poll taken during a special meeting of the Chinatown Chamber of Commerce confirmed that all kinds of businessmen were hard hit, disclosed Dr. Dennis Wong, chamber president. One idea discussed was to have Mayor Moscone "walk through Chinatown late at night" to calm public fears, like Alioto did three years ago in the Tenderloin during the notorious Zebra Murders. Moscone declined, but other politicians jumped at the gimmick.

So, two nights later, two leaders of local government arrived separately in Chinatown to demonstrate dramatically their concern by walking the streets without notifying the police beforehand—just the media. Soon, reporters were tripping over wires and cables as they schlepped along with the politicians.

Inside the Golden Dragon, County Supervisor Diane Feinstein and her husband were dining with Judge Low, Dr. Wong and other potentates. Otherwise, business remained slow there. Later, she made the short stroll to Grant

Avenue, reporters and a slowly growing collection of the curious in her wake. At Grant, fellow Supervisor Quentin Kopp was shaking hands all around. Someone stuck a microphone in his face. He sounded like Walter Matthau:

"I'm happy to see people like Judge Low, particularly," he began, "and Lim P. Lee, our great Postmaster, and Dr. Dennis Wong. . . . Is Jack Wu here? . . . The word I receive is that people seem to have been turned off on San Francisco, and . . . they shouldn't be. So, let's let the whole world know that Chinatown is alive and well."

The next evening, esteemed literary figure Alex Haley arrived for dinner at the Imperial Palace with an actress from his "Roots" series. The next night, Mayor Moscone and his family dined there, causing owner Tommy Toy to beam: "When celebrities like Mr. Haley and the mayor come in, we have turned the corner." Right around the corner, three hours later, a mah-jongg parlor was heisted and the seventh victim in fourteen days was claimed.

One day during this period, cymbals could be heard rhythmically clanging from behind the locked doors of the downstairs dining room of the Golden Dragon. It was a Buddhist ceremony for the soul of Fong Wong, who had met an accidental death.

Fong Wong's accident was that he got in the way of the grease gun during the massacre. He was forty-nine, a waiter. He came to the United States in 1969 and last year was finally able to send for his family in Hong Kong. He lived with his wife, who works as a baker in a fortune cookie factory, and their six children in a two-bedroom flat over a Chinese noodle factory in North Beach.

The family of Fong Wong is statistically typical of thousands who have flocked to Chinatown since Kennedy reopened the gates. No one knows for sure how many people live in Chinatown, not even the census taker. But the latest federal guess is that some 80,000 Chinese live in San Francisco (population 665,000). It is known, however, that

Chinatown is the largest Chinese settlement outside Asia. For Chinese immigrants all over America, it is the closest thing to home. And it is a third-world community of enormous wealth, a concept that is almost a contradiction in terms.

Forty percent of its people reportedly live below the government's official poverty line. Almost 90 percent of the elderly are believed to exist in what welfare workers call extreme poverty, living on sixty dollars a month or less. Half of the Chinese population is said to live in Chinatown's eighteen-block core. The density of nine hundred persons per acre is ten times the city's average and ranks second nationally only to some parts of Manhattan. Seventy percent of the housing is substandard, compared with 19 percent for the city as a whole. Eighty-two percent of the families live in three or fewer rooms, and 60 percent share bathrooms or have none. The TB rate is the highest in the land. The suicide rate is three times the national average. More than half the population is under twenty-one. Half the population is foreign-born, and half speak little or no English.

The 1976 annual report of the Chinese Newcomers Service Center found the following:

All premigration men who desired work were gainfully employed but postmigration unemployment for men was 54 percent. On arrival, many women found it necessary to seek work, most as seamstresses. Of the new families, 56 percent lived in one- or two-room households. Among the families visited, 43 percent paid no rent and many more were dependent on their sponsors for accommodation. The percentage of menial workers among the newcomers rose by 28 percent since coming here. And none of the 7 percent employed as professional or technical workers before migration was able to find work in the same field.

On the side streets, along Powell and Stockton and Kearny, along Pacific Avenue, are many of the sweatshops.

Around town, in some three hundred sewing factories, an estimated three thousand women produce garments for major American firms on a piecework basis.

They are called bundle shops in the rags business. Truckloads of garments, usually inexpensive cottons precut by the manufacturer, are brought in for finishing under subcontract agreements. Seventy percent of the seamstresses reportedly earn less than three thousand dollars a year. There is no vacation, no overtime pay. There are no medical or health benefits. The ten-hour day, the seven-day week, are not unknown. The Labor Department cannot effectively police the wages because the employers often claim that their women workers are family members. The employees are too fearful to complain. An ever-present supply of fresh workers, some of them illegal aliens, is available.

This is the Chinatown of Fong Wong and his family, the Chinatown beyond the neon and gold leaf trim, beyond the stone lions and tile dragons, the silk and incense, teak and porcelain, quail eggs and shark fins, bird's nest and bean curds, bamboo shoots and bamboo back-scratchers. This is the Chinatown the Chinatown establishment chooses to ignore.

As much as the Chinese have been victimized by the larger society historically, they have been equally at the mercy of their own: the Uncle Tongs, as the young have nicknamed the Chinatown establishment, the men who run the banks, the restaurants, the sweatshops, the gambling, the dope traffic, the prostitution.

Power in Chinatown is concentrated among an interlock of family associations, district associations and tongs. Family associations are clans built around a patriarch or common ancestor of the same surname. The two largest clans in America are Lee and Wong.

Since more than 90 percent of San Francisco's Chinese came from the sticks surrounding the city of Canton, they also formed district, or company, associations. Officers of district associations, incidentally, are often elected by votes cast according to family strength.

The six largest district associations combined to form Chung Wai Wui Kwoon, or the Chinese Consolidated Benevolent Associations, better known in San Francisco as the Chinese Six Companies. This is the top of the power pyramid. By general agreement, the Six Companies were empowered more than a century ago to speak and act for all California Chinese in affairs that affected the majority. Later, the Six Companies established the Chinese Hospital and Chinese School, where kids are kept two hours at the end of each day to learn the language and literature of their ancestors. In its prime, the Six Companies was the Supreme Court of America's Chinese. Today, they still fancy themselves to be the "official representatives" of America's Chinese. But their slippage is showing: in the street, kids call them the "rice tub."

With the clan and district structure came the tongs, which remained in fact what they always had been in China: semisecret societies enacting roles respectable people could not openly undertake. In times past, tongs engaged in racketeering, narcotics, murder, prostitution, extortion, gambling and blackmail. No job was too dirty. Today, some tongs still function as a Mafia. And like the Mafia, they have divided things into spheres of influence. The On Leong Tong controls east coast Chinatowns, while the Bing Kong and Hop Sing are the strength in the West. The Bing Kong is the most powerful of San Francisco's five tongs in terms of money. The Hop Sing is the most powerful in terms of muscle. The Suey Sing has the power in Oakland's Chinatown.

One tong, according to federal sources, operates a licensed gambling casino in Las Vegas under hidden ownership. It is extremely difficult to obtain inside information on illegal tong activities, the same federal sources contend.

For decades tongs have fostered the image that they are

fraternal orders, nothing more than Elks Clubs for old men. Membership in a tong, of course, is not meant to imply that a person is guilty of illicit activity. And, of course, tong officials routinely deny any illegal activities.

Perhaps as much as half of the real estate in Chinatown's core is owned by family or district associations or tongs. The Golden Dragon premises, for example, are owned by the Hop Sing tong. The restaurant itself is operated by Jack Lee, west coast president of the Lee Family Association, and Hop Sing Elder.

Down the back streets owned by the powerful, and down the eight-foot alleys, can be heard the sounds of another side of the real Chinatown, the sounds of clinking mah-jongg tiles and gambling chips rising from a dozen or more basements. Any night of the week. This is the Chinatown of another man named Wong, whose life has been far different than that of his clansman, the dead waiter, Fong Wong.

Not too long ago, Albert Yin Wong, a friend of mayors and congressmen, a former president of the Chinese Six Companies, and a power in both the Hop Sing tong and the Wong Family Association, used to give little red money envelopes, *hung bao,* every ten days to San Francisco cops Gurnie Cook and Gus Koniaris. Inside each envelope were two neatly folded hundred dollar bills. Albert Wong didn't know it, but the envelopes and their contents were going straight to the FBI. Nor did Wong know that his conversations with the two cops were being recorded.

In February, 1973, Cook and Koniaris raided Wong's gambling den at 41 Ross Alley, arrested twenty-six persons, and seized $7,300. When that happened, Wong invited the cops into the kitchen for a chat, and offered them twenty dollars a day each to allow him to operate. Once a month, he suggested, he would leave the doors of his barricaded casino open so they could make a perfunctory arrest.

All told, Wong gave Cook and Koniaris $8,100—including $500 to drop the case resulting from the February raid. The thirty-eight little red envelopes stuffed with C-notes were entered as evidence in his trial.

Part of the evidence was a tape recording made August 21, 1973, at Wong's apartment. The tape begins with small talk about the murder a week earlier of William Hoo, Joe Fong's mentor. Then, Cook clearly exclaims, "Oh, oh, . . . there's the money! Thank you." And resumes talking about the murder, asking Wong whether Hoo was a member of the Hop Sing tong and if he had been trying to see the tong's books. Later, Cook asks Wong how much his weekly operating expenses are.

"One week?" replies Wong. Cook repeats the question. "Oh, operation," Wong answers. "It takes about . . . over two thousand dollars." Cook asks, "For a week?" Wong replies, "Yeah."

The dapper gray-haired little man who came to court each day in a bow tie and dark glasses, carrying a cane and wearing a jade ring, was convicted on two counts of perjury to a federal grand jury. His attorney, Marvin Lewis, one of the nation's most successful trial lawyers, in a plea for leniency, admitted that his client had been "engaged in the gambling business for years in Chinatown." If Wong lied, it was because he feared bodily harm, Lewis explained, either from the cops or from the Chinese, who traditionally dealt harshly with informers.

"Mr. Wong is not essentially a criminal," Lewis bluffed. "He has contributed much to society. It does not make it right, but Mr. Wong was brought up in an atmosphere where the existence of gambling in Chinatown is accepted."

Wong was sentenced to three months at Lompoc, a minimum-security federal institution, and fined the maximum, twenty thousand dollars, to be paid at the rate of four hundred dollars every ten days, just like his payoffs to the cops. The day after sentencing, he turned seventy-four.

There is yet another Wong whose life has been as different from that of Albert Wong as Albert Wong's has been from that of the late Fong Wong.

About a year ago I strolled along Grant Avenue in the company of a Chinese woman, who stopped suddenly to greet an old man. She introduced him. "This is the Godfather." There was a smile on her face, but she was not joking.

Wong Yin Doon is about eighty-five now, but for much of his life he has been the most powerful Chinese in America—the late Chiang Kai-shek's right-hand man on these shores, the most powerful influence in the Bing Kong tong, the controller of the Hop Sing tong through intermediaries and protégés, and the acknowledged leader of the huge Wong Family Association whose bloc of votes he used to run the Ning Yuen District Association, and thus control the Chinese Six Companies.

Wong's special friendship with the late Generalissimo made him a wealthy man. Chiang gave Wong a virtual monopoly on the import of Taiwan mushrooms into the United States. As a member of the central executive committee of the United States branch of the Kuomintang (the KMT, Chiang's Nationalist Party) and as a director of the KMT-sponsored Anti-Communist League, he controlled Nationalist activities in America's Chinatowns, and traveled regularly to Taiwan to confer with Chiang on matters of mutual interest.

February 21, 1972, the day Air Force One touched tarmac at Peking's airport, was a sad day indeed for Wong Yin Doon. Chiang Kai-shek is gone now, too. And Wong's power ebbs day by day.

So, too, does the power decrease among Chinatown's venerable institutions. The split between the young and old, the immigrant and the native-born, the rich and poor, take their toll.

The tradition of settling disputes within the tribunal

hall of the Chinese Six Companies was shattered in 1973 when rebels within the Hop Sing tong chose to take their grievances to Superior Court rather than submit to the time-honored arbitration.

The lawsuits filed by the rebels accused "those old guys" of keeping the tong books closed, refusing to seat duly-elected new officers, and refusing to turn over the keys to the national headquarters at 141 Waverly Place.

More than that, the court actions permitted public scrutiny for the first and only time of the secret inner world of the tong—and blew the cover off the Hop Sing tong's gambling and protection empire. Public officials and law enforcement agencies, however, never pursued the opening. It seems as if nobody really cared, then as now.

The feud erupted December 15, 1972, when president K. S. Wong appointed local officers contrary to bylaws calling for their election. A new election was ordered by the courts. But when election day came, out-of-town members from Seattle, Portland, Los Angeles and Marysville came to vote. Also present were uniformed officers from Central Station and lawyers from both sides. Jack Lee, owner of the Golden Dragon, presided. Lee threatened to cancel the election unless the plaintiff's lawyer—Gordon Lau, the newly minted present-day county supervisor—left the hall. Lau agreed, on the condition that only local members be allowed to vote in what admittedly was a local election. As soon as the voting began, police summoned Lau back. The out-of-towners were casting votes.

Back to court went Lau. The court ordered yet another election, with only local members voting. Failure to do so now would result in contempt-of-court proceedings, the judge made clear.

The old guard moved quickly. Two days later, an urgent national conference was convened on the second floor of the Golden Palace restaurant in Los Angeles for the express purpose of expelling the rebels. According to the meeting's minutes, conference chairman K. S. Wong pointed out that the seven chief plaintiffs had separately violated the bylaws and rules.

William Hoo—Joe Fong's main man in the adult community—was cited in particular. Hoo, according to the charges leveled by the tong, knocked at the door of the Lee Family Association in San Francisco about 2:00 A.M., the day after the canceled election. "At that time, a Mr. Pon opened the door. Because Mr. Pon came to the door a little late, Hoo Yuen [William Hoo] ignored Mr. Pon's explanation, used his fists and his foot and assaulted Mr. Pon. Hoo Yuen also boasted at that time that he was the famous 'Lon Jai' [rotten son or tough guy] of Chinatown; anyone who does not give him 'face' [respect], even if he is as big as Hop Sing tong, can be flattened. Most of his words . . . implied threats. On the following day, the elders of the Lee Family Association came to this organization to complain . . ."

The vote to expel Hoo and the others as undesirables was unanimous, signed by K. S. Wong, Jack Lee and the leaders of Hop Sing branches in Denver, Reno, Los Angeles, Marysville, Seattle and Portland.

The court-ordered election was held, and four of the seven expelled members were elected to office. Their installation, however, was boycotted by most of the membership, and the branch chapters refused them recognition.

Then the elders changed the locks at headquarters.

Wiley Lum, one of the expelled, went public. He charged at a press conference that the century-old tong's assets totaled $6 million, but that there had been no audit of the treasury for eight years; that tong-owned buildings in San Jose and Vallejo were sold but not recorded on the tong's books; that a $10,000 war chest started in 1920 had disappeared.

The plaintiffs went back to court a third time. The allegations raised by Wiley Lum were the basis of the new complaint.

The elders, in turn, claimed the plaintiffs were a criminal minority who'd been trying to take control of the tong by threats and actual beatings. Their motive, the elders declared, was to use tong resources and influence for criminal purposes. To support this claim, the elders entered into evidence the rather lengthy criminal records of four of the plaintiffs, Bill Hoo, Jack Hoey, Kelly Chan and Poy Lim.

The elders also entered into evidence the Chinese language version of their Basic Rules and Regulations, last revised in 1960. This was done to show that, under the rules, only members in good standing could inspect tong records. The plaintiffs, they said, had been expelled as undesirables. The court ordered its official interpreter to translate the document. It was marked as Exhibit K.

Exhibit K is a remarkable document.

Chapter 12, for example, lays bare the Hop Sing tong's gambling and protection activities: who gets protection and who doesn't, and under what circumstances; and details how much money the tong levies each week on each table in a gambling operation. For example, Article 22 of that chapter spells out what is expected from its Reno branch: "For places which conduct various games of chance, each table is levied $3.50 per week. For a Long Draw place $1.50 is levied per week. For a Short Draw place $5.00 is levied per week."

Other chapters deal with the amount of benefits a widow may expect should her husband be cut down in the line of duty or die in prison; the amount of cash subsidy an imprisoned member will receive upon his release; requirements that the majority of employees in a gambling place controlled by the tong be tong members; and requirements that all gambling places in Tacoma, Vallejo, Guadalupe (Mexico), Reno and other independent areas must employ members to fill all positions "for the sake of strengthening the sphere of influence and to protect the interests of our members."

The lawsuit against the Hop Sing tong was quietly dropped somewhere along the way.

Jack Hoey is now a member of another tong, and Bill Hoo, the famous Lon Jai of Chinatown, died on August 9, 1973, of natural causes at the age of forty: gunshot wounds to the head.

Meanwhile, Hoo's protégé, Joe Fong, is completing the fifth year of his life sentence. He is now twenty-three.

"If the moon had a hole in it," Joe Fong told *San Francisco Examiner* reporter Raul Ramirez one recent day, "they would say 'the Joe Fong gang did it.' It is an easy solution to anything. . . . You have something like the Golden Dragon? The place is tong hideout. The Golden Dragon could have been done by other groups. There's four other tongs in San Francisco. How come they don't mention their names? No. Now, everybody is looking at the police and the youths in confrontation, while the real crooks stay undisturbed."

Joe Fong's bitterness toward the tongs is exceeded only by his anger at the Chinese Six Companies.

"They are supposed to represent the Chinese community. They don't speak out for poor people. Those family associations, those Six Companies—they have a lot of money. They could do something for the youth. But where are the playgrounds, where are the Kung Fu classes, where is anything? You never hear from them."

Joe Fong was wrong. The Chinese Six Companies were being heard from, at a press conference they jointly called with the Chinatown Chamber of Commerce to announce plans for a phony festival they hoped would bring the tourists back, the Mid-Autumn Festival, heretofore always celebrated privately with visits to relatives, a sort of Thanksgiving Day.

Mayor Moscone was at the press conference. So was Postmaster Lim P. Lee, and Dr. Dennis Wong and Don Po Fong, the current president of the Six Companies.

The press did not want to hear about the Mid-Autumn Festival. They wanted to hear about killings and gambling and the state of the economy.

"Let's talk about the festival," Don Po Fong insisted in hesitant English.

"Why haven't the Six Companies put up a reward?" a reporter asked. Don Po Fong conferred in Cantonese with Postmaster Lee, who announced coldly, "The answer was, he does not know."

"What are the Six Companies doing to bring the killers to justice?"

"The responsibility for solving the crimes," Don Po Fong said through his interpreter, the postmaster, "rests with the police."

"How many gambling joints are there in Chinatown?"

The Postmaster leaped to his feet. "Gentlemen, that is not a question! If there are no other questions about the festival, the meeting is adjourned."

"What about gambling?"

The Postmaster, agitated, "We're not here to have a sociological conference."

"Baloney," said a reporter. "This is the first chance we've had to talk to the Chinatown leaders about the gang killings!"

Moscone jumped into the breach and talked about beefed-up police patrols, his hopes of adding more Chinese-speaking cops, the reintroduction of a Chinatown hotline telephone at police headquarters (the last hotline was shut down in 1972 for lack of use).

"Lanterns will illuminate Chinatown like the ten suns of ancient legend," another spokesman plodded on. "Store lights will blaze until midnight and the Golden Dragon [not the restaurant!] will make a rare appearance on Grant Avenue on October 10. . . ."

On the way out, Mayor Moscone told a reporter he knew there was gambling in Chinatown because *he'd read about it in the papers*. Hot damn. Moscone was *born* in San Francisco! The festival? It was held as scheduled, from September 28 through October 10. No one came.

Chowchilla Kidnap

This story is about one of the most satanic crimes in human history. Three friends snatch a school bus—full of small children!—and bury them under the ground.

It was around eleven o'clock at night and I was in my scriptorium at Sutter and Hyde in San Francisco. Mary Chong was with me. We decided to spend the night there, rather than return to Sausalito. I put on the TV to catch the end of the ten o'clock news from Channel 2 in Oakland. They flashed a bulletin about the disappearance of all these kids. What's this? I watched all the eleven o'clock San Francisco news. They added nothing. In fact, some stations didn't have the story at all. I resolved to call the local AP bureau first thing in the morning and did. The story was still the same: The kids had vanished from the face of the earth. Incredible. I called New Times *and they reluctantly said okay. I remember that it was a hard sell and I got angry about the myopia of the people in New York. All those kids! The disappeared ones! Without a trace! Martians? Who knew! The New York people acted like it was just another bozo California story.*

I approached the assignment the way I thought an old-time, gumless, copy-paper-chewing metro reporter would. I put it together blow-by-blow and pulled out all the stops.

New Times *decided not to publish it and I got a kill fee of $250 or $300 or something. Fortunately, I was able to interest Terry McDonnell, then editor of* San Francisco *magazine, in taking a peek at it. We met at his favorite haunt, Cargo West, along the old Barbary Coast, took a* *table, ordered our Scotch, and I handed him the story. He didn't stop reading until the last line. "I want it," he said. It was an act of affirmation. I had known it was a good story and I wanted to see it in print. He gave me $500 for it. I was pleased. I needed the money. It meant I could live another few weeks.*

It was at least nine months in the planning, at a cost of at least $12,000. Yet when it was executed, it unraveled. It mocked them. They fled in panic, their panic almost antic. They seem not to grasp the enormity of the grotesque crime. They play the hick. Their grins are goofy. They stand accused of kidnapping nineteen girls and seven boys, ages five to fourteen, and a school-bus driver. They shuffle their feet. They carry on like they're straight from some God-forsaken boondock like . . . all right, go ahead and say it . . . like Chowchilla, California. Poor Chowchilla. Under the microscope so long, it turns around these days and bites itself on the ass. OD'd on excitement like some kinda Plains, Georgia.

So, in the end, why'd they do it? If, indeed, they did do it. But we must assume they did: They left behind ransom demand and kidnap plan, and children's names; and they were caught red-handed last November bulldozing the very pit. Once discovered, why didn't they abandon the pit plan? All the way down the line they made mistake upon mistake but wouldn't quit. It's as though they were seeing something through. Is the biggest kidnapping in American history just the Bumpkin Caper, after all? Or more? And why Chowchilla? Is it simply, "Well, why not Chowchilla?" Does five million dollars explain it?

What did the rich kids see when they watched jalopy pistons flutter down into valves hour after hour? Hanging out on heaps of scrap metal, what did they feel? Did they really reach Beelzebub?

On the Ides of July, in the approximate geographic center of California, in middle America, one might say, Frank Edward Ray, fifty-five, surveyed the flat roads and the flat, drought-stricken land and the ninety-five-degree late afternoon heat of the San Joaquin Valley. One more day, he knew, and he could tend his cotton, hay and alfalfa until Dairyland School reopened in September. It was the end of six weeks of summer school. The kids had been at the swimming pool at the fairgrounds. Most of them were still in their bathing suits. The final day, tomorrow, would be one of games and prizes, a whacky Olympics, topped off by a picnic. The kids were in the spirit of things as they climbed aboard the bus. Even Ed Ray was in the spirit. He had been looking droopy and acting grouchy on the ride each day lately. But now he kidded the kids about the petition many had signed for an extension of summer school. "I bet you fifty cents we won't have three more weeks of summer school," he challenged. "You're on!" some shouted back. And then Ed Ray moved his big, yellow International bus slowly away from the one-story beige brick building, onto the gravel intersection of Avenue 18½ and Road 13, more or less the way he'd been doing it for the last twenty-six years. It was ten minutes to four.

Kindergarten student Edward Gregorio, five, was dropped off on Avenue 18½, and minutes later along the same narrow road, Ed Ray stopped to let off Nancy, Debbie and Miles Tripp. Nancy, eleven, likes to stand in front of her house and watch the bus and her friends continue along Avenue 18½ until it goes around a curve and out of sight about a half mile away. She saw a white van pass the bus this day, but thought nothing of it. Ed Ray turned onto Road 16 and dropped off Susan Zylstra, seven, whose parents were in the front yard to greet her. Ed Ray came back on Avenue 21 to let off Lisa Barletta, twelve.

A white 1971 Dodge van was parked on a slant across Avenue 21, its driver's door open. Ed Ray slowed, thinking the van might have broken down. You know how it is in the country: someone looks like he needs help, and you stop.

Out of the van jumped a khaki-clad man in a stocking mask. In one white-gloved hand he carried a double-barreled shotgun, in the other he brandished a chromeplated revolver. He yelled to Ed Ray to open the bus door. Two more masked gunmen leaped from the white van.

"Get to the back of the bus!" Ed Ray was ordered. "And keep quiet."

Jeffrey Brown, twelve, thought it was a joke. He jumped up on his seat with his hands up. "We didn't do it!" he shouted.

"All of you get in the back of the bus!"

"Really funny, Jeff," his sister, Jennifer, nine, murmured.

A second gloved gunman drove the bus while the first rode shotgun over the kids. The third followed in the white van.

Pamela Barletta, thirteen, Lisa's sister, watched in amazement from the front of her house as the bus carrying Lisa went right on by.

Terror grew aboard the bus. Kids began crying, screaming their heads off. They asked if they were going to be hurt. Their captors said no. They asked if they were going to be taken home. "In a little while," they were told. The bus left Avenue 21 after a mile and turned onto a rough, dirt road. "Put your hands on the seat in front," counseled the shotgun-wielding guard, solicitous of their welfare.

"Just do what they say, and shut up," pleaded Ed Ray.

The bus stopped in a dry canal bottom, Berenda Slough, about four miles from Dairyland School, in the natural camouflage of a twenty-foot-tall bamboo thicket, between an almond orchard and a cornfield.

"Why are they doing this to us, Edward?"

"Don't talk. Just do as they say."

The white van pulled up a foot from the bus door. Another 1971 Dodge van, this one green, was parked nearby. The gunmen ignored the cries of "why?" There was little talk. Twelve children were loaded into the white van. The other fourteen and Ed Ray were ordered into the green van. Jeffrey and Jennifer Brown were separated. It was pitch black inside the vans. They could no longer see their abductors. The front seats were blocked from view by a plywood wall. The white van moved out. The green van stuck in the sand. The tires spun. Ed Ray thought maybe somebody'll find us before he gets out. Then, the tires grabbed traction, and the green van joined the white van on Avenue 21. It was hot inside. The walls were lined with tarpaulin. No one could see in or out, although cracks of sunlight could be glimpsed occasionally. The children never heard a word from up front. Jeffrey Brown believed it was all some sort of joke, that they were going to be driven around and then taken home. When he could no longer see the specks of sunlight he realized, "It couldn't be a joke . . . they haven't fed us dinner yet."

The kids were hungry. They talked in the white van about how thirsty they were, how hot it was. At times they tried to sleep. But with so many kids, it wasn't easy. Everybody was lying on top of each other. Every time the vans stopped, the kids jumped. The vans stopped three times, refueling from cans. The smaller ones grew nauseous from motion sickness and gasoline fumes. There were no toilet stops. All of the kids had to go in their pants. In the green van, Ed Ray managed to rip some tarp away from the metal walls and get some fresh air. Some of the older kids began singing to cheer up. They sang "Love Will Keep Us Together," they sang "Get Down Tonight," they sang "Boogie Fever," and they sang "If You're Happy and You Know It, Clap Your Hands." Which is when some of the kids started crying again. So they changed the words, and sang "If

You're Sad and You Know It . . ." And everybody clapped. They traveled on and on, hour after hour, and then Ed Ray felt the van run through some brush. He could hear it scratching the sides. The convoy came to a final stop. It was half past three in the morning.

About forty-five minutes after Ed Ray edged his bus away from Dairyland School, the first worried parents called Leroy Tatum, superintendent of schools in Chowchilla for the last fifteen years.

"Hey, the little guy isn't home yet."

Joan Brown, mother of Jeffrey and Jennifer, arrived home from her part-time job at the Chowchilla Insurance Agency and thought the kids were hiding from her. Sometimes they do that. Mrs. Brown went around her house for five minutes talking to them. "Come on out, you guys. I know you're fooling." Then, she noticed that the peanut-butter jar wasn't out. And there were no chairs in front of the television. First, she called Ed Ray's house. No, said Ed's wife, Odessa, a clerk at the local branch of the Bank of America, she didn't know where he was. Next, she called school. The bus had probably broken down, she was told, and the driver is not allowed to leave the bus. Superintendent Tatum sent people to check the route. They found nothing. The bus and the kids had vanished into thin air. Tatum called the sheriff's office.

A townsman, Walter Wittwer, and his son, Steven, went aloft to search for the bus. When they sighted it in the slough, well-hidden at ground level by the bamboo, they circled and dipped their wings. It was 7:30 P.M.

The bus was deserted. The ignition was locked and the key was gone. Concern became alarm. Twenty percent of Chowchilla's summer-school population had been hijacked.

It was inconceivable, all agreed, that Ed Ray was involved. Ed Ray? "Ed Ray is a tough guy," said his boss, Leroy Tatum, who has known him twenty-five years. At five-foot-six and 190 solid pounds, Ed Ray is still a grizzly, despite his years. He fixes the school bus himself, with parts he buys from Emmett McDonald's auto supply. He is a native of Chowchilla. His passengers include granchildren of his own classmates, and the children of some of his passengers of a generation past. The kids call most of the other drivers mister. They know Ray as Ed, or Edward. They *know* Ed Ray. Everyone in Chowchilla knows Ed Ray. The mayor has known him thirty years. No, it couldn't be Ed Ray.

"The kids are gone and that's our only fact," sighed weary Sheriff Ed Bates of Madera County. "There's no blood, no evidence of foul play. I absolutely can't figure it. I'm at a loss for words."

The biggest search in California history began.

Parents waited by telephones that didn't ring. Night fell. Fifty FBI agents swarmed in from all over the state and overbooked the town's two motels. Local and state police scoured the land and knocked on farm-house doors. Volunteers searched on horseback. CB radio buffs filled the air. Vigilantes wearing cowboy hats and caps that proclaim Mack, and Beef, and Cat, packed handguns in their belts and marched with shotguns through the streets.

It began to rain. The wind picked up. It began to thunder, and lightning ripped the sky. It had not rained in Chowchilla since winter. It rained on the same date a year ago, a townsman noted. Most of Chowchilla lost electrical power for three hours. Good for the crops, bad for the search.

Parents started thinking the authorities weren't providing all the facts. As the night wore on, Denver Williams, a cottonseed mill worker and the stepfather of Lisa Barletta, was permitted to enter the bus in the slough, and report to parents held back by police lines 150 feet away at the side of Avenue 21. "There's not much in there," Williams said. "Just a few towels and things."

The only clue was two sets of tire tread marks superimposed on the bus tracks. Somebody left the slough in a vehicle after the bus was ditched.

The night and the rain stopped the search until daybreak. Few in Chowchilla slept. Parents grouped at the police station, a brand-new cinder block building that also houses the fire station and courtroom, and there sipped coffee, and exchanged rumors and theories. Was it the infamous Zodiac killer, who once threatened to take a school bus? Was there a macabre link to a 1959 short story called "The Day the Children Vanished," about a school bus hijacked to divert attention from a bank heist? The Madera County Library owned a copy. Was it terrorists? A deranged person? A grudge against Chowchilla? A kidnap for money? Did one of the older kids take command by force? What was it? Sam Barletta, Lisa's natural father, arrived from Fresno and joined the vigil. Rodeo performer Bob Marshall, wrestling steers at the Calgary Stampede, was told that his son, Mike, fourteen, was missing, maybe kidnapped, and caught a plane. Bob Reynolds, whose daughters, Judy, thirteen, and Becky, nine, were gone, found himself in a nightmare. "I keep waiting to wake up." His wife, Evelyn, was under sedation. Friends came to the police station with dishes of food and buckets of chicken. A mother looked at the clock on the wall. "Come on six o'clock," she prayed. "Hurry and get here."

All day Friday the little farm town vibrated to the sound of powerful engines from the outside world: state planes, choppers, private planes. Large green National Guard machines churned dust as they settled on the airstrip, an airstrip so small that the access road leads directly onto the runway.

John Moody, a building contracter whose CB radio handle is Blue Streak, manned a command post across from the police station. Ten thousand truckers were out there, he knew, with their eyes peeled. "We pass the word on," said

Blue Streak, "and don't say anything around the parents because they might overhear and get upset." And then Blue Streak was on the airwaves: "If you're here for the glory, if you're here to take chances or get shot at, go home. We don't want you. The kids' lives are at stake. This is a situation where we don't want heroes. Don't go in and try to take them yourselves. Radio for help. When it arrives, be ten-ten on the site."

The men's softball game was canceled. The players were either out searching, or not interested. The city recreation program had no participants and Nancy Red, the director, closed shop.

President Ford expressed his personal concern in Washington and asked to be kept abreast of developments. Lieutenant Governor Mervyn Dymally arrived to take charge of informing the two-hundred-member (at least) press corps who swamped phone lines to relay an incredible story to a disbelieving nation.

Townspeople turned to prayer. More than a hundred gathered at the First Baptist Church, where the Reverend R. S. Buskirk asked "God's mercy not only for these children but for the abductors." Over at the First Assembly of God Church, the Reverend John Surratt told about the time his brother was kidnapped in Texas and driven sixty miles from his home. "All the while our mother prayed for his release. And my brother was released unharmed. Yet, another couple abducted by the same kidnapper was killed. My brother was spared because of prayer. Pray that there is no vindictiveness. Instead, have love for the abductors, as God has love for us when we sin."

But there was talk of vengeance.

"We're becoming more and more resigned to the very worst," admitted Mayor Jim Dumas. "It's just tearing this town up. Tearing it up."

The simple rural life was shattered.

One hundred miles north of Chowchilla, in Livermore, deep inside the winding rutted roads of the California Rock and Gravel Company, the back doors of the Dodge vans were opened. The bus driver was told to get out first. He was asked his name. Then he was asked for his pants and boots. In return, Ed Ray was given a flashlight. "Go down," he was ordered. A metal ladder led the way into a hole in the ground, three feet wide.

The kids were told to get up one at a time. Each was asked his or her name. The names were written down. Articles of clothing were taken from sixteen of them. The kids were sent down the ladder, girls first, to the waiting arms of Ed Ray nearly twenty feet below the earth's surface. The ladder was pulled up.

A steel plate, three-eighths of an inch thick, was placed across the hole. Two heavy-duty industrial batteries, each weighing more than a hundred pounds, were placed atop the steep plate. A thirty-inch-high wooden box, filled with dirt, was placed on top of everything. More dirt was piled on top of the crate, and dirt was packed against its sides. Dirt began to seep down into the hole.

Ed Ray knew they were in some kind of an old truck body. As he played the flashlight beam around he saw double wheel wells at the back, and double doors. He also saw a squalid interior. The walls were crudely lined with wire mesh, like cattle fencing. The sides sagged inward. The beam of light picked out a large jar of peanut butter, and twelve five-gallon jugs of water, potato chips, Cheerios and a couple of loaves of white bread. Ed Ray saw two timbers, four-by-fours, one propped against the sagging roof, the other serving as a cross brace between the sagging sides. Two six-inch holes had been torched out of the frame for a chemical toilet. There were fourteen mattresses and box springs and a dozen dirty blankets and bedspreads of purple, pink and white. Two other holes had been cut out of the roof, one in the left front, the other in the right rear. They contained battery-powered exhaust fans. A four-inch flexible hose, thirty-five feet long, extended from one of the exhausts into tree branches, where it could not be seen. Two white plastic tubes were air shafts. It was pitch black and scary. The kids began hollering and screaming again. They knew when they went down that hole that they were not going to be taken home. Twenty-seven individuals were in a twenty-five-foot-long, twelve-foot-high, eight-foot-wide tomb.

So there they were, inside an old Allied Van Lines moving van. On the outside of the buried van, unseen by all, was the plaintive message: "Find Us Fast in the Yellow Pages." They could hear the kidnappers working above, cutting wire. The kids cried to be let out, and Ed Ray begged them not to holler and scream. But they kept on crying, and begging for their mammas. The air grew fetid and roiled with dust. A girl fainted. Suffocation became a real possibility. The ceiling started to give way. Ed Ray thought they were going to die. He sat down and cried. Sometimes, he prayed. If the kids walked, inevitably they stepped on someone. If they laid down, they laid down on someone. Ed Ray tried to get them to sleep.

"Edward?"

"Yes."

"We're hungry."

"Okay. Get something to eat and then get back to bed."

The cutting sounds stopped. There was silence above. Then, a kidnapper spoke down an air tube. "We're going away now. But we'll be back."

How could the trapped be sure? Was someone posted above ground? Ed Ray figured, "We were gonna lose our lives there, same as gettin' it if we dug ourselves out." Ed and Mike Marshall, fourteen, tall and rawboned, decided they'd better start digging. They piled box springs and mattresses atop each other, climbed them, and went to work on the steel plate. The heat was stifling, and they were sweating. They kept pouring water from the jugs over each other to keep from fainting. Then, they'd scale the mattresses and dig some more. They started to budge the steel plate a little, but the two huge batteries above the plate slowed them. Together, in one final burst of sapped, gritty strength, they shoved, and the steel plate and the batteries tumbled down into the hole.

And they saw that the large wooden crate, full of dirt trickling down on them, remained, sealing them from freedom. Ed and Mike couldn't even begin to move it. Ed found a short block of wood, about eighteen inches long, a leftover from the four-by-fours that braced the insides of the moving van, and used it to bust boards from the crate. They pried with their hands. The boards loosened and a mound of dirt fell down into the bunker. They dug the dirt back, fearful all the while that their tormentors would hear them. They dug and dug. The kids beneath Ed and Mike planned what they would do when they got out. "We planned that we would walk across the street to Lisa Barletta's house," said Jeffrey. "And they would call my mom and she would get the station wagon and come and pick us up. Then we were going to bring everyone to my house. We'd take cold showers. We'd call everybody's home and if their moms didn't want to come, they could stay the night. We were going to have popcorn."

Ed Ray summoned Robert Gonzales, eight, whose tiny fingers plunged through a small hole in the side of the crate. He pulled back. A crack opened. He said he could see mountains and trees. They were not, after all, in the slough. They were not across the street from Lisa Barletta's house. They were not in Chowchilla. Then, Mike Marshall simply broke on through the box. His hair was dirty. His face was dirty. His blue corduroys were brown. He helped the girls out as Ed Ray passed them up, and then the boys. When all were free, Ed Ray came out of the hole. It was 7:30 P.M., Friday. They had been buried alive for sixteen hours. The captors had posted no guard, and Ed Ray led a ragtag band of woozy kids along the quarry roads until they found the night watchman's shack. "I know what you're talking about," said the astonished watchman. "I heard it on the news." Soon, fire engines and police cars were there, and revolving blue lights splashed across the brown Livermore hills in the dusk.

A half-moon lit a cloud-specked night sky. And, although reporters had taken over the Chowchilla firehouse, one could hear crickets chirping behind the din. The press was chirping inside on sixty emergency phone lines, borrowed by installers from dozens of Madera County pay phones. Pacific Telephone Company was selling the lines for forty dollars apiece. The phone people also rolled a station wagon up to the firehouse apron and there, amid rows of evicted fire engines, passed out free cases of soda to the press. Theo Wilson of the *New York Daily News* arrived in a taxi from Los Angeles. It cost her paper two hundred dollars. The press was now the biggest freak show ever to play town. Locals stood outside the firehouse doors in silent amusement, watching the press interview itself. Rage appeared. "You people are unbelievable," one woman chastised a reporter. "Walking to your fame on someone else's heartbreak." And surrealism crept in. Teen-agers cruising past the firehouse in cars shouted, "Are we on TV?" . . . "Is the governor coming?" Still other residents arrived with food and urns of coffee for the press.

A block away, on Robertson Boulevard, the main stem, where seven miles of royal palms are interspersed with oleander trees, some white, some red, a baffled FBI squad worked behind drawn blinds inside the one-story city hall they had commandeered the night before. Farther along Robertson, at Red's Market, across from City Park, Michael Red was equally baffled. The only event close to this magnitude in the past, he said, was the cattle rustling three years ago.

At the firehouse, by sheer numbers, the press began to destroy itself. A rumor that began on one side of the room caused mass shifts on the other. The press swayed from side to side, sometimes as the result of a simple thing, like someone going off to find a toilet. Arguments and shouting and shoving matches broke out as Lieutenant Governor Dymally appeared at any of his several news briefings, at which he usually said there was nothing to report. The TV lights would shut down when he said this, and the microphones would be untaped from the table at which he spoke. It became impossible, not to say unrewarding, to remain there.

Beyond the firehouse, one could smell poultry in the air. A freight train had rumbled through. Tumbleweed clumped in masses at a corner, like the reporters down the block. One noticed that there are no parking meters in town, anywhere. Men wear dusty Levi's and cowboy Stetsons on the street, or those caps that say Beef, Cat, Mack. It is Earl Butz country. Everyone seems to have a motorcycle of some sort. A sign on the outskirts welcomes travelers to the home of the Madera County Fair ("always in May") and the home of the Western Stampede ("always in March"). A state marker at the edge of town places the population at 4,611, and the elevation at 273. A peeling billboard a mile away on Route 99, which normally whisks traffic past, also welcomes people to Chowchilla, and promises, "Honest Injun, there's a heap of living here." A grinning cartoon redskin says so.

The first recorded mention of Chowchilla was in the 1830s. It was known as Rancheira de los Chauciles, the land of the Chauciles, an aggressive, hostile tribe vaguely remembered, mainly for their reputation as horse stealers. Rustlers, again. The high-school football team is called the Redskins. There is a Tommy Hawk Restaurant on Robertson

Boulevard, open all night. Chowchilla was officially born in 1914 when O. A. Robertson formed the U.S. Farm Land Company, and invested in the area. A year later, one of the few macadam roads in Madera County was Robertson Boulevard.

Chowchilla is about as small now as it was then. It's so small that Police Chief Gary Brown doubles as city manager. A hand-lettered sign in an empty storefront on Robertson announces that "Farmer's Hardware moved to back lot across the alley," assuming automatically that the reader knows the lay of the land. Across that alley, and across another back lot, is Dumas Furniture. Its owner, Jim Dumas, fifty-nine, has been mayor since March. The salary is seventy-five dollars a month, same as the city council.

Dumas wore a royal blue leisure suit this night, with white patent leather shoes and a white patent leather belt. His white-gray hair is fine and combed straight back in a pompadour. He's a bit of a dude. He gets his hair cut—styled, rather—at Jim's Barber Shop on Robertson, a one-chair establishment next to the Cotton Club. There's a sign in Jim's window that says "Hair Styling $7.50." The mayor shook his head in sadness under a streetlight and told a reporter that "it's all been crazy lately, anyway," not just this. And then he said he and City Councilman Alvin Acker were kidnapped themselves, briefly, last month. In Fresno. In the parking lot of the Sheraton Inn, after a meeting of the California League of Cities. "This guy . . . he was a young black, he just jumped in the car and said, 'I gotta get out of here quick. Get driving.' A couple of blocks away, he pulled out a gun and said, 'give me your wallets.' I lost eighty-two bucks." (Alvin Acker lost ten bucks.) Dumas is a native of Judsonia, Arkansas, and is a former Flying Tigers pilot. He had family here. He came for good in 1954 after a tornado destroyed Judsonia in 1952. "We're all Okies and Arkies here," he smiled. "We're all from the Dust Bowl."

The Dust Bowl is a memory. Where they live now, in the fertile San Joaquin Valley, they feed much of the nation. Stretching in all directions from town are fields of corn, soybeans, alfalfa, hay, cotton, and orchards of fruit and nut trees, dairy farms and cattle ranches. The only structures above one story are silos. The people are scorched by the blazing summer. They work with their sleeves rolled high. Their necks are red, and leathery, and creased by thick, deep lines. The average income is estimated at between $9,000 to $12,000 annually. Family reunions, such as the recent gathering of the Dickensons, quite naturally close with the singing of "God Bless America." It is a churchgoing town. There are twenty-two churches for the 4,611 residents. The children are baptized with names like Wade, Rex, Cecil. In normal times, they tell Portigee jokes to each other.

A kid ran up the street. "They found the kids!" he yelled. "I just heard it!"

Lieutenant Govenor Dymally was being mobbed in the firehouse. There was no order. Minutes passed before the lumpen press settled. Once more there was shouting and jockeying for position. It was awful. But it is always so.

Yes, it is so, Dymally finally was permitted to say.

They have been found. They are safe and well. They are being held in the San Francisco Bay Area. They will be brought back by chartered bus in a few hours. The FBI is talking to them. They are tired but they are all right. They are being fed and given a change of clothes. That's all I know. . . . "Where! Where were they found! Where!" . . . In Livermore. That's all I know at the moment. There was a loud crashing noise in the middle of the firehouse. A table upon which a dozen newsmen stood buckled under the aggregate weight. Its legs gave out. It collapsed. The Fourth Estate toppled in a heap on the cement floor, camera lenses pointing at odd angles to the ceiling.

Mrs. Frances Williams, Lisa Barletta's mother, sobbed

in the doorway, tears dropping from her cheeks, and began to collapse, like the table. "Oh, I'm so happy," she cried over and over as two women companions grabbed her and hugged her to keep her ample body upright. Earl Weiner, agent in charge of the Sacramento FBI office, joined Dymally and confirmed what had been said. Townspeople applauded. There was not a dry eye among them. Automobile horns blew on Robertson. But what is this? A wedding, amid this? The lead car carried a sign that said "Just Married." Tin cans dangled from the rear bumper on strips of bed sheet. The bride wore white and was swarthy. Ah, Friday night in the Central Valley. Life goes on.

As the town waited for the kids to return, Garland Verner, forty-six, a mechanic at the cottonseed mill, sipped coffee in the Tommy Hawk Restaurant and suggested the kidnappers "should be hung by the heels in the street. I'd like to do it myself." Three stools away, Ernest Bryant, sixty, who came to Chowchilla from Arkansas in 1932, more than agreed. "They should skin 'em an inch at a time. I could do it to 'em myself, and it wouldn't even bother me."

In Livermore, at the Santa Rita Rehabilitation Center, a women's prison that was once a Nisei detention center, hamburgers and french fries were fed to the hungry children. They received medical checks and outsized prison garb, stenciled Santa Rita, to replace their bathing suits. Serious men in dark suits questioned them for hours. One agent awakened a seven year old. "Sherry, darling, I know you're tired, angel, but we want to talk with you. Can you take your thumb out of your mouth for just a second?" Don't worry, it's fun, an older kid who'd already been processed promised a five year old. "They ask you a lot of questions and then give you stuff." From Ed Ray and the kids, a composite description of the abductors was drawn. Police were looking for a tall man in his fifties, a small man in his forties, and a small man in his mid-twenties.

With three police escort cars, the children returned to Chowchilla on a bicentenially painted Greyhound chartered bus. One girl had a nightmare during the trip, and screamed "leave me alone, leave me alone!" Another girl drew a cartoon during the ride, a happy doodle of happy little girls, smiling suns, giant mushrooms floating next to clouds, moons, trees, cats with big whiskers, and she printed across it the words, "I love you, I love you." They arrived in Chowchilla at 3:55 A.M., Saturday, thirty-six hours after they vanished.

A woman deputy carrying a little girl wrapped in a blanket was the first to leave the bus, to handclapping, whistling and popping flashbulbs from the four hundred people who waited. Some of the kids were barefoot, some bewildered. And some cried as they rushed to embrace their parents. Bill Parker beamed and lifted his daughter, Barbara, eleven, high over his shoulders for photographers, saying, "I told you she was a doll!"

Ed Ray, dressed in green coveralls and tired, stepped from the bus and waved to the cheering crowd. His wife, Odessa, ran to him and wrapped her arms around his neck. The reunion was brief and the parents left hurriedly with their children. There was little talking, just the sound of shoe leather scudding across asphalt. Several near fights broke out between parents and press. While some grinned joyously as they met the cameras and microphones, others covered the heads or hid the faces of their children. "Don't look, honey. Keep your head down!" Another instructed, "Shut your eyes. Don't open your eyes!" A TV cameraman, unable or unwilling to move from the path of a parent (and friends), was smacked to the ground. "How are you feeling?" a reporter asked. "Can you tell us what happened?" The reply from the little girl's mouth was an unexpectedly sophisticated, "No comment."

A hastily-drawn soap sign spread across a car dealer's showroom window by late morning. "Welcome back kids &

Ed." President Ford said in Washington he was "delighted." But Sheriff Ed Bates wasn't sure about that. The President, he claimed, "saw fit to give the case first class treatment after the kids disappeared. We get them back and five minutes later we go from fifty FBI agents to zilch." Chowchilla was turning in on itself. Agony was over, joy had expired, and anger and fear spread thick.

The Livermore quarry was sealed off and deputies turned away all. At the Santa Rita Rehabilitation Center, five miles away, Jack Baugh, chief of criminal investigation for Alameda County, was sure the case would crack soon. Real soon.

It must have been, detectives theorized, someone familiar with the quarry terrain, and with the pattern of security. Maybe it was someone who worked there, or used to.

When investigators first lowered themselves into the hole, they could stand it underground only for about ten minutes. It was "so unbelievably hot." Tests on the battery-powered fans that pumped exhaust air out of the moving van showed "they would have failed within forty-eight hours," creating a mass coffin. It required three days to remove the moving van from its burial place. When it was put on display, press transportation to and from the site was provided by the quarry owner, Fred Nickerson Woods III, an outgoing and robust man in his early sixties. It turned out that the van was purchased last November 21 for $2,700 from Palo Alto Transfer & Storage by a man named Mark Stewart Hall.

As it was being unearthed, investigators found an even more startling lead, in the records of Security Eye Patrol, the firm that guards the quarry from weekend incursions by dopers, beer drinkers and naked swimmers.

One night the previous November, the log stated, a guard caught three men digging a hole with a bulldozer. One man identified himself as Frederick Newhall Woods

IV, the son of the owner, and claimed he had a perfect right to be there. He dangled keys to the main quarry gate, and gave the guard his driver's license. The picture on it matched the man. He said the other two men were his friends. Their driver's licenses identified them as James Leonard Schoenfeld, twenty-four, and Richard Allen Schoenfeld, twenty-two, and their pictures matched. The guard called Fred's father at Fred's urging, for confirmation. And then he let the matter drop, other than to note it. He didn't want to be messing around with the boss's son.

Police also learned that Woods, who is twenty-four, and the Schoenfeld brothers were caught stripping a car in October 1974, in Downieville, way off in Sierra County, and were placed on probation.

A member of one of California's most powerful first families was now the prime target. Sixty deputies invaded the eighty-six-acre estate of the Woods family in Portola Valley under cover of darkness.

Portola Valley is not even in the same universe as Chowchilla. Part of the network of genteel country towns commonly known in northern California as the Peninsula, it is the horsey retreat of Bay Area wealthy living the good life. The children of the Peninsula expect fat allowances, and receive Corvettes for high-school graduation, not Bulovas. Patty Hearst grew up there. So did Woods and the Schoenfelds.

Young Woods lived in a cottage, former servant's quarters, beneath drooping live oak, about fifty feet from his grandmother's tattered gray mansion, where vines climb the shingles two and a half stories to the roof. Old Frances Woods is in the Social Register, but has had no part in the Peninsula's fashionable goings-on for years. She is tended by a full-time nurse (who asked reporters for Lana Turner's phone number in the middle of the raid!), and rarely ventures outside. When she was young, she cared for retired San Francisco police horses. They roamed her meadows, some forty of them at one time, living the good life and beating the glue factory for a token dollar each per year. Woods's father and mother, Harriet, live in another house, beyond woods and fields of yellow rye grass. Narrow dirt roads web the property.

The place is not being kept up. Money is not the problem. They are Newhalls. The Newhall Land and Farming Company, with headquarters in Valencia, north of Los Angeles, has vast holdings in agricultural, cattle and recreational operations, oil, gas, land, commerce. The company owns twenty-eight thousand acres in Madera County, about fifteen miles west of Chowchilla, and a cattle ranch in adjoining Merced County. There is even a town named Newhall, in the desert outside of Los Angeles, where some of them live. The company was formed by the five sons of Henry Mayo Newhall, who caught gold fever and left Saugus, Massachusetts, in 1850 for San Francisco. The patriarch went on to Stockton, speculated heavily on railroads, and bought all the ranch land he could. His sons made the most of it.

The cops stayed at the Woods estate for two days, searching. Each rolling hill seemed to lead into newer and larger collections of old cars lined in rows in clearings that had gone to seed. In all, they located some one hundred cars and trucks. The elder Woods is a collector himself, with a fondness for fire engines. They found a twin of the buried Allied moving van. They found a tractor, vans, Detroit sedans. Police cars, Jeeps, T-birds, trucks, a Pierce-Arrow. And, as the deputies turned his land upside down, all the father could say, with tears in his eyes, was, "I've been told not to say whether I have one son or ten." He has one, as it turns out.

Fred Woods graduated in 1969 from Woodside High School, where he was made fun of, and didn't go on to college. In high school, he carried snapshots of his jalopies in his wallet. He was a loner. He was weird. Thus, it surprised hell out of everyone when he married Songel Padget shortly after graduation. A junior at the same school, Songel was a state ward living in a foster home. Fred's father reluctantly approved the teen marriage and it took place at Calvary Baptist Church, Redwood City. The bride wore a pleated orange dress, with a sash at the waist. It was a simple Sunday afternoon wedding. They wed out of mutual insecurity, says Songel, now twenty-four, living in Covington, Georgia. Fred also felt abandoned. "His mom and dad gave him everything but love." The parents traveled frequently, leaving Fred behind in his grandmother's care. "They were so devoted to each other, they neglected him." Life in the cottage was lonely for Songel. His parents were the only visitors. Fred didn't like people coming around.

Sometimes, in the evening, Fred would take a gun and shoot windows out of his junk car fleet. Fred and Songel roamed all over California in his cars and trucks. His favorites were a gray Checker Marathon taxi, which had three hundred thousand miles on it, and a maroon Cadillac hearse. He wouldn't let Songel drive his cars, nor anyone. She bought a Nova with her thousand-dollar wedding present from her in-laws. And Fred was tight-fisted. "It upset him every time I asked for money." Songel tired of asking and began a $1.75-an-hour job at Palo Alto Cleaners. The marriage lasted a year.

Fred retreated into his obsession, his wheeled vehicles. He worked as an ambulance driver, moving van driver, and took a laborer's job loading and weighing trucks at his father's quarry. He commuted to Livermore in his Checker taxi. He quarreled frequently with his father. In the summer of 1972, he went to Martha's Vineyard, off Massachusetts, and worked in cousin Dan Whiting's gas station. The family has had a two-hundred-acre summer place in Chilmark for years. Cousin Dan says Fred was a hard worker, and reliable.

When Fred returned home, he got into serious jalopy wheeling and dealing, and formed a partnership with an old classmate, Jim Schoenfeld. Fred and Jim developed a scheme to buy some city-owned land in Mountain View, and move to the site a decayed Victorian mansion owned by Fred's family. They would restore the house, they said, and live in it. They filed a joint financial statement with the Mountain View Planning Department, listing assets at $67,000, including $32,000 in saving accounts, and eighty-eight vehicles and boats. The plan was rejected.

Fred is regarded as a cold-blooded businessman and a sharp dealer out for top dollar. One person he dealt with says Fred took an extra fifty-dollar cut after agreeing to a hundred-dollar sales commission. "I had to put on two new tires." He handed over a check for eight hundred dollars.

"He was a mean kid," says a neighborhood kid. Yet, Fred is not without supporters. Craig Hunt, eighteen, worked as a mechanic for Fred at $2.50 an hour for nine months. He estimates Fred sold fifteen to twenty cars a month. "I liked Fred a lot. He was fair about paying me and never questioned my hours. He was a good man."

Craig claims he was with Fred at the Portola Valley estate only a few hours before the 4:00 P.M. kidnap. "Between 1:00 and 2:00 P.M." Chowchilla is about three hours driving time. Fred fed the horses and then left to take care of business, according to Craig. When Fred left, Craig was out of a job. "I think they realize," says Craig of the detectives who've interviewed him, "there are more people involved in this."

Down the road from Portola Valley is affluent Atherton. It is against the law there to rent. Houses sell for $150,000 and up. The Schoenfelds lived in their parents' ranch style house amid several acres of lawns and trees. Jim and Rick grew up with horses and dogs, a swimming pool, and an ever-enlarging fleet of old cars.

These two sons of Dr. John B. Schoenfeld, a podiatrist, mended fences in the neighborhood, fixed chain saws, and looked after people's property. They shared passions for old cars, horses, cards and guns. They are considered ordinary, everyday kids.

Jim played chess and basketball at Woodside and was thought of as nice, quiet, reclusive. But after graduation, "he got into being a strange gearhead." Jim began to pay curious visits to a high-school classmate who runs a combo junkyard and commune. "He came up here three or four times just to hang out amidst the scrap iron," recalls Jimmy Wickett.

If Jim had his druthers, a closer friend says, "he would have a two-acre plot and a hundred thousand wrecked cars to work on the rest of his life." In dealing, he was the opposite of Fred Woods. He once took $750 for a Caddy, insisting that's all it was worth, refusing offers of $900 and $1000. Last semester he took a course in money management at Canada College, a local junior college. He hung around his cars and his guns and he played cards. Rick completed two years at Canada. He worked odd jobs at Stanford's linear accelerator. Jim filed papers at the U.S. Geodetic Survey office in Menlo Park. Last April 23, Jim went to Reno and got a Nevada driver's license in the name of Ralph Lester Snider, who died in 1960 at the age of five from auto injuries. He rented a trailer home under that name on the edge of Reno, and wore dark glasses when he paid the man through the end of July at $120 a month.

Jim's best friend is John Muldown, a Redwood City reserve cop. On the day of the kidnap, John and his mother drove to Madera County, home of Chowchilla, where he applied for a job with a rural police department. On his application he listed Jim Schoenfeld as a character reference. "The FBI man laughed out loud when he heard that," said John's father, Joseph Muldown, a junior-high teacher. The elder Muldown describes Jim as "apolitical, leaning toward Reagan conservatism, if anything." Jim's cultural taste ran toward Wild Kingdom, Disney, the Beach Boys.

On the day before the kidnap, Jim and Rick asked a friend to feed their horses. They were going to Fort Ord for a few days, to an auto auction, they said. That night Jim played hearts at the Muldowns' until midnight, when Rick came by, and stayed for a while.

A week later, the cops sure wanted to talk to the boys. By the time they heard about the place in Reno, the trail was cold. It had been cleaned out. All they came across were three empty beer bottles and a pair of white undershorts. The lawyers retained by the parents of the fugitives won a court gag order. But sheriffs from four counties were on the case, plus the feds, and leaks were plentiful. In Fred's cottage, police said they found a paper bag listing the scrawled names of the twenty-seven kidnap victims, detailed plans for the kidnap, and an unsigned ransom note demanding that $5 million be air-dropped in military footlockers over a rugged and almost inaccessible section of the coastal Santa Cruz Mountains. "We are Belzebub," the ransom note reportedly stated. The name, one of many for the Devil, was misspelled.

The case broke fast. Police learned about an eight-hundred-square-foot garage space in a San Jose warehouse, rented by Woods last December 19. Fred and Jim painted old cars there before selling them. The Dodge vans used in the kidnap were found there. Ed Ray came over from Chowchilla and identified them. He stayed in the warehouse three hours. Detectives stayed six days, sifting, hauling. They learned that the vans were bought last November 24, along with a third one, for eight thousand dollars cash at a Navy surplus auction in Alameda, three days after the moving van was purchased. One van received a smog control certificate June 7 at a San Jose gas station and was registered six days later in Los Gatos by Mark Stewart Hall of a nonexistent San Jose address, the same name used to buy the moving van. And it was learned that Jim Schoenfeld recently bought X-ray equipment, leading detectives to speculate that it would have been used to reveal whether ransom footlockers were booby-trapped in any way.

The boys had dropped from sight, vanished into thin air like the children of Chowchilla. They were "armed and dangerous," the all-points FBI bulletin warned. And they were, meanwhile, being sighted all over the Midwest . . . of course.

Fred and Jim drove to Reno on Saturday, July 17, as kids lined up to be fingerprinted by the FBI in Chowchilla. After closing the trailer home, Fred and Jim subdivided, and each became Ralph Lester Snider. Fred flew United from Reno to Vancouver under that name and Jim began a stupefied odyssey across the Northwest in his beige and battered 1963 Chrysler. When Woods arrived in Canada, no one bothered to ask who he was. He wore a white cowboy hat, one side pinned Aussie style, a leather jacket and blue denims when he registered as Snider at the St. Francis, a hotel on the edge of downtown. The room was $44.95 a week. The television is in the lobby. He sat there a lot and watched it, and kept to himself. Five days later, he moved next door to the Almar Hotel, where the rent is $30 a week. He watched TV in the lobby. "He was like a dumb kid off the farm who hadn't been out too much," commented Omar Lunden, the manager. "He seemed like someone who could be talked into doing almost anything." On his fifth day at the Almar, Fred buttonholed Omar Lunden for a job. He told the manager he was running low on cash. He said he'd do "anything . . . cleaning rooms, washing up the bar, just about anything."

Jim aimed the Chrysler straight for the usually bypassed border crossing at Kingsgate, British Columbia, north of Eastport, in the Idaho panhandle, where immigration officers are so lonely they automatically search just to break the routine. Jesus, look at all those guns! What're all those guns for, boy? This Ralph Snider seemed jumpy. He said he was on his way to visit a friend at a game farm near Edmonton. As happy as they were to have someone to talk with, the Canadians weren't buying. It didn't add up. Go home, they told him, and get letters attesting to your good character. Instead, he went to Spokane.

At Sportsman's Surplus Store the next day, he sold five

guns and 3,400 rounds of ammunition for $180. He said he needed the money to get back home. The guns were hidden under gear on the back seat, beneath gasoline cans, hot dogs, potato chips, bread and winter clothing. The buyer spotted an antique musket, a black powder muzzle loader, and offered $30. Jim thought the man must be kidding.

That evening, at 7:00 P.M., July 19, he fumbled again trying to enter Canada, picking Cascade, north of Colville, Washington, another little-used checkpoint. Again, the Chrysler was combed. Customs found two rifles, two pistols, identification for Fred Woods and the peripatetic Snider, and California and Montana license plates. They questioned Jim for half an hour while a check was run. He said he was on his way to the Olympics. He said he carried Woods's identification because Woods was his boss, sometimes borrowed the car, and probably left the papers there accidentally. And Snider? Well, he hemmed, it's just something to have. Immigration figured him for some kind of con man who requires multiple identity. Word came back from the United States. There were no holds on any of the persons or items listed. But Canada still wasn't buying. His guns were returned, and he was given the gate. Three days later he was declared a fugitive.

In Coeur d'Alene, Idaho, the day following the second border failure, Jim went to the town's only junkyard. He spent an hour at Jack Forest's Salvage, just being shown around. He sat on stuff, and roamed about. Later, he sold Jack Forest his toolbox, an electric drill, a set of four-inch bolt cutters and two automatic pistols for $135. He wore old camping clothes and a week's stubble of beard. He looked like he had been sleeping on the ground.

Jim netted $315 in those two days of dealing. He answered a classified ad inserted by Elmer Williams of Coeur d'Alene and bought a 1950 Chevy panel truck, green and rusted and coughing, for $250. The sales slip was made out to Snider. But Jim registered it under his own name at the

Kootenai County tax assessor's office, paid the 3 percent sales tax, received his temporary paper plates, and headed home, 1500 miles away.

Rick, though, was ever the home boy. While Fred and Jim drove north, he was in Atherton. He was home with friends as the Chowchilla kids clawed at dirt all day Friday. And that weekend he rode horseback with a girlfriend. He remained in the neighborhood seven days, and took care of a youngster whose parents were on vacation. The FBI visited Rick on Wednesday afternoon, July 21. Reporters talked with him that evening at home, until he declared he didn't want to talk about it. That night, he called the boy he'd been caring for and said he'd be leaving town. The next day, Thursday, he did.

On Friday, he turned himself in.

Bail was $1 million. His father said only, "I wish I could tell you the whole story." His lawyer said he was suicidal, bewildered, frightened. "He thought he was going home in a couple of days. It came as a shock to him."

Fred read about Rick's arrest in a Vancouver paper. Jim would later say he hadn't heard about it, he'd been on the road.

Chowchilla was relieved, but at war with itself and fighting its image. "Please don't tell them we're a God-forsaken little town," Ned Crouch, chamber of commerce manager, pleaded with a reporter. "We are not. We're a nice little town."

Down the road, in Madera, the county seat, a sign appeared on the marquee outside the Madera Methodist Church, entreating: "Dear Judge, please give the kidnappers more than 6 months suspended sentence."

And Mayor Dumas was catching hell at the city council meeting. People charged him with irresponsibility in controlling the press. He was blamed for the endless, intense scrutiny. Marty Martin, manager of Valley Fertilizer Company, told the city council to instruct Dumas about "what and what should not be released to the press." He said "the community is fed up with the stories. Every time you pick up a newspaper, there are three or four articles in it about the kidnapping." The continuing glare might attract kooks, Martin feared. "Let's go back to where our life was," he demanded.

"Frankly," said the mayor, "people want to be left alone. They think I should make no comment. They want to let it die and let the town get back to normal."

But the town was back to abnormal. Some five hundred gathered at the fairgrounds on the night of July 26, while Rick sat in isolation in the Alameda County Jail in Oakland, while Fred sat in the lobby of the Almar Hotel in Vancouver, while Jim sat in the 1950 Chevy panel truck. The five hundred went to watch a program presented by a TV station in Fresno, ninety minutes of news program first aired kidnap weekend. At 8:00 P.M. the temperature outside was a hundred. The hall was hot. Ed Ray sat in the second row and was applauded in person when he appeared on the screen. The town saw itself, friends and neighbors, as they had been seen. All the networks came to the show. The next day, on the news, they could watch themselves watching themselves. Even Hollywood turned out. A man who said he was Richard Bare, advance man for United National Pictures, Inc., drove up from Los Angeles. He said they were going to make a picture, on a budget, "just under one million," of the kidnap. He said Ed Ray would be hired as a technical advisor. He said he directed Eddie Albert and Eva Gabor in "Green Acres" for six years.

It seemed the only person not to attend the fairgrounds program was burly Bill Parker, the man who had hoisted his daughter, Barbara, atop his shoulders and declared to photographers, "I told you she was a doll," the night he got her back. He remained on his front porch and watched the Olympics on television. Too many neighbors, he said, accused him of being a publicity hound and a celebrity.

Two days later, Wenesday afternoon, July 28, Fred Woods crossed a Vancouver street to a pay phone, the Almar manager remembers, and made a lengthy call, "about fifteen or twenty minutes." That night, Jim was seen in downtown Menlo Park, a few miles from home. He was in the Chevy. The search lasted all night, yet he went a dazed way until 6:10 A.M., when a gardener from Mountain View, Lee Wallis, forty-eight, heard his description on the car radio as he drove to work. "My God, that's him!" Wallis cried out as he looked ahead on the freeway. "I mean, how many '50 Chevy panels are there with Idaho plates?" Wallis trailed Jim for ten miles in the slow lane. When he pulled abreast to check him out, Jim had on an old felt hat, "like a farmer's hat," which he pulled down low on his head. Wallis dropped back, found an exit, and saw a parked squad car. The cops took off so fast they overshot the Chevy. "I didn't get a chance to tell them he was in the slow lane."

Jim was arrested without resistance, a mile from home. "I'm James Schoenfeld," he said. "I was trying to get home." Then, he asked to speak with his lawyer. The lawyer said Jim was "unsophisticated, naive." And that he couldn't seem to comprehend the public concern over the case. "He doesn't understand the nature of the charges against him, nor what the stakes are."

When Rick was told about his brother's arrest, he was on his way to Chowchilla, for arraignment, in the middle of a three-car convoy. Each car had four deputies. More deputies, in fatigues, and wearing baseball caps and shouldering scope-sighted rifles, peered from the low rooftops. Chowchilla was seeing its first special weapons attack team, an incongruous urban presence . . . but someone had, two nights before, shotgunned the windows of the old courthouse. The lynching virus was still unchecked. Rick pleaded not guilty to the forty-three charges on Docket No. 6448. The hearing was over in fifteen minutes.

Outside, they stood for hours behind police lines to catch a glimpse of Rick. Hundreds waited grimly in the sun. Ed Ray sat on a low wooden fence in an alley behind the government center. He said he was just curious to see what Rick looked like. Someone asked him about the discrepancies between the composite drawings of the suspects and the youth who had just been whisked past. He was characteristically brief. "You pull a stocking over your head," he answered, "and see what you look like." Behind ropes nearby was Bill Parker, who "just wanted to see how big he is. Some of the pictures you see of him make him look like a nice boy." A retired farmer named Jake Pretzel, eighty, spat at the ground. "I'd like to see 'em tied to a tree and have their limbs pulled off one by one," he admitted. "That's what I'd like to see. Tie 'em to the first goddamned tree and you wouldn't have these problems." Judge Howard C. Green's wife, Jeanne, was otherwise inclined. "They have nothing to fear from us, but they don't know it yet," she said. Tourists also turned out. There was a man from Copenhagen, and a party of four touring the West. "We came to see Chowchilla make history," said Yolanda Recchia, fifty-three, of Flushing, New York.

After Rick went, the sharpshooters came down from the rooftops. A man in the crown recognized somebody. "Hey, you hog-backed Okie," he called. "Did you get dipped before you came back here? I don't want no chiggers and ticks on me." They all laughed, and the crowd melted, quickly, like the night the kids came home.

On the way back to Oakland, Rick was told Fred had been arrested. Five detectives from the Royal Canadian Mounted Police, acting on FBI information, arrested him without incident at the main Vancouver post office.

"I knew it was a mistake to go there today," Fred laughed to a reporter.

He wore his cowboy hat, but not pinned Aussie fashion

this time. He had been in Canada, he said, for a vacation. Under an assumed name.

Were you expecting to hear from anybody at the post office?

"Maybe Jim Schoenfeld, or something. . . . I wasn't sure if he had been apprehended or not, or if he had mailed something to me."

He was asked about Chowchilla.

"I got a feeling I won't get a fair trial down there."

Why is that?

"Why is that? Well, it's a small community. . . . I've heard of . . . and I would assume that in a small community people all tend to know each other, which would bring the whole thing closer to home. And in a small community like that, you would assume that if anybody is suspected of this thing at all—like not proven guilty, but suspected—that they'll just automatically say they're guilty, considering the judge knows everybody in town. And he's not really going to give us a fair trial, either. Which I would like. So, that's what I feel about that town. Definitely."

A week later, everything was in place for the arraignment of Fred and Jim, the sharpshooters were in place, so was the crowd. As Fred was led into the government center of Chowchilla, a woman gasped. "I've seen him before," Carolyn Ramsey declared. Sitting in front of her at the Stampede. "He was with another young man, two unkempt young women, and a small child. The words 'fuck you' were written on the legs of his trousers. He wanted to be the center of attention. He was swinging hand-over-hand along a girder. He came back and he kept whooping and hollering, disturbing everybody. He reeked of body odor. In my mind and in my heart, I'm sure it's the same man." Inside Judge Green's courtroom, Ed Ray sat in the front row, ten feet from the accused, and stared intently at them, chewing on his knuckles from time to time. "I just wanted to come for myself," Ed Ray said. A few rows back, Bill Parker boiled over at the end of the arraignment. Defying Judge Green's order to remain seated, he walked out quickly, brushing past deputies. "I wanna go home," Bill Parker demanded.

That's the way it played in Chowchilla. It was, over three weeks, part carnival, part bumpkin, part tragedy, part Grand Guignol, and a whole lotta rolling stock.

Sheriff Ed Bates, confident the evidence amassed is "the most complete and compelling" he's ever seen, dismissed the devil, hinting that "sometimes the facts are less damaging than the surmises." He is "more inclined to say it was more of an adventure-type thing." Up in the Alameda County jail, one of the three was said to be talking, claiming it was planned slowly over the months in order to bolster each other, and that they never actually expected it to happen. Over in Sacramento, Ed Ray received a hero's reception at the state convention of the School Employees Association, and a tumultuous standing-O when he was presented its Man-of-the-Year Award. He wore a tan leisure suit and his hands trembled when he accepted the three-hundred-dollar check that went with it. He was struck almost speechless. Getting the kids home was the main thing, he said at last, and all's he wants to do now is get back to driving that bus. Odessa helped him manage the news mob. "We're just ordinary small town people," she explained. And the bus, it's still impounded at Melvin's Garage, over in Madera.

Korczak Ziolkowski

Korczak Ziolkowski died in October 1982. He was clearly one of the most amazing and interesting men I ever met. His real name was Joe Lewis. We come from the same hometown. The piece ran in Outside *magazine, which Terry McDonell was editing for Jann Wenner. I hadn't been doing much for them. A little rewriting. Mechanic work. Sprucing up dead pieces.*

One afternoon Terry called. "I've got one right up your alley," he chuckled. There was excitement in his voice.

"What?"

"Korczak Ziolkowski."

"Sold!" I didn't have to think about it. Next thing, I was on a plane to Denver, then on one to Rapid City. My luggage was God knows where. I filled out the missing luggage form, hopped into a rental car and drove to the motel in Custer where I had been booked. The airline called. They had found my luggage and were putting it on a Greyhound. I could pick it up in front of the bowling alley in Custer at 9:30 that night.

"Which bowling alley?"

"Which bowling alley?" the airline clerk howled back at the chump.

Oh, I see.

I had a crazy time with Korczak. Up in the predawn every morning and down from the mountain around four in the afternoon. He stirred two-fisted martini cocktails and we repaired to his study and drank and drank and talked and talked. I was on the verge of turning forty and was beginning to freak about it a little bit. Korczak first went up that mountain when he was forty. I thought he might be able to help. "Your life is really just beginning now, kid," he said. "Everything that went before is more or less just bullshit." He might have been right.

Custer is the only place I've been where I saw a horse in a bar. I was having a beer and suddenly a horse and rider came through the swinging doors. Then, they were next to me. A horse inside a saloon is a very imposing thing. I did not enjoy it.

The Black Hills are so named, one is told, because of their dense, dark pine forests. They are said to be an oasis amid thirsty badlands. And they are held to be beautiful. It is hard to know if any of this is true, however. The billboards kept getting in the way.

There are live porpoise and seal acts at Marine Life Aquarium, one learns, and the Reptile Gardens had alligator wrestling. One may "drive-thru" Bear Country U.S.A., or stand on the wall and defy natural law at The Cosmos. Or visit the Parade of Presidents Wax Museum, or the Holy Land Shrine Wax Museum, both of which are nondenominational.

From Rapid City all the way to Custer, right through the heart of the Black Hills, that's the way it is.

A hundred years ago there was only a bunch of Burma Shave signs. Why, there wasn't even a road, unless you include the ruts left by Custer's wagons.

Custer found yellow metal in these hills and told about it in a big voice that brought many men. Later on, of course, he got rubbed out for doing that.

His presence was unlawful in the first place. The land belonged to the Sioux. In fact, the Black Hills were their most sacred lands, Paha Sapa, the very center of the earth.

The Great Father in Washington knew all this. Indeed, in 1868 he had signed an agreement that the land would always belong to the Sioux, and that no white person could pass through without their consent. Trouble is, they kept changing Great Fathers.

At first they told the Indians they wanted only to use a little land, as much as a wagon would take between its wheels. This became the Bozeman Trail. They asked for a little more land in another direction so they could send the Iron Road through to the far coast. Then, they asked to build forts and settlements to protect and serve those roads. Soon, the people in those outposts sent rumors back to civilization (in this case, Chicago) that there was gold aplenty in the Black Hills. Others started sneaking across the border.

The then-current Great Father, U.S. Grant, wanted fact, not rumor, and knowing that treaties are made to be broken, ordered a reconnaissance of Dakota Territory. Nobody bothered to obtain visas from the Sioux.

On July 2, 1874, the expedition crossed the Missouri with the thousand men of the Seventh Cavalry, their thousand horses and mules, their 110 wagons and ambulances, and their 300 cattle, and commenced to make 883 miles of wagon ruts. At the head of the column rode the youngest general in the history of the U.S. Army, George Armstrong Custer, the Long-Haired One, Pahuska.

They camped about three miles east of present-day Custer. A practical miner with the expedition, Horatio N. Ross, traced along a creek and after a dozen or more pans had been washed out, returned with a little yellow dust wrapped carefully in the leaf of an old account book. The dust was examined under microscope, washed with acid, mixed with mercury, cut, chewed, and tasted. It stood every test. At daybreak, officers and privates, mulewhackers and botanists were panning in the creek. From the grass roots down they struck pay dirt.

A reporter with the group, John R. Curtis of the Chicago *Inter-Ocean,* sent word to the outside that "there is gold here in quantities as rich as we ever dreamed of." Curtis neglected to mention until his final paragraph that the gold was in Sioux territory where "no one can come with any safety, or with any legal right as long as the treaties that now exist hold good."

This fact apparently bothered the rest of the expedition no more than it did the reporter. They solved the Indian question around the campfire. They decided to ignore them. The Custer Park Mining Company was formed and notice was posted inside a hardtack box placed at the claim. "It was a company of rough men—the most of them—who enjoy life on $13 a month and rations," Curtis observed in his next article.

The last important gold rush in the United States was under way. Outside the law.

The ruts Custer's wagons cut through the Black Hills ever widened to accommodate the gold seekers, and came to be known as the Thieves' Road. Today, it is a terrific stretch of four-lane highway, so smooth and unscratched as to permit the motorist a comfortably safe view of all the billboards. It is still called Thieves' Road, by the way—unless you hold to a different opinion of the Roadside Attraction.

Less than ten years later, the last of the bison herds was slaughtered by the outsiders. The Sioux nation's hoop was broken, and there no longer was any center.

The gold didn't last much longer than the buffalo.

And the little community of Custer almost became a ghost town. (The town was named for Custer "because of his being the first person here," current chamber of commerce literature explains.) Almost became a ghost town. . . .

We have Gutzon Borglum, carver of mountains, to thank or blame for reversing that trend. Today, Custer is a living, breathing, stagnant backwater and no ghost town at all. Were it not for Borglum, all those billboards would lead nowhere. As it is, they lead to Mount Rushmore. All the rest—the alligator joints and the multiple waxworks—are mere satellite chapels, pit stops for the worshipful as they Winnebago toward Rushmore.

Tourism is a greater bonanza than the yellow metal. In furtherance of the cause, the residents maintain an ersatz atmosphere of the Old West. Careful not to let their heritage lapse, they celebrate Gold Discovery Days the last weekend of July, the anniversary of Horatio N. Ross's lucky strike. Otherwise, they like to sit facing the sidewalk in diagonally-parked vee-hick-uls and regard the doings at Fly-Speck Billy's gift shop and the Custer Café. They play mostly to the Winnebago element, which is curious, since this is the heart of anti-Indian country. (Perhaps they perceive Winnebagos as good Indians, remembering that a band from that tribe accepted twenty horses and a hundred dollars from the U.S. army to betray their friend Black Hawk, who was only trying to stand and fight.)

There are thirty-three motels now in Custer (population 1,500) to serve pilgrims to Rushmore, only twenty miles up the Thieves' Road. They also have three Roadside Attractions of their own that they're proud of, plus a fourth one they'd rather forget.

A corner billboard by Custer's only traffic light lures fish to Bedrock City, where one may eat a bronto burger and ogle those lovable Flintstones, Fred and Wilma, Barney and Betty, and Pebbles and Bamm-Bamm. One is asked to remember that "this is the original." The same billboard has come-ons for Ledbetter's museum of antique cars and relics of the past, and for the talking dummies created at Western Woodcarvings, a Reader's Digest–approved attraction.

Five miles from the traffic light is the most amazing artistic endeavor of all time.

Which is the one they'd rather forget.

It is the equestrian statue of Crazy Horse, 563 feet in

height and 641 feet in length. And it is amazing on two fronts. Its dimensions all but overload human credulity, and it is the work of a single man.

For thirty years, Korczak Ziolkowski has been drilling, dynamiting and bulldozing the great Sioux chief out of a mountain. Every day, weather permitting, he repeats the cycle: more drilling, more blasting, more bulldozing.

Ziolkowski battles not only the mountain, but about half the population of the Black Hills. He refuses to set foot in Custer and has not done so in nearly eight years. Worse, he keeps threatening to make a ghost town out of the place. He is widely reputed in local circles to be a man of uneven disposition. He has been called a cheap imitator of Borglum. Even Borglum's widow claimed he was an impostor.

Mere utterance of the name "Kore-chack Jewel-*kuff*-ski" strikes raw nerves in town. To a chambermaid at the Custer Motel, he's "a phony." To a barmaid at the Skyway Lounge, he's "a foul-mouthed, vulgar man." And "he knows the mountain may fall down—that's why he's not finishing it." Across the street at the Gold Pan Saloon, the bartender chuckles at the thought of the bearded old fool up on the mountain, and it's simply that, "Arrr shit, he'll never finish it."

All of which is okay with Ziolkowski. He has frequently told them, "Look, you sons of bitches didn't invite me here. The Indians did. And that's more than they ever did for you."

Vandals have put bullet holes in his equipment, tried to set fire to his buildings, and destroyed several marble busts on display along a path leading to his studio entrance. After that happened, Ziolkowski mounted a revolving red light on the roof of a black 1955 Chevy and painted on its front doors the seal of the "Crazy Horse Police Dept." For a while, a rear bumper sticker declared Custer Had It Coming. And now at night, in one of the hemisphere's most pastoral settings, guard dogs patrol the grounds, and the sculptor and his wife pack guns.

Townspeople winced anew after Ziolkowski opened his land to AIM members (American Indian Movement) when they rampaged through Custer in February 1973. About two hundred angry Indians came in a convoy to retaliate for what they believe was a miscarriage of justice: A ruling of justifiable homicide in the death of a man named Bad Heart Bull at the hands of a white man during a barroom brawl in the outlying hamlet of Buffalo Gap. Convinced that the county legal machinery was in the hands of fork-tongued bigots, the Indians burned a covered wagon on static display at the Chute Roosers, a chuckwagon–barn dance place on the way to town, reduced the Custer Chamber of Commerce building to ashes, and started a minor fire in the 1881 Court House before they were checked by a swarm of FBI agents sent in by the then-current Great Father.

Ziolkowski admits cheerfully that he aids and abets a communal nervous breakdown. Early on, he appeared before local groups to calm skeptics, but only scared them worse by reciting his dream-plan for an Indian university, teaching hospital, museum and 7,200-foot runway. One woman was prompted to accuse a much-younger Ziolkowski of desecrating the hills with his "monstrous" carving. She warned in a letter to the *Rapid City Journal* that "its blot would spread to Mt. Rushmore, cheapening our shrine to democracy." And she predicted that if he were allowed to continue, "our Black Hills will become a paradise for idiot sculptors." She was right. After Ziolkowski, came the deluge: all those wax museums, talking wooden dummies and lovable Flintstones.

The sculptor never dreamed he'd be in the tourist business, never expected to remake his world in buckskin jacket and cowboy boots at the age of forty, gambling the rest of his life against the possibility of creating an enduring monument to his own failure.

It seemed like fate when Henry Standing Bear wrote the one-time Boston fop in November 1939, from South Dakota: "I note you have won honors at the New York World's Fair in sculptural work. A number of my fellow chiefs and I are interested in finding some sculptor who can carve a head of an Indian chief who was killed many years ago."

They had in mind Tashunka Witco, Crazy Horse.

Ironically, Ziolkowski had recently returned from the Black Hills, where he had been an assistant to Borglum on Rushmore. He was fired after two weeks for punching out Borglum's son, Lincoln. The elder Borglum, in his letter of dismissal, suggested it would be better for Ziolkowski "to pursue your creative efforts where you are not hampered by any other ways of doing things."

What better, mused Ziolkowski, than a memorial to a man who also had other ways of doing things? And where better than in the shadow of Rushmore, near enough to needle. He returned to South Dakota to look at mountains with Standing Bear. World War II intervened, and Crazy Horse was assigned to low priority as Sergeant Ziolkowski landed on Omaha Beach.

To most, Crazy Horse is known as Custer's destroyer at the Little Big Horn. To the Sioux, he is remembered as their strength.

Crazy Horse never signed a treaty, never registered at an agency, never lived on the reservation, and never permitted photograph or portrait. He submitted to no man, and sought only to preserve the old values. He chose the warpath when it became his only out. He was born about 1842, according to biographers, and was called at first the Light Haired Boy. The name Crazy Horse came from a vision in which he saw his horse standing still, yet dancing as if it were a horse made merely of shadow.

"I was just afraid of him," recalled Black Elk, a second cousin, in his book *Black Elk Speaks*. "Everybody felt that way about him." He went about the village in silence, not noticing anyone except, sometimes, children. The older he became, the more he went off alone into the mountains. He began to be called the Strange One. He had little interest in the activities most Sioux cultivated: singing, dancing, wearing paint, bragging on war stories. "He never wanted to have many things for himself, and did not have many ponies like a chief," Black Elk remembered. "But everybody liked him, and they would do anything he wanted or go anywhere he said."

He commanded their admiration and respect because nobody was afraid of being left wounded or dead to the enemy if Crazy Horse were along. The growing hero-worship of Crazy Horse led to tragic ends. Older chiefs who had accepted agency life—Red Cloud and Spotted Tail among them—grew jealous and betrayed Crazy Horse, claiming that he plotted to kill General George Crook. When the report reached General Philip Sheridan ("The Only Good Indian Is a Dead Indian"), commander of the Military Division of the Missouri, he telegraphed Crook on September 5, 1877: "I wish you to send Crazy Horse under proper guard to these headquarters."

On that day, Crazy Horse was making for Fort Robinson, under guarantee of safe conduct, to visit his wife dying of tuberculosis. Their only child, a daughter, had recently died of the same disease. Inside the post, he was asked to confer with the commanding officers. He had no idea what they planned until he saw barred windows on the building he was about to enter. Crazy Horse drew a knife and started to fight his way out. His old friend, Little Big Man, at the time an agency policeman, seized him. In the struggle for the knife, Little Big Man was slashed. Private William Gentles reacted with a bayonet thrust into Crazy Horse's stomach.

Crazy Horse was dead that night. It was just as well: The government's plan was to imprison him on the Dry Tortugas.

Indians, save for a few in the melting pot, no longer live in or around Custer. They hate the name.

But many, including Crazy Horse's cousin Black Elk, then ninety-three, returned on June 3, 1948, to dedicate the mountain memorial that Ziolkowski again had time for. As public officials and Indians beamed approval at each other and waited expectantly, Henry Standing Bear touched off the first charge. Nothing happened. Rain had dampened the dynamite. Only a few persons were still around at 4:00 P.M. when the ceremonial first blast rolled thunder through the once-sacred hills.

The first day's partial success symbolized what Ziolkowski would have to face for his entire future. He started with $174, a war-surplus truck, a wife and two assistants. For the first few months they lived in tents. He had to climb a ladder so he could see the mountain over the trees. They built sheds, a studio. Later, he acquired a dairy herd and a sawmill. He got up at 5:00 A.M. to milk the Holsteins. He lugged twenty-nine tons of lumber on his back to build a 741-step stairway to the top, and then carried equipment up piece by piece, until he rigged a cable hoist. He built a road from the highway so visitors would come. That was back when Custer had one motel. In those days, he worked with a jackhammer. He'd come down after having taken off maybe ten thousand tons in a week or two, look up, and see no sign of any work. His big breakthrough came when he hacked a road to the top. Up went Jeeps and bulldozers.

For Custer residents, the bloom is off Ziolkowski's colossal project. The mountain that changes shape almost imperceptibly year to year has blended into the pattern, just another full-fledged Roadside Attraction among many.

But to the first-time viewer it can be awesome. With a little imagination, one can see Crazy Horse riding out of the mountain, returning. More than five million tons of granite have been blasted away, fourteen times more than all of Rushmore. The rough profile is done. Some two and one-half million tons of rock are yet to fall.

The freight is paid by visitors who fork over four dollars a Winnebago-load to watch. This year Ziolkowski expects to take in about five hundred thousand dollars from a like number of people. It is a symbiotic relationship. He disdains the tourists, and has been known to call them elephants. But daily expenses are now fifteen hundred dollars, and he knows whose dollars paid for the five tons of ammonium nitrate, one and one-half tons of 45 percent Gelex, and two hundred nitro caps he just ordered to get through the next two months. He uses between four hundred and five hundred cases of dynamite a year. He can go through a ninety-dollar drill in a day if it is in the cards.

Contributions so far amount to $2.5 million, about half the projected total cost. He never touches this money for personal expenses, he insists, he works under auspices of a commission formed to make Crazy Horse a tax-free, nonprofit operation. Twice he has turned down federal grants, he says, because "they tell you what time to start, and what time to knock off—you know, Gutzon Borglum could never call his soul his own." So, in order that he may say he submits to no man, Ziolkowski sells fast food and a variety of schlock souvenirs, including plaster Crazy Horse statues at three dollars and twenty-five dollars depending on size. There is also a large wooden crate filled with rocks his sons haul from the mountain. Above the crate is a teaser that says some of the granite is flecked with gold, and to leave a donation please.

For the money, one gets to tour his studio, look at the mountain 4,800 feet away, or put a dime in a pay telescope for a close-up that reveals a "Slow Man at Work" billboard; browse among Indian artifacts in a museum wing he and his sons recently built; and visit part of the meandering fifty-seven-room house he has been enlarging with his boys during winters. The public rooms of the residence are crammed with Egyptian furniture from King Farouk's estate, Marie Antoinette mirrors, Revolutionary War fifes and drums, Victorian lamps, antique miniature toys, and several examples of his smaller, earlier sculpture.

People pay Ziolkowski and Ziolkowski pays the mountain. The toll includes worsening arthritis, a back damaged when a three-hundred-pound cable snapped, broken ribs, a heart attack, worsening deafness from all the drilling and dynamiting, a limp resulting from ligaments torn when he misstepped from his Caterpillar D-9, and near misses recorded when lightning set off a nearby box of dynamite, and when a Cat's brakes failed at cliff edge.

He is sixty-nine years old and living on pain killers. The joints of his massive fingers are bent out of shape and swollen. But under his stained and dusty old felt hat, blue eyes flash.

"Want a beer?"

His son Casimir, twenty-three, who helps on the mountain with brother Adam, twenty-five, was sent to fetch Heineken.

Ziolkowski's bedroom-study is stuffed with copies of Michelangelo busts, and shelves of books about Indians. At his bedside was a book by H. L. Mencken, and another on Chaucer. The knotty pine walls are hidden under framed and signed photos.

Visiting with Ziolkowski is like going deep into the Negev to see Ben Gurion. It is an audience. He talks. You listen. He reminisces a lot: Barbara Stanwyck, Robinson Jeffers, H. Allen Smith, John F. Kennedy. To Werner von Braun, he said, "Holy mother of God, how I once *hated* you!" With the late Senator Karl Mundt, he "used to invent drinks and get pie-eyed." Cecil B. DeMille "sat right in that chair." And Walter Brennan and Yvonne DeCarlo became good friends. Ray Kroc, McDonald's hamburger tycoon, "fell flat drunk on his face right outside that door." Henry Fonda stayed around for almost two days. And all those phone calls from Senator McGovern. He's hung up on George three times now.

On a table is a framed letter from Dennis Banks, an AIM leader who skipped to California rather than face South Dakota's music after the rampage in Custer. The letter is to one of Ziolkowski's teen-age daughters, Marinka, and Banks says in part that he is honored to know and love this family.

"Dennis Banks is a gentleman of the first water," Ziolkowski declared in a Boston accent shot through with enough broad-A preservatives to outlast a dynasty of Kennedys. "Dennis Banks is guilty of nothing." On the other hand, however, AIM leader Russell Means "is guilty of everything!" The hard feelings date to the time Ziolkowski permitted AIM to hold a sundance on his property. (The traditional sundance calls for a young man to be cut in his back or chest so that a strip of rawhide, fastened to a tree, can be inserted through the flesh and tied. The man dances to the drums, leaning on the rawhide as long as he can stand the pain, or until the flesh rips loose. Its purpose is to purify a man, and to give him power and endurance.) During the encampment, Means's young cousin was shot dead by another celebrant. "Russell came out looking for revenge at four in the morning," Ziolkowski explained. "I told him, 'No! You promised me there'd be no whiskey, guns or dope. You broke your promise!' I told Dennis the last time I saw him to stay away from Russell. That was in June 1976, at the Mark Hopkins Hotel in San Francisco." According to Ziolkowski, Dennis Banks told him that he and Marlon Brando are the only two white men Banks can trust. "But if I were an Indian, I'd never trust a white man. No way!"

Is that why you refuse to go to town?

"I'd probably have to kill somebody." There was no easy way to establish whether he was serious, or just funnin' around. He brooded briefly about the reservoir of bad blood accumulated through the years, and recounted the time he took on six guys in Custer. How long has it been since you've thrown a punch in anger? He considered his mangled, meaty fists. "Oh, about a year and a half."

Currently, he is escalating a war of letters with The

Council of Friends of the Boston Symphony Orchestra over the marble bust he carved in 1935 of his earliest benefactor, Juvenile Court Judge Frederick Pickering Cabot, who also happened to be the first president of the Orchestra's board of trustees. It seems the bust was moved last year from its specially-built niche in the first balcony foyer to a less desirable location. In the niche, The Council of Friends placed a potted plant.

This came as an unbelievable shock to Ziolkowski. As far as he's concerned, there would be no Crazy Horse monument—there would be no Ziolkowski, period!—were it not for Judge Cabot, who introduced him to museums, antique shops and the symphony. New worlds opened for the lad who had endured a Dickensian early life of orphanages, foster parents and heavy labor in the shipyard. At night, the young Ziolkowski became a man-about-Boston, sometimes affecting spats, bowler and walking stick. He also began to make money as a woodcarver, a talent he discovered while repairing a ship's figurehead. Ziolkowski was never what might be called a starving artist, but executed many commissions and prospered. At twenty-five, he married Dorothy Brewster Comstock, eleven years his senior, and moved into the twenty-two-room home she shared with her mother in West Hartford, Connecticut.

In West Hartford he made his first unknowing giant steps toward the Black Hills by undertaking a most ambitious project, a thirteen-foot statue of Noah Webster that would require almost two years to complete.

Ziolkowski had been living in that quiet and well-heeled village six years when he learned to his surprise at a cocktail party one evening that he was standing in the house of Webster's birth. He expressed dismay that no memorial to the lexicographer existed in town, and offered to carve one on the green, for expenses only. He was applauded by town fathers and local press, a drive for funds was started, and he went off to obtain a thirty-two-ton block of Tennessee marble. Stripped to the waist, he set to work night and day, under floodlights and on Sunday. He was denounced in pulpits for working on the Sabbath, and for shattering the night calm with chattering electric drills, and the fund-raising lagged. A group of youngsters, mostly schoolgirls, rallied to his side and stuck with him to the end in open defiance of public sentiment. The carving became the biggest show in town. The kids hawked peanuts and soda pop as nineteen tons of chips fell on the green, and then sold the chips as doorstops and bookends.

At the unveiling, West Hartford hollered foul. They did not like the beetle-browed Webster. Ziolkowski was criticized for giving the forgotten native son too small a head, and "a rather short neck." Nor did they appreciate the pageant he and his girls presented at the ceremony, in which witches jeered at Webster's dictionary in terms similar to those of Ziolkowski's opponents. Least of all, they liked the inscription he chiseled on the statue's base: "For you I labored, not for my own day. That by the Word men should know brotherhood. My Fellow Men! You have not understood. Since each of you would go his separate way." The sculptor asserted that the lines were paraphrased from an unpublished letter Webster wrote to John Jay in May 1813. Insulted townspeople demanded their removal, however, and attacked Ziolkowski as an "arrogant, temperamental" man who "thinks he is the original genius." The statue and the inscription are still there today. The sculptor checked it out when he returned to accept an honorary doctor of arts degree from Fairfield University. But the denunciations echo through time and leap today from the lips of Custer dwellers.

"Michelangelo himself couldn't come in here and please these people," Ziolkowski claims. "It was the same way with Gutzon Borglum over on Rushmore. Now they don't hate him quite so much because I'm here, and I'm worse than he was. I'm a crazy Polack with a name they cahn't pronounce, and I'm twice as insolent as Borglum. How about another beer? Have another beer."

The admission is indeed true. Almost from the start, Ziolkowski had rows with commission members. Back when Custer had one motel, his wife left him, and so did the two assistants. And then, a furious argument developed over his marble model of the memorial. Even Henry Standing Bear admitted before his death in 1953 that he didn't like it. He wanted Crazy Horse's hair to be braided. Ziolkowski wanted it to be streaming loose. The sculptor remembers that period as the darkest of his life.

But life begins at forty. Ruth Ross, one of the schoolgirls who had fought the Noah Webster battle—but of no known kin to Horatio N. Ross, practical miner—returned to his side. They married on Thanksgiving Day, 1950. After that, came the deluge: boy, girl, boy, girl, boy, girl, boy, boy, girl, girl. "I married Fertile Myrtle," he likes to say, especially, one gathers, when she is within earshot. Ruth is a slight woman of scrubbed and rosy appearance, who tries to keep the world away from Korczak, and Korczak on the mountain. It is a difficult task. He is easily led astray.

She manages not only his affairs, and those of their home, but also runs the Roadside Attraction, supervising thirty employees, including four daughters. Despite the load, she maintains a serenity and cheerfulness, even in the face of his constant demands. He seems always to be on the intercom to her: "Mother, please find me the Boston Symphony letters." On the mountain, he uses a walkie-talkie to communicate his needs, but for some reason they do not always have their receiver open. In the old days, he used to communicate from above by firing a .45 in the air. That was much better, one feels.

Wild, roaring rain fell this night on the Black Hills, up to five inches in places, forcing the Winnebagos to cancel their customary bologna with the works on Wonder Bread outdoor repast. Driven inside, they rampaged through the

Custer Café, turning the place into a feed lot. Their offspring—even the babes in arms—screamed wild threats of dire ends the parents would meet if they resisted for just one more moment the savage squeak-voice demands to do this or that and to gimme this or gimme that. The parents, it was seen, did not resist. They merely assumed stony sullenness and permitted the tads to disappear beneath tables, or climb over their own unyielding forms like miniature mountain carvers, as all the while they fattened themselves. A goddamn feed lot for sure, and not a speck of civilization could survive. To remain within those stockyard precincts five more minutes would certainly lead, one realized, to becoming totally Winnebagoed.

Mount Rushmore, at least, would be empty on a night such as this. And so it was. Hard hailstones strafed the parking lot there, and ricocheted madly across the lonely pavement. Thunder was directly overhead. Because of the energy crisis, the shrine is no longer eternally illuminated, but lightning now raked the sky from corner to corner, strobe-lighting the mute, darkened faces of the four Great Fathers pictured there. For long moments there was vision. Jefferson, it was plain to see, was haranguing the others. But from that distance, of course, it was not possible to make out what he was saying, or even to determine if this is always the pattern.

More than a foot of rain collected outside the sculptor's studio overnight. In the clear morning, he considered the results. It was bad for his work, and good for his wells. The tourists had been Winnebagoing eleven thousand gallons of water a day from him, and for the first time in his life the sculptor had been forced to buy water. Ruth came out to remind the sculptor that Johnny Cash was coming in the afternoon. The sculptor wondered aloud what it would be like on the mountain. He turned to his son Adam. "You got the vehicles ready?" Adam pointed to three Jeeps. "Right there," he said. "Okie-dokie," said the sculptor, "you'd better get them—and get Casimir, too." Adam said, "yes sir," and departed. The sons generally say "yes sir" when answering their father.

The Jeeps began a slow ascent, the father in the lead. "Oh, look at my poor road!" he moaned. "Jumping God!" The road had washed away. The lead Jeep became stuck. The sculptor told his sons to get out of their Jeeps, and fill the washout with boulders from the sides. As the sculptor waited, he pointed to a cavelike opening in the base of the mountain. "That's my tomb," he announced. "Adam and I blasted it out. When the time comes, all they have to do is put me in there, stick in some dynamite, and BLAM!" When that time comes, his wife and children will be given two hundred acres of residence land, according to terms of the will.

Slowly, the Jeeps sought the heights, churning, dipping, wishing they were tanks or turtles. A large mountain goat, rummaging at the work site, shot past scaffolding and debris and fled down a sharp embankment. The view from the top is a panorama of three states. The billboards are too far away to be seen from the crest, but one may glimpse an eagle.

A stream of tourists could already be seen arriving in the parking lot. "The people down there, they think you just come up here with a hammer and chisel, and that's all there is to it," the sculptor remarked. His hammer, of course, is dynamite, and the chisel a bulldozer blade. He is not yet near the wedging (splitting off rock with wedges) and bumping (smoothing what's left by chipping and grinding), let alone the ultimate act of actual hammer and chisel. "It took six hundred years to build Notre Dame in Paris," the sculptor counseled. "You can put ten of them in this mountain. It took thirty thousand slaves to build the pyramid at Giza. You can put five of them in it. I am a man working with his two sons. What do they expect, miracles?"

Adam started the two compressors that synchronize to

feed enormous air pressure through hundreds of feet of hose to the Air-Trac drill rig that bores a three-and-one-half-inch hole into the granite at the rate of a foot a minute. "You're going to have to lift the boom, honey . . . or bend the steel," the sculptor warned. He calls his sons honey and dear as often as he calls them by name. "Yes, sir," replied Adam as he began to raise the boom. "You have water in it? You'd better put water in it," the sculptor called out. Adam answered that he had, "twice."

Twenty feet of pounding steel chewed into the mountain. Granite dust swirled in clouds. Adam wore mufflers, the ones airport ground crews use. But to the unprotected eardrum, the roar was deafening. "This isn't sculpture!" Ziolkowski shouted. "It's mining!" What? "I said it's mining! What's the matter, you deaf? It's hard rock! I have to blow it out!"

He was asked how he knows what he is doing. "What?" he answered. The question was repeated: How do you know what you are doing? What's the matter, you deaf? "I know the mountain!" No, what is meant is, how do you know when you cut that you won't be making a mistake? "I cahn't answer that! I know the goddamn mountain, I told you! I'm not trying to be rude. . . ." Ziolkowski eventually explained that he works by the sun and the shape of the mountain. A dynamite error of fifteen feet would not be noticed, he claimed. "One of Washington's eyes on Rushmore is five feet lower than the other, and nobody minds." He hasn't taken a measurement in some twenty-two years. Detailed specifications are contained in three books. "Mother has them! Any damn engineer can take it from there! But I don't know who in the hell would want to!"

Suddenly, a section of new hose blew apart at a coupling with explosive force, snaking and whooshing along the ground until limp. Quiet was at hand. "Is that a new coupling you're using?" he asked Adam. "No, sir," answered Adam, "an old one." Ziolkowski turned to mention that he bought the new hose at a bargain, two dollars a foot instead of four dollars. Casimir came from the compressor shack to report that a transformer had blown, possibly hit by lightning the night before. The compressors would not be worth operating. Ziolkowski assumed a pained expression.

"Well," he sighed, "let's get the nine going." He meant the Caterpillar D-9, the biggest bulldozer made.

"This is the son of a bitch I broke my Achilles tendon on last year. And I've been in misery ever since. The goddamn butcher that sewed me up! Wires are coming through the skin and everything. I should've gone to Boston!" The rain-soaked Cat would not start. "Adam, where's the can of ether? Use the ether on it, dear." He turned away to murmur, "At least Adam can start the Cats. Casimir cahn't even do that!" He lightened, and corrected himself, paternally. "Aw, they're good kids, really. They're good with the Cats and the dynamite. But the other stuff: nothing. No talent." Despite Adam's ether ministrations, the Cat would not start.

"You know, God, you're a good friend," Ziolkowski implored the sky as he banged his Jeep down the mountain for lunch, "but don't pour it on so much, okay?"

Lunch began with dry Beefeater martinis he mixed on a scale of ten-to-one. The vermouth bottle lasts several years that way. He took a deep swallow, leaned forward in his kitchen chair, and made a strange admission. "I gave up twice today," he said. No, he was told, he did not. "Oh, I'll get them going," he agreed quickly. Ruth entered with a tray of cheese, but could not stay for lunch. She was needed out on the floor. He passed a plate of dark Russian rye. "Do you like bleu cheese?" he asked. "Good. Have some." He mixed fresh martinis to go with the bread and cheese, and became expansive again, trying to explain just what it is that he is doing with his life. "I'm telling a story about a race of people who used to live here, and we destroyed. And it doesn't cost the taxpayer a fucking dime."

He grew to wondering why his lifetime job is never reviewed, but supplied his own explanation in the next moment. "I work for the public. I *do not* work for the critics." He poured more martinis, sipped a while, and sprang back catlike. "Aw, you can all go to hell. . . . I'm gonna win, anyway."

Ruth returned with the largest steak ever seen. It was from their own herd and was tender and delicious with vegetables fresh from the garden. This time Ruth could sit a minute. She picked up a fly swatter, and began combating the buzzing pests. The body count mounted steadily while she remained.

Casimir entered through the back kitchen door and stood at attention until his father looked up from his meal. "Harold took down the flagpole," Casimir announced as matter-of-factly as possible, suppressing a grin. Harold is Ziolkowski's mechanic. He used to have a machine shop in Custer but sold it. His retirement lasted for a year. He couldn't stand it, and came to work at the mountain.

The flagpole had been up since 1948. It was one of Ziolkowski's premier efforts. The sculptor took a long drink from his martini. "So you want to build a memorial to the American Indian?" he shrugged. "This whole goddamn thing is Keystone Kops."

A cuckoo clock erupted along the far wall, flinging open its miniature door for the spring-driven showoff within.

Ziolkowski asked for a bottle of liqueur. He settled on Chartreuse, and poured some. "I will not be whipped," he protested. "No way!" Ruth came back to say Johnny Cash and his wife were waiting in the bedroom-study. Ziolkowski said he didn't want to meet Johnny Cash. Ruth quietly stated that they had come a long way. He turned to his drinking partner to ask if he should go. Why not? he was answered. He turned back to Ruth and announced he would go only if his drinking buddy went, too. The pal argued that Cash was here to see the sculptor. Ziolkowski considered the options, then hammered a compromise. He would go meet Johnny Cash, and his pal would join them all later.

Later, a drunkard clutching a glass of sticky green liquid was led onto a patio. Mr. and Mrs. Cash rose. "This is John Cash?" she said, pointing to the Man in Black, but phrasing the introduction more like a question. "And I'm June Carter Cash?" The drunkard plopped into a chair, but in so doing, spilled some of his drink. He attempted to cover up by fumbling in pockets for his pack of cigarettes. The Man in Black observed these proceedings. He recognized the cigarette package, and acknowledged that he, too, once smoked that brand. "I smoked Picayunes for six years," he revealed in his familiar baritone.

The sculptor asked Cash, himself part Indian, whether he had felt anything when he first saw Crazy Horse. "Could you see him?" The Man in Black didn't hesitate. "Oh yeah," he replied, "I got full when I drove up that road a few minutes ago." Mr. and Mrs. Cash talked for a while about their own sizable family of seven children, about life on the road, and about where they were off to from here. The Man in Black stood. It was time to leave. He put his arm around Ziolkowski's shoulder. "Don't be discouraged," he advised. With that, they were away, plunging through the mass of bug-eyed tourists, who parted for them.

Ziolkowski decided he wanted to do a little more drinking with his pal, in the bedroom-study. "What do you think of Johnny Cash?" he wanted to know. He was pretty tall, the pal said. "Yeah," agreed Ziolkowski. "He must've been wearing boots." They drank some more, and soon the sun was setting. The sculptor claimed that not even his own wife and children understand the mountain. Nor could he even explain it himself. "I'm gonna get that mountain looking pretty goddamn good, though. I'm not gonna finish it. . . ."

Who, then?

"A mining engineer." He sounded positive of this. He

grew more pensive. "But I'm gonna work like a son of a bitch, and that thing is going to come out, and come out, and come out, and come out. . . ." He was perking up again. "You know what I'd really like to have? It would cost me about two million bucks. A laser beam! I could sit right down here and do it." He lifted his arms and took imaginary aim. "Boil that rock right straight through."

Outside, in the parking lot, a young tourist couple took a final look at the mountain. Their two children ran and skipped ahead of them. The man put his arm lovingly around his woman. "Just think," he ventured, "when our kids grow up and get married, they can come back and see it just like it is now." They laughed all the way back to their car, the remark so leveled them.

In the morning, the gold horse that is "colored by a unique and secret process" began the parade that opens Gold Discovery Days in Custer. The gold horse, marchers and rolling stock assembled at 9:00 A.M. over at the Flintstones' place, as they do every year, and proceeded down Rushmore Road, passing the town traffic light on schedule an hour later. The Angus Queen, the High School Rodeo Queen, the 4-H Queen and various other queens passed in review. Gubernatorial candidate LeRoy Hoffman drove a tractor in his business suit, and waved. The public address announcer noted the presence of "the usual historical, beautiful, religious and commercial entries." All the local Roadside Attractions entered floats, save for one. The Senior Citizens entered a float, as did the Black Hills Power and Light Company, the Historical Society and the Forestry Service. At the end of the line of march, 4-H members on horseback carried all fifty state flags. Custer is proud at having assembled the collection. And so they ask visitors to honk their Winnebagos as they hear their state called. The roar became deafening, worse even than twenty feet of steel biting into some mountain, more than enough to drive a soul right out of his cotton-pickin' Winnebago.

Oregon: Sometimes a Great Nation

This is my Stay-Out-of-Oregon piece. Bob Sherrill at New Times *asked me to do it but I can't remember why. The story is a chestnut. Almost every magazine in America had taken a crack. I couldn't understand why anybody would want another Oregon piece. But I didn't argue. I needed the money. I went to the San Francisco Public Library and checked the clips on all the Oregon pieces. Then I grabbed Tim Page, the battered and daft British war photographer, and we set out by car. Page had been to Oregon on a lecture tour a year before and was a font of useless information.*

We toured the state for a week, interviewing its people. What I remember most gladly is interviewing Governor Tom McCall and former Senator Wayne Morse back-to-back an hour apart. Seldom has this nation produced statesmen of their stature. Giants!

McCall's appointments secretary had scheduled me for fifteen minutes—that turned into well over an hour. Which was characteristic of McCall. We left Salem eventually and drove to Corvallis, where Morse, attempting to regain his Senate seat, was speaking. After the speech we sat down at a very small table and talked. He kept poking me on the hand with his index finger, emphasizing points. Very intimate man. I couldn't help but notice the little liver spots that had spread across his hands. Old age. Weeks later he was dead. I still keep his phone number. And I'm not sure why.

As per custom, I had trouble with Page. While I was interviewing McCall, Page suddenly stopped taking pictures and began asking questions of his own, damaging the rhythm and pattern I had established and ruining my train of thought. Page got an earful on the way to Corvallis. Why photographers behave thus is beyond my ken. Suffice to say, however, that they do. Years ago I realized that I had to let photographers know unequivocally that I am boss-of-assignment. To do this, one simply assumes a command presence and suggests: Keep your mouth shut during the interview! Understand? Not one peep! One peep and I snap your neck! Get it? They get it. Better believe they do. Writers in their secret hearts hate photographers. A photographer clicks his camera and then hands the film to someone for processing. A writer, meanwhile, is just beginning the hard part. The writer must sit down somewhere and attempt to make order out of chaos, sense out of nonsense. A nerve-wracking challenge.

After I filed this piece I reread all the others that had been done on Oregon and realized I had beaten silly every writer who had ever tried the assignment. It was a perfect feeling. Tim Cahill, I remember, was particularly impressed. He told me that I had written a story about nothing, had had the temerity to tell the reader up front that I was writing a story about nothing, and somehow had pulled it off.

The fancy of Norman J. Nibblett took wing one day four years ago. The unofficial mayor of unincorporated Lookingglass, Oregon, seized by the whimsies, installed a parking meter outside his store, the hub of his picayune community. The AP put the story on its state wire, then moved it on the national trunk. A manhole cover arrived in Lookingglass, compliments of the citizens of Cedar Rapids, Iowa. Tourists arrived to marvel at the meter and stuff it with nickels. Some became transfixed. Accommodating farmers sold five-acre plots and the population swelled to 450. There was talk of getting a post office. "I used to know everyone and now I don't know anyone," a Lookingglass lifer lamented.

Most of the newcomers are from California. "I want to keep them away," Mayor Nibblett recently said. So, he is running for Douglas County Commissioner to dam the boom and resolve the karma in his southern Oregon neighborhood.

Too late. All Oregon has become a magnet. And Oregonians have become positively xenophobic about the arrivals from the promised land. These people will do anything now to keep you out. They even send their governor around to say you wouldn't want to live there. If you come to visit, don't forget your passport, you're told. And your umbrella.

The 2.2 million ecology freaks who live there are reminded by their Highway Division to "thank Heaven we live in God's Country." But there's trouble in God's Country, a place that up till now did quite nicely, thank you, with twenty-one persons to the square mile. The growth rate is double California's and Oregon is the eleventh fastest-growing state. According to the U.S. Census Bureau, Oregon gained 134,000 new residents during the last three years (by comparison, New York, with the nation's lowest growth rate, gained 24,000) and if the present rate continues, the population will double in three decades.

Worse, Oregonians know that 29 percent of all Californians want to leave and that Oregon is first choice of these new seekers. The California Department of Finance confirmed this in May. The trend appears in statistics of driver's licenses swapped between the states. In the ten months prior to April, 18,873 Californians turned in their licenses to Oregon (5,184 Oregonians turned in their licenses to California).

Nightmares, then, of an avalanche; 7 million Californians salivating at the border; megatons of white flesh stomping the roses from Roseburg in the south clear up to the City of Roses, Portland; farting in the stillness of the wheatfields of the eastern plateau. No wonder the talk of a great plywood wall (Oregon produces 57 percent of the United States supply) eight feet high at the California border; no wonder the talk of hauling out Susquatch—Bigfoot, the legendary abominable who roams the forests.

Wherein the author slips across the border and gets his feet wet

"Welcome to Oregon," read the sign. It began to rain. Har-har, they were right about that much. Where's the fence? Maybe they take it down at night—you know, roll it up at nine o'clock? Har-har. Where's Bigfoot? A station wagon emblazoned with the CBS eye pulled up. Two men jumped out and started shooting film of the sign. We overnighted in Roseburg (population 14,530). The photographer ordered pan-fried oysters and got deep-fried prawns. He sneered and called the town Pick-Your-Noseburg. What matter. With martinis going for a dollar (you specify the brand), were we to quibble? (Oregon has no sales tax; everything is cheaper.) Recreation was in order after the long overland journey. Where's the dancing? "Live Music," the sign at Horsefeathers claimed. But "Harriet and Pappy" only play weekends, the new owner said. Is there any live music? "They got four colored guys playing across the street at the Roseburg Hotel, in the Rose Room." Blues in the night.

Rain in the morning. There's a town called Drain between Roseburg and Eugene. Annual precipitation there is thirty-four inches, nothing compared with the ten feet of rain that falls along the coast at Cascade Head.

Oregon's second city, Eugene, is the southern terminal of the Willamette Valley—don't say *Will*amette, stranger; Wil*lam*ette . . . and let us not discuss Oreg*one*. Nearly 70 percent of the people live along the Willamette River watershed on roughly 12 percent of the land. It is Oregon's heartland; to some, a Los Angeles in the making. Eugene's population was estimated at 81,000 three years ago, though City Councilman Neil Murray places it now at 91,000. It can be unpleasant in late summer when they burn the grass seed fields just north (most United States grass seed grows here) and the polluted air streams down the V-shaped valley into Eugene. A legislator lost his seat over the flap last election, which brought some satisfaction to a citizenry that practices a responsibility hard to find elsewhere, with the possible exception of New England. Eugene can also be pleasant. A derelict downtown was reclaimed as an enormous shopping mall for pedestrians only. Too bad they didn't put up more awnings, though. You have to stonewall it. Just go out and get wet.

"I would guess," Councilman Murray said in his ground floor corner office at the University of Oregon, where he is assistant dean of students, "Eugene has more meetings per capita than any other city I know." He traces the strong political climate to a strong rural tradition. Pioneers built Oregon 130 years ago with a bible and an ax. (A twenty-four-foot-tall gold-leafed pioneer, a Bunyan in hollow bronze, stands atop the capitol dome.)

"It comes out of the people," Murray, thirty-two, a transplanted Washingtonian, added. "Plus, we've got good leaders." He mentioned Neil Goldschmidt, mayor of Portland, at thirty-three the nation's youngest big city mayor; Tom McCall, the governor . . . ah yes, McCall; and Wayne Morse, the celebrated maverick, jettisoned from the fond embrace of the national collective unconscious in 1968 by paradoxical Oregonians after a quarter century in the U.S. Senate.

Betty Coed passed by outside, unmindful of the drizzle and the heart that skipped a beat behind windows. Mention was made of such pleasant surroundings. Dean Murray swiveled his chair and surveyed the river and greensward across the road, idyllic in the mist. "Yes, it is pleasant, isn't it. I guess you could say the message seems clear: Oregonians can look around and see that we have the life other people bemoan they've lost."

A duck waddled out of the river and along the lawn, then another, then a third. How long, dean, does it take to grow webs on your feet? Har-har, he said. How long does it take to get your lanolin up? Har-har, he said. No, no kidding, dean. . . . "You'll want to see a guy named Ron Abell for that, up in Portland. He's got all that information."

Eugene is also the home of the Oregon Ungreeting Card Company ("Last Year in Oregon 677 People Fell Off Their Bikes . . . And Drowned," etc.).

Caramba, what rain! Recently, they tell, an old-timer admonished the governor to "stop picking on Nixon and concentrate on stopping this rain." He probably could: walking on water ain't hard here. Say he's a strange sort, the governor. Not only goes around telling on Oregon, stirring up the outsiders, but campaigns—actually campaigns—for Democrats! Six-foot-five, too! Wears a size twelve shoe! Sumbitch might even be Bigfoot!

Containing a few remarks by the governor on "sagebrush subdivisions and coastal condomania."

For seven years this nominal Republican has given his neighbors easy access to the most open administration in Oregon history by regularly holding open house in his office, where informality is the rule (an estimated hundred thousand persons, individuals and groups, have visited him), and by holding town-hall sessions across the state to get his public's opinion. His morning staff conferences are open to the press. Open about his private self, too: wrote a Sunday piece for the Portland *Oregonian* last year ("My Head-on Confrontation with Cancer") after an operation for cancer of the prostate and a testicle; and went on TV with his son Sam to tell the story of Sam's addiction, what was done about it and of the prospects for a methadone program.

For all this, they love Tom McCall.

He was elected Oregon's thirtieth governor in 1966 by the largest vote ever cast and reelected in 1970 by almost the same margin. If Oregon law didn't prohibit a third consecutive term, he'd win again.

"No, he's in Georgia making a speech," said Deputy Press Secretary Gene Maudlin. "You can have him Thursday morning at eleven. You get fifteen minutes. The secretary will have to see your visa, of course."

Out speechifying again, huh . . . one could almost see the *Salem Capital Journal* editorial writers revving up: "McCall stayaway speeches draw more and ore attention to the state and in the end discourage no one"; karmic son of Lookingglass, of 7 million Losers hunkering at the California line.

In Georgia this day, McCall will be in agreement. "More people are coming just to see what it is we are trying to hide," he will tell the Garden Club of America in convention assembled. "It may be a great mistake to purposely attract more tourists to trample our environment into oblivion." That's right: stompin' on the roses, fartin' in the wheatfields. He will rail against "sagebrush subdivisions, coastal condomania and rampaging Willamette Valley suburbia" that mock Oregon's role as the national environmental model. He will also say the Oregon Story inspires people to believe they can influence the law-making process in their own states and will cite the bottle bill as an example, saying roadside litter has been reduced by 90 percent. Putting a price on the head of beer and soft drink containers works. "The bottle bill," he will say, "is a pivotal antidote, a key domino, for the national disease of over-consumption; having it in practice proves that we can have beautification, we can reduce solid waste and we can save energy by simple, practical measures. It takes four times as much energy to deliver drinks in an aluminum can as in a reusable glass bottle. This is an indictment of the throwaway society." (An economic impact study by two Oregon State professors shows the law has had no real effect on the cost of beverages and that it has created some 365 jobs for teamsters and handlers.)

McCall credits the legislature controlled by Democrats. "I wouldn't be able to do what I'm doing without an enlightened legislature," he often says. Together, they have enacted laws so progressive as to render all other states Victorian. The bottle bill, the bicycle bill (1 percent of highway funds are used to build bicycle ways) and the billboard removal bill are all national models. The cleanup of the Willamette River is hailed as "our ecological Easter" and salmon have been seen there after years of absence. Now there are plans for a Willamette greenway. The entire coastline is barred to developers. Last season they passed a law to open to the press all gatherings at which a legislative decision could theoretically be made—at a cocktail party, for instance.

The most divisive battle last session was not the bottle bill with its epic special interest lobby pressure, but the land use law in which all combatants were scarred. With Portland's suburban Washington County the nation's fastest-growing, and with supermarkets in the Willamette Valley being built over gravel beds needed to build supermarkets, something had to be done, McCall and the legislature insisted, despite the opposition of the state Grange and large landholding interests. So, land use is regulated by the state.

Nearly half the legislature was born in other states, as was McCall and half of Oregon's six-member congressional delegation. The age of state legislators was dramatically reduced during the past four years, from an average of fifty to forty-five. In 1969 only three of the eighty-nine members were under thirty. Today there are eleven. Four years ago none was under twenty-five. Now there are five. But it was a sixty-one-year-old Republican, Stafford Hansell, operator of the biggest hog farm outside of Poland, who successfully led the decriminalization of marijuana, another first-in-the-nation law. These days, if you're caught with less than ounce, you get a traffic ticket.

In which the reader is brought into communication with several natives

They *are* answering a different drummer, Dale Osborn, administrative assistant to the senate Republican leader and a Michigan native, agreed at the Black Angus, a politicians' hangout in Salem. "No tell what's going to happen at next year's session. Last year they passed a bill extending the territorial waters to two hundred miles. Because of Japanese and Russian mother-ship fishing. McCall vetoed it because it would be a joke to enforce. But they overrode it!"

Kitty, a Black Angus waitress, told the reporter to "write a terrible Oregon story." Well, your climate's terrible, anyway. "That's one of the things we've got going for us," replied the waitress, yet another California native. Toledo! Are there no Oregon natives? Writer Ken Kesey is one. Unfortunately, he was in New York.

"If you're pulling a trailer with California plates," Dale Osborn resumed, "the first question is, 'Where are you going in Washington?' " The only Californian they want, they just got: basketball's Bill Walton.

"Yes, sir," said Osborn, giving the matter more thought, "we could do it . . . we can sell lumber [the nation's number one lumber state since 1938] . . . shelter is no problem . . . food is no problem . . . we have more than enough hydroelectric energy [they sell it to California] . . . we've got oil shale for petroleum needs . . . we could be a little New Zealand. . . ."

The streets and gutters of Portland are always clean. The rain washes them. Smog from automobile pollution rolls in all summer long and the winter weather is not what you'd call chamber of commerce. Yet, she grows. There are now an estimated four hundred thousand residents and metro-Portland is thought to have 1.3 million. Some inspired high-rise architecture has gone up, but the danger of skyline overload is present. Contented inhabitants suggest a long and prosperous municipal run.

"You're just part of the string of people who drift through town doing the Oregon story," Todd Engdahl of the *Oregonian* said over coffee in Portland. "And the story you're after is about a mental attitude. Have you seen Ron Abell yet? Oregonians don't want the state to become like the rest of the country. By that," the California native asserted, "they mean California."

It rains, he said, relighting his pipe, from October to May.

Predator clouds muscled the trespassing sun as we left the restaurant. There is a rain tradition. Even the names of sports teams—the Ducks, the Beavers, the Storm—imply a liquid state.

Rain is the most important element in the arsenal of the James G. Blaine Society, a "vague but sinister" anti-growth force that grew like a "vicious amoeba" when revived two years ago by Ron Abell. In 1971, the Society's newsletter reports, the race track in Portland endured thirty-five consecutive days of rain or mud, a western record. The sun will rust you, the Society warns. All paper in Oregon is watermarked, it reveals. The Society originated in the 1940s, the creation of a Portland writer, Stewart Holbrook, who sought to glorify the 1884 Republican presidential candidate for never setting foot in the state. (Despite, or because of this, James Gillespie Blaine edged Stephen Grover Cleveland in Oregon, 26,860 to 24,604.) Now Abell's vehicle, the Society doesn't hesitate to unleash more alarming propaganda. Pass this ammunition, Abell tells members: The FBI says Portland's crime rate is higher than that of Chicago, Newark or St. Louis. And pass this: Oregon's second most communicable disease is gonorrhea; disease-carrying mosquitoes are rampant; in the last generation, more than fifty positive animal carriers of bubonic plague were located. And this: The biggest pile of radioactive waste in the world is stored along the Columbia River's banks.

The Oregon Motor Hotel Association frowns on Ron Abell. Tourism was down 15 percent last summer, according to the Highway Division, after years of increase. The decline was due mostly to the gasoline shortage. But the *Eugene Register–Guard* also attributes the drop to the Blaines and reports that a tourist bureau worker admitted, "We spent a lot of extra time talking to people from out of state to assure them that they were welcome, regardless of what they have heard or read." It looks, the *Register-Gūard* editorialized, like the time has come to bury James G. Blaine. Hoteliers hosanna'd.

Ron Abell was in a sour mood.

"I'm tired and I'm beat," said media's official state side show over the phone, declining an invitation to dinner. "And I'm tired of the Oregon story. It's been done by everybody and his dog. The national press has been on this for three years. Thirty major pieces have been done. It's been written up by everyone from the *New York Times* to the

L.A. *Times* to the *Denver Post* to papers in Ventura County, California. At the moment (that is, within the last three days) I've been contacted by a columnist for the Vancouver, British Columbia, *Sun,* the CBS affiliate in Sacramento, and the *Wall Street Journal* office in San Francisco. And they all want the same story. What if I said it doesn't exist—it's a media creation?"

Furthermore, he said, "I've disaffiliated myself from the Society because it stopped being a lot of fun for me. It took an awful lot of time and energy and it got very confused by the sorts of things that the governor says, that the Oregon Ungreeting Card Company does, and my role got very complicated. And I end up spending a lot of time not entertaining people but explaining myself. My attitude now is that this is just another place. There's not much coming in or going out. Somebody wanting an urban life would go bananas. I feel like I've been in a logging camp for a long time."

During dinner at Jake's Famous Crawfish, one of Portland's oldest eating establishments, Abell was told about the experience at the border, how it was raining on the other side of the Welcome to Oregon sign. "It's happened to me about ten times," he confided. "Typically, it's forty degrees, overcast and drizzling."

A newspaperman turned free lance, the "seems" ever coiled, clamping his teeth in vise fashion around the filters of his cigarettes. He is a native of Los Angeles who fled that urb sixteen years ago at the age of twenty-five when he determined megalopolis was amok. He thinks Oregon has passed the point of no return, too, and talks of leaving. But he can't go home again because, like the lyric says, Look What They've Done to My Song, Ma.

A beautiful woman dined at a nearby table, unmindful of the heart that skipped a beat a few feet away. "She's a professor at Mount Hood Community College," helpful Abell disclosed. "She's from Kansas City." You know her, huh? "Yeah." Small town this, Bob, the headwaiter, was kind enough to tender her the reporter's card and compliments.

Bob is thirty-four, a Phoenix native, and hit Portland four years ago, up from San Francisco, part of the perpendicular migration. It was the best move he ever made, he said. What is it about Oregon that causes him to stay? "Just the people themselves, I guess you could say. They're outgoing and friendly. The people of Portland are the nicest I've ever met. I don't know why, but there's a warmth here I've never found anywhere else." Portland is a good, wide-open town, he said. Portland even has the baths, he said. Anything goes. Yet, the law forbids Bob from bringing us our cocktails, he said. Beer or wine, yes. But for cocktails, he must summon a waitress. The reporter's notebook became impossibly martini-stained, rending futile further interviewing of Ron Abell under the circumstances. We resumed at the motel with a tape recorder.

Concerning the strange and wondrous growth of the Blaine Society

"The story began when I wrote an article in 1970 for *Old Oregon*, the University of Oregon alumni magazine, explaining the James Blaine Society. The article appears and somehow it gets from Eugene, Oregon, to Los Angeles—to Jack Perkins of NBC News. And he comes up on a hot August summer day and says, 'Where's your raincoat?' I said, 'What do you mean?' and he says, 'We're going to do this number under the garden hoses.' And then the piece appeared a month later and Brinkley closed the show with it and gave one of his little laughs, you know—that one only he can give. And then my phone started ringing. People wanting to know how they can join the Blaine Society. Well, there is no Blaine Society, I said. A lady called from Aspen, Colorado. How can we start one here? How can we affiliate? This kind of thing. I got trapped. I got sandbagged, really. Then AP put my picture on the national wire. I'm leaning against a stop sign and it ran in hundreds of papers. And about that time the *New Republic*, Peter Barnes, did a story. Then came the *Washington Post* and the *Christian Science Monitor* and *Newsweek* and everybody."

Ron has role-played for every network, including the educational one.

"Okay, meanwhile, McCall is making a lot of noise and Oregon gets the reputation of being a most progressive state. And it is such a crazy place, by the way," he said in aside, allowing the last phrase to tumble slowly, emphatically. That's right: a blues band in Roseburg.

"By mid-1973 the national media picked up on the story in its entirety. Basically, what they say is . . . they come here and say Oregon is paradise, it's Eden, and McCall is a wonderful governor, and this is the only place to live, and there's one freak who runs around saying don't come. That's me. I usually get one graph. *Time* gave me a footnote. They drag me out of the closet and always tag me onto the story as kind of an appendage.

"Actually, I never said stay away. What I say is, before you go and write your story, because you saw the rainbow and you saw a wave come in, don't write your story based on that. I'm saying, imagine what it would be like to live here. This is the story that I think people ought to be writing. As far as I'm concerned, I think it's past time for some revisionist to take a look at what Oregon really is. The climate is the worst you'll find because of the rain and the clouds all the time. We don't have a major university and we don't have any of the amenities of urban life. People go around saying *Hair* was here! *Mame* was here! You know, it's three years later. The press is not good. We have bad TV and paper. It's hard to find anything out. The inflow and outflow of ideas is less here than it would be in any decent city. The schools are okay but not great. The employment picture here is probably slightly worse than in the rest of the country.

"So, I say is this the kind of place where you want to live? And if a guy says, 'Yeah, because my wife and I got mugged last night in Manhattan on our way home and I don't want a fractured skull for anything,' well, I guess you could be happy in Oregon. But you've got to ask yourself whether what you've got is worth trading for Oregon."

"It's got nice scenery compared to some places. It's a relatively empty place, rural and agricultural, basically, with only one city in the whole state, which is up on the Washington border. For people with a pastoral frame of mind who want to get some R & R, or go on vacation, it's a nice place to come, you know? In the summer the popular places are crowded, but most of the year you can get into the parks and camps and go to the mountains or ocean . . . all this. It isn't paradise and it's not purgatory. I think from a lot of points of view it's got more minuses than pluses. You know, I'm going to leave. . . . I'm thinking I might leave one of these times. It's not because it's something I don't like. I'm tired. I feel like I'm in a run. Like I told you, I feel like I've been in a logging camp for sixteen years. And I think this attitude would get to some. The funny thing is the reporters who've been out here are sophisticated city people and they're the ones who get suckered by this. . . ."

In the morning the photographer considered the rainscape. "You need *high speed* Ektachrome here," he muttered. "There's never enough light."

At last the reader learns of the governor's birthplace

McCall awaited our pleasure. Oregonians felt they knew Tom McCall personally when they elected him in 1964 to their second most powerful office, secretary of state (no lieutenant governor), for he had spent years in their living rooms as Lawson McCall, political commentator for KGW-TV in Portland. He metamorphosed into Tom when he first sought political office in 1954. The name change, they say, backfired. He was called a phony and Portland's ten-term congresswoman, Mrs. Edith Green (born in South Dakota), was able to beat him silly in her own maiden congressional campaign.

McCall was born March 22, 1913, in Egypt, Massachusetts, and spent his first eight years there on his maternal grandfather's thousand-acre South Shore estate. He likes to point out, though, that he was conceived in Oregon and was reared from the fourth grade at the same granddad's ranch near Prineville, in the center of the state. His mother, an extraordinary woman, went to Oregon as a twenty-two-year-old bride but always returned to her native South Shore to give birth. Today, Mrs. Dorothy Lawson McCall, age eighty-five, is a political power in her right. She wrote her first book *(Ranch Under the Rimrock)* five years ago and two years later published her second *(Copper King's Daughter)*, about her father, Tom T. Lawson, a wealthy financier and sometimes muckraking author *(Frenzied Finance)*. McCall's paternal grandfather, Samuel W. McCall, publisher of the *Boston Advertiser* (defunct), was for twenty years a member of Congress, a three-term Massachusetts governor and a contemporary of Honey Fitz, storied Boston mayor.

The governor graduated from the University of Oregon in 1936 with a degree in journalism and knocked about in the trade most of his life. His "Pollution in Paradise," about the Willamette River, was named an outstanding TV documentary in 1962 by Sigma Delta Chi, the national journalistic society. Newsman at heart, he enjoys being unofficial pool man for the press at governors conferences and likes to tell a Spiro Agnew story: "Tom," he quotes the former vice-president as saying at a GOP governors conference, "you couldn't have said this! You're quoted here as saying I gave a rotten, bigoted, little speech last night!" To which

McCall remembers answering: "I'm not positive I used the word 'little.' " The terrible thing, McCall continues, was that none of the other governors laughed. "I was all set until then to be the chairman of the next conference, but my candidacy suddenly disappeared."

Most of the national attention McCall receives is for his environmental work. He alerted Oregonians to the energy problem by establishing the nation's first gasoline rationing program and reduced the speed limit to 55 mph before anyone else (last August). He banned outdoor lighting, cut back temperatures, eliminated hot water and air conditioning in state buildings and put janitorial work on a daytime basis. "It takes six hundred pounds of coal to provide the energy to operate one sixty-watt bulb for a year," he said. "Turn off that bulb!" He gave up his Lincoln Continental for an Audi during the gas crisis.

He is back in the Lincoln now and the lights are on again.

The hot TV lights of the CBS team from Sacramento went on in the governor's large, ceremonial office.

". . . Congress, they're all highly intelligent, articulate people. There's a preconception of whether the president is guilty or not. Right now. So, if they impeach him, and the Senate follows through, the people are gonna say, what do you expect, anyhow? It's a Democratic Congress and a Republican president. And if they don't impeach him, a lot of people are gonna say he acted so suspiciously I'm not gonna trust him anyway. We could have a long, drawn-out trial that isn't gonna prove anything. So, that's why I favor resignation, or a swap between the president and the vice-President. You could eliminate that part of the president the people don't trust, which more than half of the people don't trust, and put him in charge of foreign policy with Henry Kissinger, which is the thing most people in the United States says he does very well, in all the polls. And then Gerald Ford could come on as president. He's not a brilliant tactician, or a brilliant diplomat, or a brilliant politician, but he is honest and he does have dignity and a certain amount of ability. I think in that way we could get the nation going again and get unhung up on Watergate. . . ."

He was saying this to school kids—little ones, eight, nine years old. The pieties noticeable by their absence. The man, it seems, just doesn't know how to talk down to people.

A child is asking him if he wants to be president.

"I'm sort of testing myself to see if I could move around the nation and still do this job. Or run on the basis not really of being a full-fledged candidate, because I couldn't get the nomination of my party. My party is much more conservative in its apparatus than I am. Just like the Democratic Party is much more liberal than its rank and file. I come from a party whose state and county chairmen overwhelmingly favor Governor Reagan for the presidency. Would not even spit on me. We would move ahead as an independent, maybe. Cuz we are independent. Most people in Oregon *are* independent. They're free thinkers. And most people, according to the Gallup and Harris polls, feel that the political parties aren't doing their job. Frank Mankiewicz, who is really very good tactician and politician, even though he had a debacle with George McGovern . . . . Frank Mankiewicz said that a guy like Tom McCall is a strong contender who could bust down the middle and win all the marbles. So, God help us all. I'm not ready for that and I sure don't want to do it. But we're going to bust down the middle and talk sane and make sure the right people give the right answers to the right questions and that's good enough for me. I don't think I'll ever be elected to anything else. . . . I might run for governor again, though . . . someday. . . ."

Mentioning Mankiewicz in front of prepubescents? Finally, has this man no sense of decency!

The governor's working office adjoins the ceremonial

one. It is walnut paneled and larger than a phone booth. It overflows with memorabilia. There is a yellowed, autographed baseball, an old, deflating football, a model of the *Thomas W. Lawson*, reputedly the only seven-masted clipper ship ever built. When the tallest governor in the nation sits here, the room seems very small.

"This darn thing about going around and telling the Oregon story, I mean this isn't fatuous," he is saying to his guest. "Their comments are very revealing about what people want: I mean, you get the same reaction from the board of directors of John Deere, or J. C. Penney, as you get out of Stanford. They're awfully tired of BS . . . they really are. I went down there and talked to their communications course. . . . Just a minute . . . Doris! Hey, Doris!"

"Yes, sir," answered a woman in the next room.

"Do you have a copy of Lyle's letter, Nelson's?"

He has the long jaw, this man, and the broad vowels of the brahmin Yankee. The way he looks and talks, could as likely be a Saltonstall or a Worcester or a Forbes sitting there.

"You might be interested in . . . let's see, what'd I think was good. . . . I gave a good speech to the Commonwealth Club, which is a pretty fancy outfit. I called for Nixon's resignation in front of that conservative group and I got a standing ovation. I . . . that's quite a speech and really gave it with . . . my heart."

Doris appeared with the Stanford letter. It contains comments by students after McCall lectured. One anonymous collegian remarked that McCall "has a personal touch; has sincerity; his enthusiasm reminds you of an American spirit that once was."

McCall took advantage of Doris's presence. "You might just haul that Commonwealth Club speech out. If that's all right. Is that all right, Doris?"

"Oh, yes," replied Doris, and returned to the files.

"Oh! Another you might like is the speech I made in March in Idaho for Governor Andrus." McCall tells this story: "I kept seeing one of the Republican governors looking at me in a mournful way at the last national governors conference, so I asked him if it was because I was going to Idaho to campaign for Cecil Andrus. He said it was, so I said don't you like Cecil? And he said, oh, no. He's the nicest guy there is. But he's a Democrat! This, to me, is an indictment of politics. Issues are more significant than party labels."

Governor, you made reference to Frank Mankiewicz when you were talking to the school kids. . . .

"Hey, Doris!" Too late. She was out of earshot. "I'll get you that interview with Mankiewicz. They ask him how about McCall running *with* Rockefeller and he says McCall is the real Rockefeller . . . sure, yeah, Rockefeller no longer is, you know, he isn't. . . . Want to see that interview?" Sure, yeah.

A peek into the file marked "Presidency"

"Yup," he says. "Say, a letter of Bill Moyers's you might want to see. He says McCall is absolutely my candidate in seventy-six. Let me get you that one."

McCall has a bulging file marked "Presidency."

Doris returned with the material. McCall asked her to fetch the Moyers quote. Which she did. McCall reread the letter. "Don't embarrass him any, but this is true. He [Moyers] and I both have a great mutual friend. His name is Osgood Nichols, who's a helluva PR man in New York and Washington. As a Harvard student, came out to the ranch to pitch hay. My dad used to have . . . he's an old Harvard man. . . . And so Moyers wrote him November 28, 1973. And then he wrote me."

McCall began to read aloud. " 'McCall is my candidate for President in 1976 irrespective of his party, a man of singular integrity, with his ideals intact, although he moves neatly in the confines of pragmatism.'

"Isn't that a helluva piece of writing? Mmm-mmmmmm," he added in a coda of satisfaction, the way Sidney Greenstreet might have.

But will you chase the nomination even though, as you say, the party apparatus is against you?

"Oh, God, no. I'm not going to demean and besmirch myself to try to capture it." He seemed genuinely aghast at the thought, the way patrician pedigree ought to be.

"What I'll probably do is, the thing closest to my heart ever since I heard of it, was . . . some officials from Oregon State came in to see me and said how about an endowed chair, the distinguished chair of electronic journalism and government? The Governor Tom McCall, the former governor. . . . So I would teach on a nine-month contract, that is, if the thing goes through. It's almost consummated. I believe it would be a great object lesson, a great experiment, for the full professor teaching the course to be a candidate for president. . . . Because I think all the artificial barriers that we've run into that inhibit somebody from running . . . he's gotta look like and sound like Ronald Reagan. But he can't win if he does! But he can't get nominated unless he does! This sort of thing."

What happened to the eight-foot plywood wall that you're supposed to have down at the border? It wasn't there. . . .

"Hah!" he said. "California people, once they're established in Oregon, want an eighty-foot fence! They're absolutely the most isolationist people you'd ever want to meet, once they get in here. God, you'd think Oregonians are fierce! Transplanted Californians are absolutely paranoid about letting anybody else in. It's funny.

"But this whole thing is as serious as I can make it. It's gotta be tongue-in-cheek when you say, okay, visit us but don't, for heaven's sake, move in. That's as far as you can go. It's gotta be light. Some people have told me they felt they were being turned on by Oregonians. So what happened to western hospitality? What is this strange sound coming from someone who must indeed be the personification of western hospitality as the chief host of the state of Oregon? It's the toughest line to follow . . . you're darn right. It's really a tough position because you insult people, alienate people, even though all the reasons for their not being wanted are impersonal. And all the reasons lie in the fact that in too many cases what they came to enjoy is dead. And that's the whole damn thing."

That's the message?

"Yup."

Governor, your mother said she wanted to run for governor to keep the seat warm for you, sort of like Lurleen Wallace did, until you could run again four years later.

"She finally . . . she just . . . she's screwing everything else up. The night before the filing deadline in April she issued a statement that she was satisfied that the candidates in the field were going to carry out her views. So she wasn't at age eighty-five going to 'get in the muck of politics.' But she can absolutely be the most destructive person . . . even after not running! After withdrawing! She's going to make an endorsement that is gonna screw up politics for the next twenty years. [Laughter] And I mean it. God, how do you get her to endorse someone *after* the primary. She's that powerful a figure! She's a feisty old girl. So, how do you handle her? If I said, Mother, for God's sake, don't run, why she'd probably be running for the White House. She's a contrary old girl. Yes, indeed."

The tiny office filled with aides. It was noon. Our scheduled fifteen minutes had dissolved into an hour. They wanted to spirit him away. But the conversation was now about newspapering and McCall was telling how it all began. "God, jobs were hard to get. But a friend of mine wrote from Idaho on a paper there, the *Moscow Star-Mirror*, and so I went over there for about five years and got into the greatest newspaper fight you ever saw. There was a guy named Dr. Frank B. Robinson, who had a mail-order religion called Psychiana, and he turned Moscow from a third-class post office into a first-class one, this was such a tremendous mail-order religion. So the *Star-Mirror* was the only publishing house in town and they doubled the price of his printing. So he says you sonsabitches, I'll fix you. I'll run my own printing press and my own paper. So we had the greatest training ground you ever saw. Two daily papers in a town of seven thousand!"

The aides fidgeted. It was time to go. McCall rose from his chair. Jesus Christ! Look at those brogans!

With McCall, there always seems to be time for one more question. Governor, are you Bigfoot?

He stared down at his feet. A smile crept up his face. "No," he said. "I don't think there is a Bigfoot. But if you see him, tell him he's welcome to visit but not to stay."

Leaving the capitol, Ron Schmidt, the press secretary, mentioned the governor would lead a rattlesnake hunt that afternoon on the state house lawn.

The CBS man raced for the phone.

"And make sure you tell the truth about the weather!" Schmidt called to the departing figure.

Wherein the author bids a fowl farewell to a liquid state

There was supposed to be a secession going on over at Otter Rock, dubbed Cape Foulweather by Captain James Cook. Secession within secession, a fitting end. Our informant erred. It turned out to be one man's secession, unsupported. The layover was Newport, the nearest town of consequence. The photographer said he was too tired to go out for a few cold ones. The reporter was on his own. Leaving one oceanside tavern that night, he spied huge footprints in the sand. Bill Walton? At another place he heard a combination country-mariachi band. A lumberjack there, after long minutes on the dance floor and out of breath, nevertheless allowed he'd "stay around for another mess." All the taverns displayed Loyalty Day signs, a big deal in Newport. Not the place for this agent.

The sun was out in the morning. Last day. We watched a solitary bicyclist pedal for miles along the shoreline near Dunes City. Well, whaddya wanna do? the photographer was asked. Wanna go find Lookingglass and stuff some nickels in the meter? Naw, he said. Let's go buy some cooked crabs and get a few cold ones and sit some place. We chose Siltcoos Lake. A fisherman worked the end of the boat ramp. Some folks pulled up in a Winnebago, then left. The fisherman departed. Then there was solitude, plain and simple. Just the sound of crab shells cracking, just the smell of crab juices dripping from hands. A duck waddled out of the lake toward us. Then a brace. Soon, many brace of ducks, nay, a nuisance of ducks. Surrounded. Throw them some meat! screamed the photographer. They wanted more. They wanted it all. Let them have it all! he shouted. We fled. Mugged by ducks.

"She flies with her own wings"—

Oregon Territory Motto

The Carnival of Crusader-Quacks

This is the piece that nearly did in David Felton when he was at the Los Angeles Times. *Born and raised in Pasadena, and with inner knowledge of the workings of the Tournament of Roses, he had no trouble pitching the idea for a series to his editors. They placed him on detached assignment. Felton spent the next eight months researching. When the time came to put it together he couldn't. Which is how Felton earned the nickname The Stonecutter at the L.A.* Times. *And it is how monumental writer's block came to be known in the craft as Felton's Disease. The only way he got this story off his back was by resigning from the staff. He soon went to work for* Rolling Stone *and moved to San Francisco. Years later he still had all his research sitting around in crates in our flat. One day he proposed to Jann Wenner that the Pasadena story would be perfect for me. I was coming off a great success with my San Francisco Red Sox pieces at the time and was, as they say, hot again.*

My endeavor did not win the praise of Paul Scanlon, then the managing editor; though Felton and Tim Cahill fought for it. Wenner never bothered to read it (he was in the process of moving the operation to New York and was spending all his time there) and I wound up with another kill fee. Once more I was becoming the undisputed King-of-the-Kill-Fee. I offered it to Lewis Lapham at Harper's *and he said he loved it . . . but was having some difficulty deciding how to use it until Peter McCabe, who was trying to revive* Harper's Weekly, *walked into Lapham's office, picked the piece off the desk, started reading, and declared he wanted it for the* Weekly. *Lapham was only too happy to be rid of it. The piece led to another assignment. McCabe asked me to cover the 1976 Republican Convention in Kansas City. All was arranged: credentials, reservations, plane tickets, expense money. I was about to leave for the airport when the phone rang. It was McCabe, telling me the* Weekly *was dead.*

> *"The Tournament of Roses is like nothing else under the sun. It can be compared to no military or civil pageant. It is a fiesta impossible to accomplish anywhere else in the world. It is unique; it is Southern Californiaesque; it is Pasadena's New Year's gift to mankind, and it is worthwhile."*
>
> from a 1913 Santa Fe Railroad brochure

Yeah, it's all of the psychobabble in that blunt summary; it's also the meeting ground of Babbitt and Costello, and a ton of plop dropped on boulevards in two hours by 272 horses.

In all, I spent ten days in the smooth clutches of the Tournament of Roses Association, an enduring organization of nearly fourteen hundred men whose sole avowed purpose is to put on a parade and a football game every January first. They could sleepwalk through their annual caper, so refined are the details. Even as I arrived, two days before Christmas, all the bleachers were up. In fact, the whole enchilada was in place: We can count on this after eighty-seven years of such goings on.

They were wary at first of my observations of them in their natural habitat, but shed their suspicions after a time, or appeared to, and permitted me to approach. I was allowed to study their activities, to mark their dos and don'ts. I witnessed them in their abiding places. On occasion, a few acted friendly toward me.

Their history is not without controversy, however, and is marred by the frequent flowering of a recidivistic strain in their body genetic; a robust and energetic strain that thrusts undeniably upward in a mysterious way—as if directed from without!—until it emerges into the cathedrals of power, having suffered in its quest little or no opposition from the generally docile majority, and remains there unconfronted—indeed, abetted—by the silence, until final reward. Carriers of this strain are characterized not only by this marked urge to show the way, but by an irresistible impulse to "tell it like it is." Advanced carriers always manifest this pronounced tendency to know what's best, and are known to take matters in hand, stopping at nothing to get their way. For purposes of classification until a more formal study is undertaken, I will label carriers of this strain crusader-quacks, after the manner in which they operate.

Playing anthropology is but way of preamble.

Yet, when we apply other disciplines, the Tournament shreds into the same dope. Viewed as antic behavior, we see reflected the passage of dingbatry to sublime heights. Inspected in its rose-colored light, we find public-spirited fellows suggesting their community pride and well-being as they portray their version of America. This is false light, for in it we do not see the rest of America. In such vain aspect, they become self-appointed custodians of Americanism, planting seeds and dabbling in manipulation of the senses; and we see the thorn that pricks at the soft rose underbelly.

Would you believe the thorn is stroking the rose? It is almost as if the Tournament is hustling gospel with mirrors. Like the illusionist covering up his act, these merchants of a troubled dream will use whatever cosmetic necessary. They camouflage the taint, dealing, as it were, from behind potted palms. But they are serious in their ephemeral business. There is much at stake in containing the citizens in awe, lest they fade to the side of the restives.

Their true calling, they fancy, was to build a house in which to observe the playing of football once a year; and to paint a five-and-one-half-mile pink line down the middle of Orange Grove and Colorado boulevards over which some sixty floral vehicles, twenty-two marching bands, and all those horses tread. When done, they repair to Tournament House, once the mansion of chewing gum tycoon William Wrigley, gratified at having brought joy to an estimated 125 million viewers. Then, they hibernate briefly before boosting up the torque for another go at a more perfect parade, aiming for a better sameness. That is all they do: put on a parade and a football game, and promote patriotism. Which is well and good, except that the Little Old Lady in Tennis Shoes (a most dreadful symbol for a city) isn't what she used to be; nor is her uncle, Sam.

In the infancy of the world's greatest floral spectacle, the Tournament had to send a committee around the country to solicit entries. Now, there is a committee that politely turns down the more than two hundred applicants for the six-or-so float and four band vacancies each year. It is not unusual for would-be participants to wait five years in a fierce competition wherein names of mayors, governors and celebrities are invoked.

The Tournament is now beamed by satellite around the world. Today, floats cost an average of twenty-five thousand dollars . . . cheap at the price: For this investment, corporations like Western Airlines or Rand-McNally get a minimum five-second exposure over two networks before one of the largest TV audiences of any year. The evangelist Aimee Semple McPherson raised eyebrows in 1925, long before TV, by spending four thousand dollars on her Angelus Temple float, but she knew a value. Los Angeles Mayor Tom Bradley, unlike the priestess, felt the high cost of float construction was a waste of money, and tried to withdraw from the 1974 parade. A delegation visited city hall and told Bradley it might be a long time before Los Angeles could get back in. What an embarrassment to your city not to be in the 1976 Bicentennial parade. Bradley yielded.

Under-financed entries these days are asked to drop out or rotate with other strapped weaklings. Bands pay their own expenses, which may run between $25,000 and $40,000. Equestrians spend about $1,000 per entry to ship, feed, and stable their stock, which alone is said to be worth $1.75 million, and they invest an average $3,000 in silver trappings (a parade requirement) per horse. The motorized floats are said to be valued at $2 million, and their garlands of the world's rarest, most exotic and most expensive flowers are said to be worth $250,000. Seven firms bid for contracts in the year-round construction of these festooned fantasies. Andy Anderson of Fiesta Floats may not be kidding when he says he's going bananas because ninety thousand orchids didn't arrive today from Hawaii, and that this could spell the difference between profit and loss if he has to hunt elsewhere.

The first Rose Bowl game in 1902 made money with gate receipts of $4,000. Today, the game brings in $4 million. NBC alone coughs up half that figure for TV rights. For that kind of cash, NBC can and does interrupt game action by dictating unscheduled time-outs to sell advertising. And sponsors get a fine return on their investments: This year's game between Ohio State and UCLA attracted 71,750,000 TV viewers, according to Nielsen data, making it the most-witnessed college football game in history, and the second most-witnessed sports event ever, exceeded only by the seventh game of the 1975 World Series. Of today's $4 million annual sales, 85 percent normally goes to the Big Ten and Pacific Eight (the two conferences represented in the Rose Bowl game) and the Tournament splits the remaining 15 percent with the Pasadena city treasury. In years earmarked for stadium improvements, the colleges' take is cut to 75 percent. The split with the city comes after expenses are deducted, and the annual surplus is placed in a trust fund jointly administered with the city. It is used by the Tournament for capital improvements.

Our natural human desire to be part of a tribal success only partly explains why so many willingly contribute fifty thousand man-hours of labor a year. A more likely reason is the self-awareness that one may be an everyday palooka, yet receive powerful ego massage as a Tournament big wheel.

Some say they are members because the Tournament is a neat way to relieve life's ongoing pressures: pure fun with nothing serious at stake. (In advancing this, they are fond of quoting pop futurist Alvin Toffler, who states in *Future Shock* that pageants provide a cushion, a sanity-preserving continuity, against the social fragmentation wrought by overindustrialization.) Some join for personal reasons. One novice admitted cheerfully during lunch that he is in it to make career points: his boss is chairman of a Tournament committee. Like other sly newcomers accumulating business or social connections, he readily spent $150 out-of-pocket for the obligatory white suit, white shoes, and rose-and-white official necktie that members don at dawn each New Year's Day.

To succeed in this society of professed funsters a man must be on the make. If the Tournament is not at least his year-long obsession, he can't advance; and there's a long list of screened applicants waiting to sign on. The novice begins by guarding a sawhorse New Year's Eve on some freezing street corner. He must be totally committed to guarding his barricade. He is graded in his work, and if he guards well, is appointed to a committee. The reward is a better committee assignment each year. If he misses one meeting too many, or performs below par in his chairman's eyes, he is subject to a discreet expulsion: The bill for his annual dues simply is not mailed out. As it is, 90 percent of the members pay their ten to twenty-five dollars within four days of receiving notice. (The dues pay for the upkeep of Tournament House.) At the top are the gerontocrats: the twenty-five-member board of directors and, within that, the ten-member executive committee, the policy-making power elite. Having achieved all this, one is assured of the presidency in nine years—the immediate past president sits on the executive committee—or less. (In 1971, less than an hour after being installed, John J. Cabot died of a heart attack in Tournament House. Vice-president Virgil J. White became president a year ahead of schedule. White's first order of business was to name Lawrence Welk his grand marshal.)

Highest holy day in their calendar is, of course, the annual New Year's show-off, but crusader-quacks congress year-round.

The first important muster is in late December. Black-tied men and their gowned women assemble in the Pasadena Civic Center Auditorium. Values float in the air on that night. A point of view is reintegrated. In the pit, the Tournament Orchestra commences a "Medley Americana," and soon we will behold majesty: the coronation of the 1976 rose queen, the luck of 754 local aspirants, Anne Elizabeth Martin. It is very heady, this sweet smell of self-appreciation.

Backstage, a square-dance group called the Liberty Assembly loosens thighs and threatens to entertain shortly. Off to a side, the six princesses—and, hey, they've got another black one this year!—and their queen rehearse inspirational lines. Nearby, a pilgrim to Pasadena, tuxedoed and feeling at peer (boob that he is), though somehow at sea in all this goodness, listens to a Tournament man, a member of the prestigious queen and court committee, one of thirty-four standing committees within this volunteer, but private, white world.

"This whole thing," suggests the committeeman of the nubiles in his charge, "is for them." Get off it, you old coot, the pilgrim wanted to challenge, we're here for far more than the ritual crowning of a wholesome teen . . . but was pre-empted when a second codger approached, patted one of the girls on the rump, and declared, "Let's go. You're on." (Appointment to this committee is not lightly achieved. It takes years for a prospect to be nominated, and then only after a most rigid morals inspection. The Tournament is discreet and does not want just any oaf patting the girls' fannies. "One time on a TV show," the 1959 queen, the former Pamela Prather, recalled of her clucking chaperones in an interview two years ago, "they told me to stay away from Tennessee Ernie Ford because he was supposed to be a dirty old man. Can you believe that? Tennessee Ernie Ford?") Just as well, though, not to gainsay. Be a good guest. When in the lion's den, permit the lion to lick-shine his coat with self-congratulatory spittle. Don't escalate. Under scrutiny, they're liable to get grouchy. You can't argue with success. They've got a tradition, perhaps an institution, going. Far from dead, it thrives.

The Tournament seems forever to remain in its salad days. It is the most-photographed event in the world, and Kodak dresses hundreds in full clown drag to hawk film. One might think the record number of queen contestants was set in some bygone day, that fewer girls of today would be interested, but not so: the record was broken two years ago when 858 girls between the ages of seventeen and twenty-one tried out from twenty-two Pasadena-area schools.

Through gelatine filters the Civic Center stage is bathed icy blue, the Liberty Assembly gone without encore. To the microphone comes Carl E. Wopschall, Pasadena attorney and the Tournament's vice-president, who, barring calamity, ascends in rote maneuver to the 1977 presidency. Too bad for Wopschall, though, for this year is *the* year, the Bicentennial year, and the 1976 Tournament of Roses is the official first event of this nation's two-hundredth anniversary, so designated by the American Revolution Bicentennial Administration, which was created by Congress to supervise the cornpone. The Tournament is pleased to have been accorded the official kickoff, and has selected a special theme to go with the honor: America, Let's Celebrate! The theme is always the same, however. The variation this year was reportedly chosen from three thousand slogans submitted. Now, Wopschall is testing our fiber: "What if there were one sunset every twenty years? Suppose there were only ten seashells on earth? How much would they be worth? And yet, how many Americas are there on earth?"

How many Americas could one stand at this rate? This first day of pilgrimage long since had stamped itself sullen. First omen was an abused Hertzacar—but was nothing compared with the innkeeper's terse greeting: "Oh yes, I just threw your reservation in the wastebasket. Fifteen minutes ago." The fact that I carried documents confirming arrangements made no difference. And why? Because the travel agency had not prepaid the four days of premium rates gouged around New Year's. (Regular rate was $14; the days of roses, $32 . . . part of the estimated $8 million flowing into town each New Year's.) Pasadena's three major hotels are booked months in advance. This motel, the travel agency insisted, was the best that could be had.

Actually, I could not see my disputatious host, standing as I was outside in the unseasonably hot noonday, separated from the disembodied voice by a thick security window that accepted the sun's glint, then hurled it back full into my own face. All that I could occasionally glimpse was a sky-blue golfing cap bobbing and weaving behind the plate glass. Not only was the voice unincorporated, it was metallic: It conducted itself through loudspeakers in the parking lot, a strange and stereophonic oracular golfing cap. At its mandate, I slid a twenty-five-dollar cash deposit through an inch-high opening under the glass divide, in the general direction of the bobbing blue, and was shown to a room. The innkeeper with the metallic voice revealed himself as a jumpy sixty-year-old, the gaunt fruit of some apparent dust bowl breed.

The dungeon had a nice black-and-white TV, a miniature bar of soap, and a paper bath mat proclaiming California a four-season wonderland. On the bath mat were depicted a trout angler, a goggled downhill skier and a bathing beauty in a tank suit beneath a parasol. The bath mat also carried a nifty suggestion: that it be taken as a souvenir. I showered and, at length, dried myself with the single available towelette, a mill-end remnant that I could not draw around my body; drops of water blotting my souvenir. Then, for half an hour, I tried to make phone calls, obtaining only busy signals. I could not even reach the front desk, so went there in person.

"Oh, you're not doing anything wrong," admitted the golfing cap. "I'm not letting you make any calls, that's all."

Submitting to a second Delphic command, I slid twenty dollars through the tiny opening to purchase some calls.

"Go to your room. And make your calls," instructed the voice. The phone went on the blink after the third call. But of what concern could such peculiarity be to Carl Wopschall on a limelighted stage, surrounded by tiers of flowers, prattling Bicentennial hoopla? None, because for him, life is but a rose.

Queen Martin eventually received her lend-lease diadem. We learned that Anne of 365 Days is a freshman at Pasadena City College, a traditional proving ground of rose queens; a former high-school cheerleader and present part-time restaurant hostess in nearby La Cañada, a foothills enclave and realtors' dream after the blockbusting black tide swept out of the north end and across Pasadena a decade ago; that she won a thousand dollars recently on "Hollywood Squares"; wants to transfer to the University of Southern California and pursue a career in public relations; is a fourth-generation Californian whose great-grandfather—and I'm sure they didn't mean it to come out this way—"subdivided Orange Grove Boulevard," a main thoroughfare once known as Millionaire's Row, since subdivided again into condominiums, but which, through it all, from the unpaved past of 1890 to the present, remains the starting point of the Rose Parade.

A queen more perfectly rooted could not have been chosen. Great-granddad, the land-grabber, founded Martin's Camp and Switzer's Camp in the San Gabriel Mountains above Pasadena, and grandfather was born there on Mount Wilson. Nor could the Tournament have chosen a more perfect queen archetype. In judging, they seek a stylized sweet look, a perfection of the girl-next-door confection. They look for "the capacity to glitter, bloom, and light up." Other factors are appearance, carriage, complexion, teeth. Most important, they want glitterability. They want girls who are brimming, smiling, glittering into the yonder, evermore twinkling back from aloft, smiling. ("I smiled for so long—I truly felt like smiling—that when we arrived at the end of the parade route, I could not stop smiling. The muscles in my face wouldn't relax," recalled a queen alumna.) I found it a little difficult to know what to talk about with Anne, and so seldom did, other than to inquire after her general health when we came within range of each other at some of the 183 events.

The program wore to a close with Skiles & Henderson, noisome clowns "just off a tour with the Carpenters," and with The Young Americans, who opened with "Yankee Doodle" before slipping comfortably into the vexing "Dixie." But how are they to know the song is nettlesome, sealed as they are, like the audience, in the chauvinist's cocoon?

There was a coronation ball afterward, but the orchestra played reluctantly, and only Pepsi was served (by Boy Scouts).

In the morning I learned the awful truth: The phone in my dank chamber was on the fritz because the man with the metallic voice shut down the switchboard at whim. Thus confronted, his cap was told to prepare my bill.

"Go to your room. And pack!" crackled the loudspeaker.

Which I did. Returning to the thick window, I told the cap where to go. With no phone service in or out, and though I might have the last available room in Pasadena, I had no choice, I told it, but to check out and retreat to Los Angeles. However, I was ignorant, and did not know that one is never rude to an oracle cap.

The cap bobbed toward the window. I was being called ten ways a bastard over the loudspeaker, and worse: "You're the worst guest we ever had! The worst! I can't stand the sight of you! Get out of here! We—they—were talking about you all night! What is it with these goddamn phones!"

Through the angled glare of the sun I could see a gaunt forearm coming toward the window, then a hand. In that sunlit hand, through the glass, I could see a large lead bar, the size of a gold brick. The lead weight crashed down. Suddenly, I was amid my own personal *Kristallnacht*, shards and slivers exploding all over. In that stop-second when the hand came away from the brick, in that moment before I fled in fear of Pasadena's 120,000 denizens, I saw that the weapon was engraved with these words: Pasadena Tournament of Roses Association.

There was a time when a visitor would have been enthusiastically praised for setting foot on this once and virgin soil, now a snug haven for tories and oracles that blow their marbles.

Pasadena was called the Indiana Colony when it was

founded in 1873 by well-to-do farmers in search of a less demanding climate than that of the midwestern wilderness they had cleared with a Bible and an ax.

The Mediterranean winter lured tourists by 1877, after the railroad fare from Missouri Valley points to Los Angeles dropped to a dollar in a rate war between the entrenched Southern Pacific and the newer Santa Fe. The railroads, land speculators and burgeoning tourist hotels blitzed residents of other climes with promotional campaigns. The hotels employed prototypical PR men, referred to in histories of the period as troubadours. These publicists doubled as writers, artists and otherwise cultivated men of the world, and were called upon by the hotels to provide entertainments for the wealthy guests, usually lectures on Shakespeare, or flora-and-fauna expeditions.

One such troubadour was Professor Charles William Holder, summoned in 1885 from Lynn, Massachusetts, to the Raymond Hotel. Holder, a biographer of Darwin and Agassiz, a prolific writer on many subjects, and a man variously described as a zoologist, naturalist, newsman, professor, and world-traveler, saw in Pasadena, "a city built rapidly yet without a vestige of the rough element that is to be found in the new cities of the inter-oceanic region. This is due to the fact that Pasadena has been built up by wealthy, refined, and cultivated people from the great cities of the East."

Before long, Holder organized a series of hunts with hounds for the Raymond's patrons. He tightened his relationship with the town's elite by opening the hunt to them, creating the Valley Hunt Club, the oldest social club in southern California. By so doing, Holder set in motion the Tournament of Roses.

One day in 1889, Pasadena pioneer Walter Raymond told his troubadour, "We need visitors from the East to fill up our hotels."

"I think I know how to help you," the professor replied.

Holder suggested that the club on New Year's Day celebrate the ripening of the citrus crop by holding a procession of flowered buggies for Pasadena's 4,882 residents, and others.

"Go home and pick your natural flowers and turn them into displays," Holder announced, perhaps in the manner of the man with the metallic voice.

The idea was to demonstrate that flowers bloomed in Pasadena in midwinter; here fecundity, elsewhere chilblains. And underneath it all, the persuasive troubadour was following a simple business motive: off-loading Eastern tourists at local hotels, especially the Raymond.

Valley Hunt Club hounds were proudly led on leashes by their masters that first day of 1890. Part of the lure was an afternoon of sports, and the young men of town played football for twenty minutes before three thousand spectators. Football had been played for thirty years in the East, but the event was so unfamiliar in these environs that announcer C. C. Brown introduced it as a football race. It failed, and no football races were played for the next twelve years. Instead, there were pony races, donkey races and steeplechases.

But that first Tournament realized a cash profit of $229.30, and a pageant was born. In 1901, the first automotive float chugged along—at the end of the line of march so horses wouldn't scare. (Today, the horses are at the end in hopes their leavings discourage people from flooding into the street at parade's end.) Then, in 1902, football returned. It was the first Rose Bowl game and the first postseason intersectional football game in United States history. Fielding Yost's famous point-a-minute Michigan team, winner of ten consecutive games by a combined score of 501—0 came out to play Stanford, best in the West. Pasadena was strung with blue-and-gold banners, the official Tournament colors. They were also Michigan's colors. But worse, they were the colors of the University of California. Stanford fans rioted. "Those colors we hate—they are too much like

University of California's," inflamed partisans were quoted as saying while they tore down banners. An estimated 8,500 people stampeded the football grounds and knocked down fences to see Michigan defeat Stanford, 49–0, setting in that original Rose Bowl game the standing record for most points scored (which it tied in 1948 against USC by the same score).

After Stanford's humiliation, no western team was willing to play and football was dropped from the program for another fourteen years. In its place, at Professor Holder's urging, a pastime of Rome in moral decline, chariot racing, was held (General Lew Wallace's *Ben Hur* being hot off the press). In 1907, however, horse thieves raided the stables before the start of the parade and made off with several rigs.

The first rose queen, Hallie Woods, was chosen in 1905 by schoolmates at Pasadena High. Hallie Woods made her own gown and helped decorate the float she rode in that parade. Somewhere between the sewing of that gown and this morning after Christmas, the Tournament lost what innocence it had.

And now, in the artificial light of a cathedral, the Hyatt Regency, my new home in downtown Los Angeles, I looked at queen and court and knew that, even if they could sew or lend decorative hand, the Tournament could no longer spare the time. There are miles to go before they sleep, and they may not make the next stop, a TV station, on schedule. ("How do I get to Melrose?" a committeeman asked, looking at his watch. Or was he simply timing the length of his question? One can never tell with these people.) A pizza parlor banjo band played in the background. The queen spoke in that vaulted lobby to a curious few, and was met with silence. "You may applaud," an astonished committeeman encouraged. Thus alerted, a few of the few did. Then, queen and court, committee and minstrels, were gone, leaving me to contemplate in their wake a nine-foot

Louis Armstrong, part of last year's FTD (Florists' Transworld Delivery Association) float. His skin was covered with coffee grounds, his shirt with gladiola petals and silver leaf, his pants with onion seed. An operator rode inside him during the parade and was able to make him tap his right foot to the music, and puff out his cheeks when he played. For the operator, Louis would drop his trumpet to his lap, and turn his head from side to side, smiling and nodding. I could make him do none of that.

For the Tournament, though, the ersatz Satchmo would yield again, should that be their desire. All yield: wives, those gowned people demothballed in December to escort their absentee husbands to a couple of dances; mayors of Los Angeles; the City of Pasadena, which still goes in the financial hole each year from the parade, despite its share of the money; even sleeping owners of parked cars. One recent year, when a radiator on a float somehow punctured at 4:30 A.M. while en route to the formation area, the Tournament commandeered a replacement. They left a note on the car saying they'd replace the radiator later; meanwhile, if the owner had to go anywhere that day, take a cab and bill the Tournament.

The unforeseen requires no contemplation when it happens; it is immediately finessed. Of no more difficulty than the arrogant removal of a radiator was the retrieval of former President Dwight D. Eisenhower from self-created exile moments before he was to lead the 1964 parade. It seems Ike thought it wise to oil himself against the early morning chill by retiring with his personal flask to a toilet in the four-story Tournament House. The sliding door of his cubicle slid from its track, imprisoning him. He was found thus compromised by an anxious search party. A crowbar was produced, and the derailed door yielded.

In an off-lobby bar at the Hyatt Regency, I joined two straggling Tournament men in their official nectar, which they call a flu-driver, being three fingers of cognac over ice and orange juice to fill. I tried to comprehend the strong arm of their power as we talked of golfing cap and borrowed crown; of many things, their nectar always before us on the bar. "I can remember," said one, "when the queen looked just like she stepped out of a flying saucer—you don't know how far they've come." Added the other, "It used to be the president's daughter, or someone who looked like his wife used to. But look, if you're going to do a story, make sure you capture the soul of it. We may be a stuffy, old group to some of you, but with all those people watching us on TV every year, we must be doing something right. Here, have another flu-driver."

Yes, they must be doing something right. But what?

Albert Einstein had been impressed, I knew. As honored guest of the 1931 Tournament he saw General C. S. Farnsworth, the last grand marshal to ride horseback, lead the way of Rudolph Valentino's old mount, the Arabian stallion, Jadaan. Einstein watched all this from the seclusion of a bank president's private office and, upon emerging, announced, "This was one of the most delightful days I've experienced since leaving Berlin." Richard Nixon had been impressed. He came with his family the twenty miles from Whittier at age nine and saw his first Rose Parade at curbside. So impressed was he that in 1939 he brought back Patricia Ryan for their first date. Dick and Pat saw Shirley Temple, then ten and at the height of her box office popularity, serve as grand marshal. So tired was the kiddo from waving to the crowds that she could not raise her arm the next day, forcing production of her current movie to suspend.

Nixon himself fared well as grand marshal in 1953 and 1960. (Bob Hope, the late Earl Warren and Nixon are the only repeat grand marshals in modern times. Dr. Billy Graham, with one down, is a good bet to join the team; and John Wayne could be a two-timer, if healthy.) In his two terms as grand marshal, Nixon was no less a curious figure than he was in the White House. His sister-in-law, consulting on seating arrangements for the 1953 Rose Bowl game, described Nixon as "a violent rooter," and warned the Tournament not to seat his elderly in-laws in front. The description was accurate: Nixon "started bopping the people in front of him with his program," remembered that year's Tournament president. In 1960, Nixon addressed the annual kickoff luncheon the day before the game. After his speech, the Secret Service advised the Tournament that Nixon would not attend the postluncheon reception and tea. But he turned up in the receiving line and shook hands for two hours with some nine hundred people. It was, after all, an election year. In 1970, Nixon called from Washington to say he could not attend the game. Based on past performance, this meant he would appear. After arriving in San Clemente, he called again to confirm that he would not be present. Such verification could only mean that Nixon definitely would be there. But the game went on without the man. Perhaps he became lost along the way? He wouldn't have been the first. In 1955, the West Point band got lost during the parade and didn't finish the route. It was the first time the West Point band ever traveled west of the Mississippi, but still . . . all they had to do was follow a pink line painted down the middle of two boulevards.

Like variations on the Tournament theme, the grand marshal is always the same, and comes either from the reliquary or from that which bubbles up in the Tin Pan Alleys of the president's psyche.

The president this year is Ralph Sayre (Speedy) Helpbringer, fifty-seven, who swept streets in his native Akron, Ohio, six nights a week for four years while working his way through Ohio Wesleyan University's business school. He came to Pasadena in 1946, sold tires at Tobias General Tire Company, joined the Tournament eight years later, and acquired his nickname after receiving two speeding tickets the same day. More recently, he became a sales-and-management consultant in the industrial exhibits field.

As his grand marshal, Speedy went with a blast from

the past: cold-storaged songstress Kate Smith, a known quantity once, of uncertain mornings of late, comebacking at sixty-six chiefly as a good-luck charm for the feral Flyers, savage exponents of *A Clockwork Orange* style of ice hockey, and their fans who come to the Philadelphia Spectrum for the red meat.

"I could think of no one more fitting," Speedy declared. In his choice he exhibited characteristics of the crusader-quack: Kate Smith introduced "God Bless America" to the nation on her Armistice Day radio show in 1938. The sheet music had sat for twenty years in the files of Irving Berlin, who composed the song while stationed as a soldier on Long Island, New York, during World War I. "The times have changed since I introduced that song," Kate said recently. "That kind of song just wouldn't go today. Young people nowadays are embarrassed, if not hostile, if you sing anything patriotic." But not at the Sprectrum.

Her mojo for the Flyers began working on December 11, 1969, when a recorded version of "God Bless America" was played in place of the national anthem at the start of a game against Toronto, won by the predators, 6–3. A spell was cast, and the Flyers lost only three of the next fifty games that the song was played at. With Kate's in person presence, they won the Stanley Cup, professional hockey's championship, the last two seasons. She was well paid for her help, but the affiliation is more than show business: She has an entire room in her Lake Placid, New York, home devoted to paraphernalia of her loathsome brutes.

Kathryn Smith is the third woman grand marshal in Tournament annals, preceded by Mary Pickford in 1933, and Temple. There might have been a fourth, had the Tournament its wits.

"I am seventy-five years old and my birthday is January first," wrote Mary Martenson of Alta Vista, Kansas, prior to the 1964 Tournament, which likewise was celebrating its seventy-fifth anniversary. She was especially proud, she wrote, that a native son of Kansas, Dwight Eisenhower, was grand marshal. "I would like to celebrate by seeing the Tournament of Roses in person."

"Congratulations," the Tournament replied. "If ever you are here on New Year's Day, we will be happy to help you enjoy your visit."

Ten days before New Year's, Mary Martenson arrived at the Pasadena bus depot, with no reservations and no money. An agent there called Tournament House: "Your distinguished visitor is here." What? The Tournament reacted: Mary Martenson was put up at the Pasadena Athletic Club; they passed the hat for spending money, and even Ike kicked in twenty dollars; and she was given a great time and sent back to Kansas three days after the parade.

Five years later Mary wrote again: "My eightieth birthday coincides with your eightieth Tournament. I will be very happy to come to Pasadena as your honored guest. I hope I can ride in the first or second car of the parade. I will have my hair combed and I will wear my white shoes. Should I come to Pasadena by train, or will you send an airplane for me this time?"

They replied: "It is not our custom to invite distinguished guests twice. If we ever change our policy and invite General Eisenhower to return, we will include you."

The Tournament thinks a lot of this anecdote. They begin their eighteen-dollar hardcover, three-hundred-page pictorial history with it.

In stiffing Mary Martenson they demonstrated fuzzy thinking and lost a public relations bonanza. Mary could have become the living symbol of Pasadena. She could have been on TV, in the newspapers. She could have been named honorary grand marshal. (There was precedent: a queen mother was named for the 1947 parade.) They're not the sports they say they are, the way they treated that old lady.

On the last day of the year, I entered Pasadena Civic Center once more, for the largest Kiwanis Club luncheon in the history of the world, the forty-sixth annual Rose Bowl Kick-off Luncheon. Box lunches were distributed to four thousand men. We pledged allegiance to the flag. A monk from the nearest Spanish mission rambled an invocation in which the Rose Bowl game was hailed as heaven-sent. It was an unwieldy affair: The official Tournament band (the Pasadena City College Lancer band) unaccountably struck up at will, even as speakers spoke. "Gentlemen and seven ladies," said the first speaker, smiling down to queen and court at the second and lower head table. "Eight! Eight!" many shrieked, pointing at Kate Smith at the upper head table. "Gentlemen and *eight* ladies," the speaker resumed, focusing on the grand marshal, who blew him a kiss, "welcome to the biggest stag party in the world!"

Speedy Helpbringer took the microphone to introduce Kate Smith, recalling the words of Franklin D. Roosevelt: "This is America. This is Kate Smith." Kate received a standing-O. She rose and said, "God bless you all."

Next speaker was NBC announcer Al DeRogatis, an old Duke all-American. (The 1942 Rose Bowl was played on Duke's campus in Durham, North Carolina, because a Japanese attack was feared on the West Coast; meanwhile, back in Pasadena, bandleader Kay Kyser was grand marshal of the parade that never was.) "The meaning of this great event," DeRogatis began—only to drop the matter, shifting abruptly to a technical discussion of backfield formations. So, DeRogatis also knew! And they got to him! I stared in disbelief at the words in my notebook: "DeRogatis, the meaning of this great event . . . the I-formation of Ohio State and the slant-veer formation of UCLA."

Curt Gowdy, DeRogatis's NBC sidekick, sanitized the air. So, Gowdy's in cahoots! He covered up by talking about what a great job referees do, and how their judgment on controversial plays is more often than not backed up by instant video replay. "You know," said Gowdy, "the Japanese invented the instant replay. They're very good at technology. . . ." At the lower head table sat service club bigwigs from the world over. They turned and beamed at Kensuke Suzuki, international president of the Y's Men's Club. C'mon, Gowdy. Get the Jap to take a bow. They're good at that, too, you know.

Gowdy was ready to introduce the main man, Wayne Woodrow Hayes, for twenty-five years head football coach at Ohio State, fourth on the all-time coaching list with 213 career victories, a regular New Year's commuter to Pasadena, making his eighth trip and fifth in the last six years. (His first appearance was 1955, the year the West Point band got lost.) This year, his Buckeyes were undefeated in eleven games, including a convincing victory over bowl rival UCLA, and were ranked number one in the nation.

Woody Hayes, a man fascinated by military history and tactics, is revered by the assembled for his views on discipline and for his pungent exposition of the hard line. They like to call him The General. Although sixty-three, Woody has tantrums on the practice field and is known to punch and insult his players, and grind his wristwatch into the turf with his heel. Woody is also known to splinter sideline markers. Two years ago at the Rose Bowl, Woody slugged L.A. *Times* photographer Art Rogers. In the postgame interview he was asked about the incident and replied that he only wanted to talk about football. But *Times* reporter Mal Florence badgered him. Woody swatted a five-foot-tall microphone to the floor, scattering reporters. In the world of Woody Hayes, he is the only free spirit; everyone else is a number, and some are more the cipher.

"Woody," said Gowdy, "is one of the most cooperative men I've ever met." Few eyebrows raised at that, and I swallowed the sound of one voice chuckling.

Woody took over and described his coaching philosophy. "I kick their rumps on the practice field and scrub their backs in the shower." So, that's what it is! He described his politics. "I'm a little farther right than Barry

Goldwater." He spoke Greek. *"Enthios,"* he said. "To render above oneself. It is the Greek derivation of enthusiasm. Our society seems to lose enthusiasm along the way. But the reverse is true with the Tournament of Roses. And Kate Smith, you've been one of those positive factors." He recalled seeing Kate "in an old 1933 movie about land-grabbers." He introduced by name his assistant coaches seated in the audience and asked each to stand. But then he was off on another topic. "All right, you men may be seated now, thank you," he barked in afterthought. The command evoked a flurry of laughter from the four thousand. Good ol' Woody, still The General. The devotees were pleased as they departed. "God, he's got tremendous enthusiasm," enthused one. *"Enthios,"* quipped his partner.

I left Pasadena to spend New Year's Eve privately. On my way to Los Angeles I heard past grand marshal Dr. Billy Graham on the radio: "At least Nixon never had naked women running around the White House." True; Graham's fellow past grand marshal had had other tricks in mind. I returned to Pasadena at 2:00 A.M., to quiet streets and to a temperature at the freezing point.

The only known event of import during my absence came when an off-duty L.A. cop shot himself in the leg while guarding a sawhorse. South Orange Grove and Colorado boulevards pulsed with rowdy youth camping overnight in sleeping bags, lighting fires in oil drums to keep warm, spilling wine. Some had staked curbsides as early as noon, even as I sat among Kiwanians. Near the formation area, sixty-foot-long floats were massing, directed around difficult corners by walkie-talkie. Revolving lights from police motorcycles sprayed silent buildings red. Down the block moved long-necked dinosaurs with petal skins, telephone brains and bones of chicken wire. The Calgary float was jockeyed toward position. The *C* was missing. It read "algary." I ran into the street to warn of the loss. What was I doing? Then, I fraternized more! As an excuse to get out of the sweeping chill, I took refuge in a Winnebago, and there warmed and drank flu-drivers with Tournament men until 6:00 A.M., when a millionaire threw open his mansion, a few doors from Tournament House, one of the last mansions on Millionaire's Row, for a preparade breakfast and drinks, a party his family has hosted for forty-five years. Elsewhere, 120 members of NBC's Rose Bowl crew were getting out of bed. On the lawn of Tournament House, I spotted Speedy Helpbringer and grabbed him for a quick interview. Jesus Christ, where the hell did you get this goddamn weather? I asked him. Speedy pulled up his pantleg and pointed to woolen Bicentennial socks.

The parade began precisely at 8:30 A.M., as always, before the one million live viewers always estimated. The Long Beach mounted police, on twenty-six matching palominos, moved ahead to clear stragglers. Kate Smith, riding in an open 1906 Rolls-Royce, and cologned in its fumes, proclaimed a cheery, "Happy New Year, everybody!" The parade will be over in exactly two hours. (TV long ago told the Tournament that two hours is about all a viewer will sit still for.) I can see navigators in some floats, telephoning directions back to drivers to keep astride the pink line; drivers who can see nothing else for five and one-half miles but a pink stripe crawling under them at three miles per hour.

I am watching the parade from ground zero, the operations command post. The networks have men here, too. They all have stopwatches. The City of Glendale float ("America, Let's Show our Colors"), "is off thirty seconds, Fred." The first European band ever to participate, the ninety-piece Musique Municipale de la Ville de Genève, oompahs past. "Slow 'em down, Fred."

Fred Soldwedel, parade operations committee chairman, rushes into the street. The TV men are absorbed in their own clocking, as Fred and his partner in the booth jabber messages. Fred relays instructions to a navigator.

"Smile," he counsels lovelies on a float through his megaphone. An insurance company float, wistfully titled "Let's Have an Old-Fashioned Rose Parade," passes. "How we doing?" Fred asks the booth. "We've got forty-five seconds in the bank, Fred," comes the reply. "Good, we need it." Drum-and-bugle corps pass. I begin to tingle. "Damn! The Salvation Army band is having trouble making the corner! We'll lose a minute!" Children leap into the street to grab an occasional fallen flower as trophy. (In yore, did farmers rush to shovel the plop? Would Pasadena have permitted?) The more the spirited marching bands pass in review, the more I tingle. Have I been manchurianized? How else to explain my helpful behavior with the algary float, the fraternizations, and now these tingles? Could it have been the flu-drivers? If allowed to breathe properly in a Courvoisier bed for a few minutes, they did possess, I had observed, a pretentious little something—that full nuttiness of the elixir. This nectar of theirs, is this the absinthe of the crusader-quack?

And then, number 124 in the line of march, bringing up the rear, a wagon train of sixteen horses and four wagons, rolling by in a reverse replay of history, traveling eastward to Pennsylvania, their Bicentennial journey to end July 4 at Valley Forge. The plop began to build.

It was all over but the shouting. "That's it!" cried Fred, clicking his stopwatch. "How'd we do?" he asked the booth. "We did it! We did it!" the joyous reply rang down. "Right on the button! Twenty seconds in the bank!" The crowd burst across the restraining rope at curbside, snaked into the street, and crisscrossed the plop. Everyone loves a parade.

Yin became yang two hours later. Woody Hayes's Buckeyes figured to repeat their earlier 41–20 conquest of UCLA, but at half time led the Rose Bowl game by only 3–0. UCLA was aware in its locker room that teams with two or more defeats during the season (UCLA was 8–2–1 this year) have won the Rose Bowl fourteen times, defeating previously unbeaten teams twelve of those times. UCLA had done it before, under similar circumstances, beating undefeated Michigan State in the 1966 Rose Bowl after losing to them in the regular season. That had been UCLA's last Rose Bowl appearance.

This day, ten years later, history repeated. UCLA took control in the second half and won, 23–10. Ohio State lost the mythical national championship.

The press waited fifty-one minutes for Woody in the postgame interview area, on the promise he would appear, before learning he had snuck out a back door and had boarded the team bus. There sat Woody on the seat behind the driver, full of sound and fury a day earlier with Kiwanians, buried now in seething thought, no mask upon his emotions, glaring bitterly down at us. Nor would The General allow his players to speak.

Bicentennial New Year's was past and the Republic moved on toward its third century. As January became February, the Tournament was hard at work on the 1977 model, making up for what the rest of us lack in *enthios*, rendering above itself as usual. Back home in Columbus, Woody was skewered by the student newspaper for his silence, but remained uncharacteristically mute. Perhaps, he, too, had lost his enthusiasm along the way.

The San Francisco Bosox

I was living in a sublet along the panhandle of Golden Gate Park and was nearly broke. I had something like twenty-eight dollars in ready cash and a couple of cans of sardines. No booze, no drugs, no toys. Worse, Tim Page was homeless again and I had no recourse but to offer him the living-room couch. Page earned his keep, however. Each morning between 8:30 and 8:45 he would hear me turn over in bed, a sign that I was waking. A few minutes later he would enter my bedroom. "Cup of coffee, mate?" he would ask, setting it down on the night table. Ah, steaming hot black coffee! That's the ticket! There would also be a package of Picayune cigarettes, a lighter and a clean ashtray. Plus a copy of the Chronicle, *which Page, being an early riser, had already bought at the corner. I would prop up in bed, smoke Picayunes, drink coffee and read the paper. The Good Life!*

One midafternoon the phone rang. It was Warren Hinckle, who had recently assumed editorship of Francis Ford Coppola's experiment in journalism, the ill-fated but beautifully produced magazine known as City of San Francisco. *"I understand that you are the only man in the world qualified to review Norman Mailer's book on the fight in Zaire," he bellowed.*

"That's correct," I agreed.

He said he was sending a messenger over with a copy of the book. "When do you need it?" I asked.

"Yesterday," he said.

Hold on, I cautioned. "I've got Page laying about. I won't be able to do it here. If you need it immediately you'll have to book me into the Claremont Hotel for a couple of days." He consented and I had a gladsome time in that wonderful Victorian relic in the Oakland hills. I called Hinckle when I finished and told him he could have the piece that evening if he took me to dinner. Okay, he said. I was to meet him at six at the Washington Square Bar & Grille. We had a few martini cocktails at the bar and went into the dining room. Dinner came and went and the armagnac arrived. I slid the packet across the table. Hinckle opened it and read without comment. When he finished he said, simply, "Great!"

He looked at me a moment, obviously pleased, and then said, "All right, Cardoso, what do you want to do for us next?"

"Well, Warren, I think I should get to Boston as soon as possible and cover the Red Sox for the rest of the season. I think we should adopt them as the official San Francisco team."

"Great! Great!" he roared. "When can you go?" (If there is one thing Warren Hinckle knows how to do well, it is spend other people's money.)

I was stunned. I hadn't expected this. "Uh, uh," I stammered, "tomorrow?"

"Great! Great!" he said.

Boston, the home of the bean and the cod,
Where the Cabots speak only to the Lowells,
And the Lowells speak only to God.

Anon.

To Fenway, to see baseball played the way our fathers played it, on real grass, come the humble and the Lowells.

Take Jimmy Lowell.

A lawyer by profession, and Jasie to his friends, he always managed to get to his regular seat in time for batting practice. Being a Lowell, he was accorded certain privileges at Fenway, and so kept an overcoat in a locker there. In chill or damp weather, an usher would appear with the raiment. Jasie knew everything about baseball.

"You would hardly have expected it in a Lowell born in the bright stream of poets, educators and the literary great," recalled an old friend. "But let's face it, Jimmy was something of a maverick Lowell, the like of which it is doubtful the clan will ever produce again." (The writer would like to submit that the poet, Robert, is odd; but this has no place here.)

The story about Jasie best-loved was one circulated by his Back Bay doctor, a world-famous ophthalmologist. Seems Jasie had reached a point in life when he couldn't see well enough to discern whether or not the second baseman had put the tag on the sliding runner. The doctor, naturally a Sox fan, was understanding, and did everything that good practice would allow.

Yet, Jasie remained unhappy sitting in Fenway, the world between the foul lines blurring.

Then it happened. He bought a box of Cracker Jack one evening. About the second inning, he got down to the prize: a cardboard eye frame into which were mounted two pink isinglass lenses. Jasie put them on and looked out toward the left field scoreboard, where the out-of-town scores are posted. For two years he hadn't been able to distinguish a name or a number on the board.

Suddenly, he *could* see, he *could* read: Cincinnati 3, St. Louis 1 . . . New York 8, Chicago 2.

It was considered a miracle.

More on miracles in a moment, but first this important time-out: Folks, do you realize that Horace Stoneham will have a cool million in the till next year before the first pitch is thrown, just from the Giants' share of network TV cash?

That's right, $990,000 from NBC and ABC, for a team that will appear on networks only by accident (i.e., when the scheduled game-of-the-week is rained out, replaced by a backup game from the dry West).

A pretty good running start, wouldn't you agree: a cool million?

And he'll still field a terrible team! (If he hasn't yet sold the club—which he should, being as he is in apparent dotage.)

Stoneham has an historical parallel in Boston, a man named Harry Frazee, damned in perpetuity, who, like Squire Horace, sold his best players in order to get operating funds. More on that later, if I may, simply because it's such a distasteful topic.

Permit me to set forth the game plan. I propose to consider the following in this and subsequent pieces: the Red Sox in particular, with occasional references to the Giants; African witch doctors and whammies (a subject about which I have some knowledge); teeth, of course; racialism; road games; press boxes; and the Portuguese. If space requirements allow, I plan to reveal certain entries from my Rutter. I may also bring in for spot relief passages from the Melvin Maddocks's article on Fenway Park in the September 15 *Sports Illustrated*.

You say you're unsatisfied, you say you want a miracle? Well, there is no exploding electronic gimmickry at Fenway, where the organist would never lead a charge! during a Red Sox rally. Not small miracles, in this age.

And, miracle or not, the Sox seem to be surviving September without doing their famous El Foldo act.

The key games are the next two nights, history when

you read this, against the pursuing Baltimore Orioles. Luis Tiant, who pitched a near no-hitter last week against weak Detroit, opposes Baltimore ace Jim Palmer in the opener. Not a ticket is to be had. The two-game series will push home attendance over 1.6 million in this second smallest of twenty-four major league parks. (Check the sporting green—Jesus, I almost gagged on that!—to see how many the Giants have drawn to their much larger monument to the winds.)

Did I tell you that pitcher Dick Pole was married on Sunday? Can you, in your most liberal moment, imagine one of the Giants being wed? Who would want one! (Heh-heh, only kidding, fellahs).

No, let's begin anew. Give me another chance to get off on the right foot. Let me backtrack to the actual beginning. Which also gives me an opportunity to consult my Rutter.

September 9 entries: enroute to Boston on the day schools open, to be picked up at Logan by a Jew and his black African wife. Will the Irish stone their car? Will the blacks? Am I nearing the epicenter? The *Golden Hind* may well have been the first English ship to circumnavigate the globe, but it must be marked that Drake captured a Portuguese pilot and forced him to take her through the secret Magellan passage into the Pacific. This pilot here said there's light rain in Boston. What is rain like in the summer? It's been so long . . . perhaps I'll hear thunder. Felton, Westerners are afraid of thunder. Watching *Return of the Pink Panther* aloft, when—behold! I feel a tingle and a twitch in my left bum. Do you hear that, San Francisco, mecca of the inner peace industry? I am in touch with my body! Eureka! Novick and Victoria at the airport. Their car had not been stoned, but they were about to be, on some Colombian leaf, courtesy of San Francisco's fledgling Dope Conspiracy.

So much for my Rutter for the nonce.

To bring you to date, I have witnessed, since arriving,

seven games in five days. The images collide, and my head is confused. But let's investigate those tilts, hopscotching, as it were, for highlights.

The Sox have taken five of the seven and maintain a four game lead over Baltimore. At the end of this most-crucial two-game test, the Sox will either have wrapped it up, or will face a photo finish with the Birds. The Orioles have been whacking hell out of the ball lately, surprising because they've got three regulars batting round .210. Maybe they're getting all the hits out of their bats and will be patsies the rest of the way. (Many ball players believe that each bat has only so many base hits in it.)

Left-hander Bill Lee, out of USC, has resurrected the eephus pitch, a high, slow floater last used in 1946 right here at Fenway by its inventor, Rip Sewell, in the all-star game. Ted Williams slammed it more than four hundred feet. A couple of weeks ago in Milwaukee, Lee used it against Hank Aaron, who stepped out of the box, insulted and disgusted. A debate ensued among writers. It is a disgrace, some held, to do that to Aaron. Ah, what the fug, held others; it's only a game, it's not sacred.

Quote from Billy Martin, manager of the Yankees: "From what I've seen in Boston, the only people nervous are the writers; certainly not the players." Is true: no stuffed shirts, no racial problems, banter in the clubhouse.

Rookies Fred Lynn and Jim Ed Rice are the main reasons why the Sox are on top. Back-to-back last night against the Brewers they each batted in their one hundredth run of the year, an incredible feat for first-year players. Their offensive stats are fantastic.

But for all the interest in the young players, Carl Yastrzemski's willingness to keep playing with his painful shoulder and Americo Petrocelli's willingness to play with the threat of permanent injury if beaned deserve credit. Captain Carl is but a shell of a once-great player, yet he still looks menacing at the plate—and is a dangerous batter because the pitchers have to pitch to him, if only to avoid Lynn and Rice, next in the order. This may be the end for Rico, the last hurrah for a great third baseman. "He is suffering from 'ostronaut' problems—inner ear difficulties," according to H. Bibesco, professor of Red Sox at a girls' school in the Wellesley area.

Eddie Andleman, who hosts a TV sports talk show, still hits the streets occasionally with a camera crew to offer a five-dollar bill to anyone who can spell Yastrzemski.

John Claiborne, who maintained a productive farm system on five dollars a day, it is said, for Charlie Finley, before quitting, is now scouting his old club for the Sox. His observations on Oakland: Sal Bando was bothered by his bitter arbitration case but is now hitting and fielding well; Joe Rudi's status, with his thumb injury, is touch-and-go for the playoffs; and things may be different without Catfish Hunter.

What's this? The Giants have routed baseball's best team, the Cincinnati Reds, 9–2, to end an eight-game losing streak. Candlestick attendance was 5,453 for the surprise.

Here, many of the home games are on television, but anywhere from fifteen to thirty-five thousand still come out to Fenway. (The Red Sox have $3 million in the till next year before the first pitch is thrown: $990,000 from the network TV contract; $1.9 million from local TV; and the remainder from radio rights locally.)

I see that the Japanese group interested in buying the Giants has called off the deal because of financial problems and feelings.

The Japanese suggested their purchase of the team might arouse the anti-Japanese sentiment among sports fans. So, while whites and blacks are fighting in the corridors of Boston schools, you should not point any fingers, San Francisco, y'hear?

Baltimore disc jockey Johnny Walker has gone to Nairobi, Kenya, and has met with witch doctor John Agunga in order to put the whammy on the Red Sox. The hex was placed on the Sox sometime on the morning of September 13. Immediately, the Sox lost the first game of a double-header to the lowly Brewers (but won the second, hey!).

Walker gave Doctor Agunga a baseball autographed by the Red Sox and some team pictures. The doctor then cursed the Red Sox. "They will temporarily go blind, they cannot see the ball," predicted Dr. Agunga. "They'll have trouble running, they'll get dizzy and can't run as fast and the ball will seem to swerve a little bit." Dr. Agunga also cursed the ball, so that it will seem to go toward one location and then will move a bit.

It is said that Dr. Agunga once made a soccer ball disappear. Having once resided in the Congo, I believe. Oh, yes!

Went to the pro shop across from Fenway and got properly togged: bought me a three-dollar straw sky that says Red Sox on the hatband; also bought me a coffee mug; bought me a poster of Carlton Fisk, our all-star catcher; but turned down the eight-dollar official cap, which is double-knit (ugh!) . . . what happened to felt? What happened to Felton? The new Sox caps are red, with a blue visor; a concession to color television. I miss the old true blue cap with red *B*.

Sox manager Darrell Johnson has a can of Coors and a frosted beer mug waiting on his desk after each game. Coors, as you know, is something of a status drink in the East, as it is not sold here but must be brought in special. I must educate Johnson politically.

I introduced myself to Jack McKeon, deposed Kansas City manager, who is now scouting the Sox for Charlie Finley. McKeon was easy to pick out: white shoes, which one would never wear in Boston after Labor Day.

Of the 162 games, 101 are telecast, including all weekend games, whether home or away.

September in Boston belongs to the Red Sox, not to

school busing turmoil. 'Twas ever thus. The month of El Foldo.

Will not need relief help from Melvin Maddocks this time out, but, rather, will close with an object lesson.

In 1957, Joe Cronin, a native San Franciscan, then the general manager of the Red Sox and later president of the American League, suggested to a properly credulous Boston TV audience one midwinter night that the problem with the team was Harry Frazee, who has been dead since 1929.

Who was this Frazee whose name pops out of Boston history like that of Benedict Arnold? Frazee was yester-year's Horace Stoneham.

Frazee bought the Red Sox in December 1916, and was forced to sell less than seven years later. In between, he decimated the ball club. It turns out that Frazee had an eye for the well-turned ankle and could identify twenty-six varieties of the chorus girl. (The present owner, Tom Yawkey, who has owned the club longer than any man has owned any team, can identify twenty-six kinds of spider.)

Well, Frazee was smitten with Broadway and produced, among, other things, the original *No, No, Nanette*.

His need for money had him saying, "Yes, Yes," to Colonel Jake Ruppert, the Knickerbocker beer baron and owner of the Yankees, who kept shoving wads of bills into Frazee's pockets in exchange for star players.

Most infamous was the deal that sent Babe Ruth to New York for $100,000 cash and a $350,000 personal loan in the form of a mortgage on Fenway Park. Listen to some of these other deals:

Frazee traded Dutch Leonard and Duffy Lewis for nonentities; he traded Carl Mays for someone named Rubber-arm Russell; traded Waite Hoyt and Wally Schang for Muddy Ruel and three corpses; gave cash for Ping Bodie, who did not play a game; traded Joe Dugan for Lefty O'Doul (hey, San Francisco!); gave Herb Pennock for someone named Camp Skinner; dealt George Pipgras for cash.

These were all deals to the Yankees, who then put a lock on the pennant for a generation.

When Frazee died in his Park Avenue, New York, apartment, Mayor Jimmy Walker was at his bedside. That is the best that can be said of the man.

Do I hear echoes of Candlestick, or is it merely the wind: Is that the ghost of Bobby Bonds in center field? Where is Kingman? Ah, knocking home runs for the Mets, you say. McCovey and Mays, dealt in their twilight for operating funds. Baah!

So, too, Squire Stoneham awaits his historical fate, as did Frazee. Meanwhile, I await Baltimore.

Baseball Beaver Tales

"Success in looking for George Kimball is not finding him."

Nick Browne

It is warm and moist in Skippers Dock, so I enter that alehouse. She is up there on her tiny stage, stripping. One notes that she is discreetly sliding her left index finger inside her G-string and is playing with herself. So, too, I circumspectly diddle at the bar, and consider the fatties who are as neighbors. One has homemade tattoos on her left hand and wrist. Another, a hag whose face wrinkles when she laughs, giving her the appearance of a Mayan at a ceremonial rite, gags on her draught beer and . . . Jesus, would you believe? . . . spits out a tooth. These are women who didn't move to Norfolk when the Navy shipped out two years ago; leftover. We are in Newport, Rhode Island. The Red Sox are in Detroit. I missed connections, but that is because I am not a well man.

A talcum representative in Boston bestowed a stomach-strangling virus. First of the season, he assured.

Worse, I am spreading this bastard venom all over the house. Great guest! It is the house of Jim McGrath, a tenor who makes a living at singing sea chanties and IRA songs, and who must work a club tonight.

Still worse, word arrived from California that my new Fell Street crib has been knocked over; gone are the heirlooms.

McGrath shares his house with George Kimball, the notorious one-eyed sporting writer. When well, I hunt the elusive Kimball. I need him to interpret the Red Sox metaphysically.

However, he does not appear. (I slept in his bed last night, waiting for him.)

In Boston, he has bartenders—even ball players—lying for him. It is as though he is avoiding me; yet he *does* speak with me on the telephone. When I ask him to background the Red Sox, he rhapsodizes about their sexcapades. Beaver stories, they're called in baseball. (Pitching control is now called location; speed is velocity.)

A few nights ago in the clubhouse, pitcher Bill Lee whispered that "Kimball told me to tell you he'd meet you in the Eliot Lounge after the game."

He was not there.

Next day, during batting practice at Fenway Park, I asked Lee what happened to Kimball. Have you seen him?

"No," he said, "but I saw his eye at the bottom of a swimming pool in Oakland." (Groupies, please note: Edgewater Hyatt House.) "Sunny side up. It was worse than *Jaws*."

In a separate reality a thousand miles away the score was 4–4. Bill Lee, winner of seventeen games for the Sox, chased in the second inning. We would go on to win, 7–4, however. But in Baltimore, the Orioles would stay in hot pursuit, defeating Milwaukee. ("We are the Bela Lugosis," O's manager Earl Weaver intoned. "We keep coming out of the coffin at ya.") Next night, our Bostons would be handcuffed by fatman Mickey Lolich in Detroit, who forced them into fifteen ground ball outs; while the Orioles' gifted Jim Palmer—loser to Luis Tiant, 2–0, earlier in the week at Fenway in a classic pitching duel—would tame Milwaukee.

Poor Bill Lee.

A few weeks ago he suggested that U.S. Judge Arthur Garrity was the only man in Boston with any guts. Garrity is the person who created and force-fed the Boston school busing program. A native of Southie, he is no longer popular there. Nor is Bill Lee. When you're outspoken, you've got to stay a winner . . . right, Muhammad? And Lee has had a sore elbow for a month now. (Recently, watching Uri Geller perform healing feats on television, Lee rushed the set and rubbed his left elbow all over it. It was of no value, which says something about Uri Geller.)

If Lee is not popular in South Boston and other Irish bailiwicks hereabouts, he also is not popular on the mound.

In Chicago recently, while winning handily, he resorted to the long-lost eephus pitch. Other players consider the eephus to be strictly bush. And the Chicagos were particularly annoyed this day. Bad enough to be losing to a confidence man pitcher, but this hot dog out there is making monkeys outta us! White Sox manager Chuck Tanner subsequently protested to the League office. But now, on the diamond, the game out of reach, his players took turns trying to hit hot shots back through the mound. Lee fielded all these wounding line drives successfully. In the locker room after the game, when he stripped, he was bruised all over.

No Neck & A Crazy Grin

One time in Cleveland a couple of years ago, Lee was pitching to Walt (No-Neck) Williams, then of the Indians. Lee began circling the mound, scrunching up his shoulders, hiding his neck. No-Neck protested. The umpire ruled that nothing in the canons of major league baseball prohibits a pitcher from shrinking.

When I introduced myself to Lee, I told him that I would be covering the Sox for the remainder of the year; that, because the Giants suck, and so does Candlestick (Bleakmoor), this ragazine (thanks, Margaret) had adopted the Sox as the official stretch drive team, and that this was largely because they played baseball the way it ought to be . . . on real grass.

"There's lots of grass in Massachusetts," Lee replied. He looked right into my eyes when he said this, his own eyes twinkling.

What the fuck was this? A provocateur? I was taking no chances. I was already in dutch with the Red Sox official family, so I walked on him. I left him there, in front of his locker, number thirty-seven, toweling himself, grinning crazily at me.

So where is the cyclops Kimball? Asleep in his cups out there in Section 42 of the right field bleachers, waiting for the final home series against Cleveland next week? When I arrived in town a few weeks ago, I asked him over the phone if he would be at that night's game. (A game against Detroit; one of the sides being victorious.)

"Yes," Kimball responded. "Meet me in Section 42."

"Section 42? You must be persona non grata in the press box, huh?"

"No, I'm with the People! Section 42, or meet me in the Eliot Lounge after the game. That's the way it is." After the game, in the Eliot Lounge, he was not there again.

The Big 86

J. D. Reed of *Sports Illustrated,* in Boston to cover the important two-game test against Baltimore for first place in the American League East, admitted that Kimball had been barred.

"I understand," said Reed, "that the final straw was when he threw an empty bottle of Three Feathers down on the field. But it had been building for two weeks. He had been leaning out of the press box and yelling down to the players."

Two other versions of the Eighty-Six exist:

One has it that Kimball was sitting down in the box seats one day, carrying on loutishly, peppering his observations with colorful language. Behind him was a family man with his little son. The father reported the offense to an usher, who carried it up the chain of command, and—*voilà!*—the Red Sox official family had what they had prayed for, the goods on Kimball.

The other version has it that two years ago, during a road trip to Kansas City, the Sox were being romanced by Holiday Inns of America, which had just opened a new lodge in that town and were trying to take business away from the ancient and honorable Hotel Mulenbach. And Kimball, an old U of Kansas boy, had invited a bunch of Old Boys to the hotel. (Kimball once ran for sheriff of Douglas County, Kansas, against an incumbent who had a withered arm. The Kimball campaign posters exhorted the citizens to "vote for a two-fisted sheriff." Not to be out-grossed, the incumbent countered with: "Re-elect Vern Miller. He'll keep both eyes on the law." And into the Holiday Inn came not only U of Kansas Old Boys, but aging politicos from an old freak power campaign.) Seems they had a grand time: a booze-up, wafts of marihuana (Portuguese spelling) smoke from the room. That sort of stuff. Then, some of Kimball's cowboy friends ran naked through the corridors. He might have gotten away with it, but—there had been ball players in the room! Red Sox traveling secretary Jack Rogers reported back to Boston . . . and that was that for Kimball.

Me, I prefer the J. D. Reed version, if only because *Sports Illustrated* has credibility.

Now, the Sox lost tonight in Detroit, while the Bela Lugosis continued victorious in Baltimore against Milwaukee. (In Milwaukee County Stadium, when a local player knocks a home run, as we in baseball say, a beer mug in the outfield lights up and spouts hundreds of—are you ready for this?—balloons! Such *declassé* horseshit could never occur at Fenway, owing to the matchless good taste of Sox owner Tom Yawkey; more on this later, but first this bulletin: prize rookie Jim Rice is out for the season with a broken left hand, the result of a pitched ball. Winning the pennant will be that much harder without this poised twenty-two-year-old and his .309 batting average, 102 RBIs and 22 homers. He is also a heads-up left fielder, left field at Fenway being perhaps the most difficult in all baseball—Ted Williams and Carl Yastrzemski are two who understand that Great Wall.)

Probation in the Press Box

Because Boston lost and Baltimore won, Kimball has sent word through housemate Sunny Jim McGrath that he'll meet me in New York for the final week series against the Pinstripes in the role of spoilers, Yanks close at home vs. contesting Baltimore. Which is just what I need: to have traveling secretary Jack Rogers report back to chief publicist (and press box executive officer) Bill Crowley that the new guy from San Francisco kept company with Kimball in the Shea Stadium press box. I am, you see, already on disciplinary probation with the official family.

It happened the first night. For being lushed.

"I'm going to give it to you cold turkey, Bill," Crowley growled. "I'm going to be watching you carefully the next couple of days. You're on probation up here as of now."

There is a ranking system in the press box. The regulars gather behind home plate; irregulars, such as your correspondent, are forced to find seats at the extreme right end, toward first base. There was an empty seat to my right. I was approached by someone and asked if the seat was taken. No, I said.

So she sat down. Folks, do you know what I am telling you? A woman in the press box!

Damn pretty one, too; an intern in the *Globe* sports department. Delighted by her company, I did my best. Remember, I was drunk.

But a woman in the press box is a . . . is a whore!

And these fat, balding Boys of Summer seated all around me . . . well, I don't need eyes in the back of my head to know where their vision was focused: why that fuckin' drunk from San Francisco is gonna cop the beaver! I think it was secretly *that*, rather than being drunk, which sent all of these duffers prattling to Bill Crowley about my deportment.

Be that as it may. I got the caution when I walked down to Crowley's seat behind home plate to discuss the matter of parking privileges. Now I had to stumble back to my seat, red-faced and ashamed, all evil eyes on me as I groped along the aisle. To the left of my chair sat a visiting writer from the *Detroit Free Press*. Apparently, I forgot that he was there; for, as I tried to sit, I pitched forward and slightly to port. This man from Motown propped me, and eased me into my rightful place. Else, I would have tumbled into the reserved grandstand below, ending not only my life . . . but my correspondency. He saved my life, my correspondency . . . and I can't even remember his name, egad. Gratitude.

For I truly was lushed. Here's the proof:

The next night a *Globe* copyboy wanted to make sure I remembered the wager. Wager? "Yeah, you bet me five dollars straight up last night that Rico would hit eight more home runs this year."

I did? Jesus Christ, but there're only eighteen games left.

"Yeah, well, Frank O'Brien [*Globe* photographer] was a witness. Five bucks, man."

And, you know, Americo Petrocelli, our third baseman, had knocked only six home runs all year . . . to that moment. This was not my darling Long Ball Rico of yesteryear, not the man who knocked forty home runs in 1969. Ah, but Americo knocked a mighty blast into the net in left that first drunken night of mine.

Bleachers & Basilicas

It wasn't long ago that people in the right field bleachers, Kimball presumably among them, rose to sing:

Amer-i-co, Amer-i-co
Let loose thy mighty swing
And pound the ball
O'er left field's wall
And make the big screen ring.

When Americo knocked his seventh homer of the year, I made the bet, the copyboy reminded me. That's pennant fever for you. And ignorant oil.

But Kimball's "People" out in right field no longer sing that song. And if I am not careful, I will be out among those sullens.

For the press box at Fenway is not less than a basilica.

Oh, yes.

There is even arcane language. For example, when one enters the men's room off the press dining room and cocktail lounge, one says, "full house." Why, I am not sure. But that is what one says.

There are two urinals there and a toilet. One day, whom should I bump into in that sanctum but none other than Tom Yawkey. (In the timely and wonderful portrait of Fenway Park by Melvin Maddocks in the September 15

Sports Illustrated, which I endorse, there is only one mistake, decided Ray Fitzgerald of the *Globe*: Maddocks's claim that the Red Sox owner, who bought the club in 1933 as a thirtieth birthday present to himself, is inaccessible to writers. Not so. I mean, how more accessible can a man make himself?)

"Full house!" I shouted at Yawkey in my zeal.

Yeah, yeah, he replied.

What treatment for writers, indeed! The open bar! The steaks Yawkey serves us! (Andy Griffith, please note.) I understand that Horace Stoneham serves chicken-in-the-basket to writers at Candlestick Park (Sullenmoor). But what the hey! He needs to save every penny he's got. You would not believe the chunks of Roquefort in the dressing, the spunky wedges of Boston Cream Pie. No, it is not easy to yield those perks. I do not want to forfeit that.

(Food editors, please note: I have been food-freaking, eating brown-skinned eggs, y'know, and stuff like that; fried clams with yum-yum bellies, ersters on the half-shell, baked stuffed quahogs, buckets of steamers, Cape scallops sautéed, boiled live lobster at reasonably-priced secret restaurants remembered, beans in molasses baked.)

(Health faddists, please note: Kimball one weird vegetarian, oh boy. Walks into a McDonald's and gets greasy french fries and pours packets of chemical catsup all over them; eats Hostess Twinkies. Says Nick Browne of the *Village Voice*: "Yeah, and he does all this in the hope that he'll add another year or two onto his miserable life." Bill Lee, on the other hand, according to *W.*, a mutant creation of cheeky *Women's Wear Daily*, eats royal jelly, honey, ginseng, yogurt fish.)

Ave, Ave, Sanctum Plurissimus

Fortunately, we of the Church of Rome have a perfect little out: the Confession.

So it was that I approached publicist Crowley on the third day of my probation: I'm sorry, Bill, I told him, that I was so high-spirited the other night; being back and all that, and seeing a bunch of fellers I hadn't seen in a few years . . . it all went to my head.

"That's all right, Bill," Crowley forgave. "It happens to all of us."

Bless me, Father, for I have sinned.

Late update: Sox beat Yankees last night at Shea in downpour; Orioles idle and now four games out in the loss column; only six games left to play; finally, after all these years, the Baltimores can no longer do it, even with the League's best pitching; the Red Sox have unbelievably survived the annual September El Foldo; San Franciscans have a right to be proud of their adopted team; I can confidently predict that our Sox will meet Oakland's A's for the pennant; Kimball was a New York no-show, for which the habitués of the Lion's Head are grateful.

I am sorry that I will not be able to tell you, because of space limitations, about that marvelous pitching duel between Luis Tiant and Jim Palmer. Suffice to say it was classic. Two money pitchers in a money game. Palmer made two bad pitches: one to Long Ball Rico, who knocked it into the net; another to Carlton Fisk, who is carved from New Hampshire granite (ah, what a splendid New England name for a New England hero: Carlton Fisk), who also knocked it into the net. Tiant was superb. "Two ears and the tail," declared Roger Angell of *The New Yorker*.

All guile, he. Listed in the roster as thirty-four years of age, I am sure he is nearer to forty. How wonderful that Fidel Castro recently let his mom and dad out of Cuba to see him pitch major league baseball, though it be in the twilight of his career.

His fast ball hummed against Palmer's mates. He gave them his—as we in baseball say—assortment, including wraparound delivery, in which he looks out at Kimball in the right field bleachers while in full wind-up motion, thus flashing the number of his back to the batter, then wheels around with chin fakes. . . .

One time a few years ago in West Hollywood I watched an Angels game being televised from Boston. Tiant was dueling Nolan Ryan, an all-time great. A tight game, Sox ahead 2–1 in the eighth inning, the Angels with a runner in scoring position and their slugger, Bob Oliver, at bat, the count three-and-one, Tiant in the hole. Oliver fouled the next pitch. One bad pitch here and, well, you know. . . . So it was a money pitch coming up. Working out of a stretch, he flashed his numbers at Oliver, whipped around, fed Oliver two chin fakes in rapid succession at the moment before delivery, causing the slugger to commit himself. Poor Oliver corkscrewed himself in the batter's box as he fanned on an off-speed mesmerizer. And the Sox prevailed.

I also wanted to hip you to the Cuban Triple Play (which is always worth five dollars in a barroom bet) but am out of space, so will utilize Tom Yawkey for this week's walk-off.

The other day, late in the afternoon, during batting practice, I came upon the seventy-three-year-old owner. He was dressed as usual: twelve-dollar Sears windbreaker, eight-dollar Robert Hall slacks. Can you imagine what an embarrassment this man must be to the Ritz-Carlton, where he has maintained a suite for many years? (Yawkey winters at his private island off the coast of South Carolina.) There we were, the two of us. There is a question to put to Tom Austin Yawkey, and I did:

What I would like to know, I began, is how you have been able to resist all these years the forces who would have you gimmick up this wonderful ball yard, this—in the words of *Sports Illustrated*—"monument to admirable taste."

Yawkey looked at me. He moved his head up-and-down in apparent agreement and sounded a faint "yeah, yeah." Then he put his hands in his trouser pockets, looked down at his ten-dollar shoes (or kicks as we in baseball prefer to say) for a few moments, as if in thought, raised his head and looked at me again, smiling.

"Well," he said, "I guess I gotta get my ass upstairs."

The Secret of How the Red Sox Came to Oakland

no meat, sweets, beer or sex twelve hours before the game for the Orioles

The line-up posted on the wall of the Red Sox dugout at Fenway Park was worth photographing, and someone did. Of the nine names listed, only three could be termed regulars: a pair of substitute outfielders and the second-string catcher, who was posted at first base. So, it was the Baby Red Sox who would take the field the final day, scrubs . . . nonroster players up from the Pawtucket affiliate for the end of the long season. No matter, for the Sox had won the American League East championship the day before; and now, Manager Darrell Johnson wanted to look at the kids under game conditions. Nothing was at stake: Baltimore was dead, mathematically eliminated.

For the finale, the faithful came to Fenway 25,991 strong, increasing the year's attendance to 1,748,605, third largest in the team's history. The average for eighty-one games in this second smallest of all major league parks was 22,709. (We won't even bother to compare this with Candlestick Park statistics.)

A week of wall-to-wall rain along the East Coast, but now the Baby Red Sox were proud young lions as they filed through the dank tunnel to the dugout and the sunshine above, looking so cool in their suits of the champions, the pure white elegance of the Red Sox uniform. . . .

Let *Women's Wear Daily* tell it, it's their expertise: "They rise above the gimcrackery of other, lesser teams. No gaudy green and gold uniforms for them—instead, the pure white and road-trip gray of baseball as our fathers played it." (By "gaudy green and gold," *WWD* meant, of course, the Oaklands, who take the field looking like some volunteer fire department softball team from Carbondale, Illinois.)

One would have to be a Red Sox fanatic to recognize the names posted on that last line-up card in the dugout: Dillard, Merchant, Blackwell, Hobson, Heise, Miller. Only one name might mean anything to noncognoscenti: Bernardo Carbo, journeyman outfielder.

During a two-month period earlier this year, Bernardo went absolutely gonzo, knocking (as we in baseball say) fifteen home runs in that short span. When Bernie cooled, he went to the bench. And he could not get back in the line-up because, by then, the Red Sox were fielding the best young outfield in baseball: the sensational rookies Jim Ed Rice in left, Fred Lynn in center, and second-year man Dwight (Dewey) Evans, a babe at twenty-three, in right.

All summer long Bernardo offered incense and prayers to the images of Buddha positioned atop his locker. Yet, he remained on the bench, slightly to the left of the chewing tobacco, as we in baseball say; forgotten. But this last, meaningless day, he was listed as cleanup batter—fourth in the order. And he was ready.

"I'm batting fourth," Bernardo acknowledged before game time, "and I'm going deep."

The Baby Red Sox were mauled badly by Cleveland, 11–4, through no fault of Carbo's (he batted in runs his first two times up, sparking the Sox to a brief 4–2 lead). Late in the game, Cleveland Manager Frank Robinson inserted his own Baby Indians. Carbo came to bat for the final time in the ninth inning, with two out, and the game hopelessly out of reach. An unknown quantity, Jim Strickland, was on the mound. Catching Strickland was another kid, Rick Cerone. And Carbo still yearned to go deep. Which, after all, befits a cleanup hitter.

"Tell him," Carbo pleaded with Cerone, "to throw a fuckin' fast ball—and I'll swing. Tell him I *promise* to swing."

Out of the corner of his eye, Carbo watched Cerone pump signals to the mound. He was pumping for a fast ball, all right, Bernardo noticed. But Strickland wouldn't take the dare. Instead, he kept throwing stuff—in Carbo's case, the fork ball.

Carbo complained later, beneath the many visages of Buddha. "He wouldn't throw me a fast ball. He's leading by a dozen runs in the ninth and all he throws me is the forker, the fucker!" (Carbo popped up that final pitch; and beery louts rushed the field for souvenirs.)

According to the official Elgin clock in center field at Shea Stadium, in Flushing, Baltimore expired at 7:27 P.M. on September 27.

After their frenzied chase of the Red Sox, winning day after day, Baltimore lost their first doubleheader of the season, and along with it their pennant chances. Game after game, the Baltimores came at our Red Sox, playing .686 baseball after the all-star break in July, winning fifteen out of eighteen before self-destructing at Shea Stadium. The trouble with Baltimore was that the Sox kept winning, too, taking eleven of the seventeen games I witnessed since leaving San Francisco to chronicle our adopted team.

The Orioles accepted defeat philosophically. Said All-Star third baseman Brooks Robinson in the aftermath: "Well, my wife is going to like it. She hasn't seen home in October in a while."

(Oakland won ninety-eight games this season, including a 5–0 no-hitter hurled by four [count 'em] four men on the final day.)

In front of the dugout, Orioles catcher Dave Duncan posed with a monkey's paw that had been sent by Dr. John

Agunga of Nairobi, Kenya, the team physician. The monkey paw was to help Baltimore overtake the Sox.

Duncan was saying the paw looked like something from Colonel Sanders, and that it hadn't seemed to work too well. Perhaps it was because Dr. Agunga had asked too much of the Orioles: He had asked them to forsake completely, for the remainder of the season, meat, sweets and beer, and to have no sex for at least twelve hours before every game. (After the Agunga dictum, Weaver benched outfielder Jim Northrup, an apparent womanizer . . . or glutton.)

Perhaps the Orioles had been faithful to the Agunga requirement. Perhaps it was something else . . . perhaps it was Laurie Cabot, a Salem witch (and Red Sox fan), who nullified the Agunga whammy by spreading "a blue veil over the Atlantic."

Whatever. The Orioles, unable to hold a 3–1 lead after six innings in the nightcap, died. At 7:27 P.M., according to Elgin.

By then, the Red Sox had all left Fenway Park. Not one stayed around the locker room, tuned to the radio, to hear the death of Baltimore. There was no champagne celebration. In fact, no one was there, save for the clubhouse man vacuuming the carpet.

In the press room atop Fenway, only seven persons were around to congratulate Manager Darrell Johnson when the Associated Press machine ticked the final score from New York.

Idolizes His Team

Owner Tom Yawkey, who idolizes his team and gives them everything (in turn, they have given him two pennants and *no* World Series championships in forty-two years), was listening in his Ritz-Carlton suite to a New York station. ("It fades in and out," Yawkey explained later.)

When he heard the Orioles lose, he rang room service and ordered a dish of chocolate ice cream.

Star pitcher Luis Tiant said he went out and had a pizza; pitcher Bill Lee said he fulfilled a speaking engagement; star rookie Cecil (Flash) Cooper, who finished with a .311 batting average, said he went bowling. And the greatest rookie star of all, Fred Lynn, came to grips with the intricacies of his new Buick, given by fans in appreciation of his services: he topped the American League in doubles, with 47; runs scored, with 103; and slugging percentage, with .566; was second in batting average, at .331; and was third in runs batted in, with 105, and total bases, with 299. By contrast, on the same date a year ago, as a nonroster rookie up from Pawtucket at season's end, he was calling Boston police to report that his van had been stolen from around the corner at Fenway Park.

Carl Yastrzemski, the anchor of this team for the last fifteen years, was off to his new Florida home to rest his sore left shoulder for a few days, and to anguish over his financial problems. (No longer is there a Yaz Ford; gone, too, is Big Yaz Bread, which surfaced in 1967, the year of the Impossible Dream, in which the Red Sox captured the pennant . . . or the old gonfalon, as we in baseball say . . . after finishing ninth in a ten-team league the year before.)

Harrah's Reno and Tahoe race books had already named Oakland a seven-to-five favorite over the Sox to win the pennant, although the two clubs split twelve games this year. Oakland, bloody Oakland: World Series champions three consecutive years. They've got it all: speed afoot, pitching dangerous hitters, and that tangible called experience. You know, "they've been there before." Yes, there's enough of a there, there now.

The man who regularly tosses batting practice to the Red Sox is—and you're not going to believe this!—Martin Stone, the wealthy industrialist from Los Angeles who has been bankrolling the Democratic Party for almost a decade.

Stone used to throw batting practice for the Dodgers, until he moved East two years ago after a marital breakup.

Stone tried to buy the L.A. Rams football team, but Carroll Rosenbloom wouldn't sell. He also tried to buy the S.F. Giants, but Horace Stoneham insisted that the deal include his Casa Grande, Arizona, real estate, and his shopping center in Bloomington, Minnesota, none of which Stone particularly wanted.

Nor did he want Candlestick Park. "And it would cost too much to build a new one," Stone believes.

Stone knows that if baseball is to survive in San Francisco, it must move into an intimate ball yard . . . like Fenway Park.

"A nice wooden stadium," he suggested. Like old Seals Stadium. Well, folks, you've got that parcel of Yerba Buena land sitting there gathering dirt and hoboes.

You know, I've got a hunch that Stone can be had; for, after all, isn't San Francisco the Paris of the West, while Boston is merely the Hub of the Universe? Seduce Stone with your many charms. Let's see now, what've we got: Well, we got Trader Vic's, and, uh, Ernie's. . . .

No, I'm serious! If you're interested in having the Giants remain in San Francisco, in having them rescued from the dotage of Horace Stoneham, then, by all means, write or wire Martin Stone at his home in Weston, Massachusetts. Or call his West Coast offices in Los Angeles, at (213) 879-2003.

Believe me, the Chicago White Sox will move to Seattle (which has been *promised* an American League team; said promise being all that has kept the lid on a messy court case filed by the city of Seattle, who now want the promise kept). When that happens, Charlie Finley will move his Oakland A's to Chicago, his hometown, where he lives and works, leaving the Bay Area with one creaky old club playing in a wind tunnel. Believe me.

Look, Candlestick Park is unplayable!

Don't accept my word for it, take a ball player's.

Here's Red Sox reliever Jim Willoughby, who pitched for the Giants last year: "Toes," he said, "got frostbite."

Willoughby, a native of Gustine, California (which he assures me is 95 percent Portuguese) and a Berkeley man, sometimes dares not believe what's happened to him. "Here I am in Boston with all these people in the park. After being at Candlestick, it's a culture shock."

So, build a little wooden ball yard downtown with a seating capacity of . . . oh, about twenty to twenty-five thousand. Nice and intimate. All the pensioners who live in the Tenderloin around Market and Mission will be there every day; pensioners do love baseball so. Do something for the old folks, you buzzards. Let Angelina Alioto throw out the first ball, if that's what it takes to make the Happy Mayor shake a lame-duck leg.

Fidel Castro Boo-Boo

Is it time to hep you to the Cuban Triple Play? Okay. It went: Camillo Pascual to Jose Valdevielso to Julio Becquer, for the old Washington Senators. Remember that, because is good five-dollar stump-em barroom bet, hey. Quiz: Who was the major league club owner who took a look-see at a young Cuban pitcher named Fidel Castro and didn't like what he saw? Yes, Horace Stoneham could've changed the face of history by inking the Big Cigar.

Sara Jane Moore living across the street from me on Guerrero all that time? For nearly two years I told Dave Felton that 565 Guerrero (we live at 520) was an SLA safe house. He'd just laugh at me. How do you know? he'd ask. Because interracial couples go in there, I'd say. Felton would snicker.

Crazy little place, Fenway. First came here in 1946. Ted was back from the war. Father brought me. We sat in the third base grandstand. They played Chicago. The Bosox vs. the Chisox. Ted lined a single to right. I'll never forget it. And who will forget the last time Ted Williams stepped to the plate as a major leaguer, and knocked Dizzy Trout's grooved fast ball deep into the right field bleachers (that was before Kimball's time)? Ah, Fenway. . . .

Baltimore was gone, Dr. Agunga notwithstanding. And then there was Oakland.

The Altamont of Baseball

"Third base at Fenway," Bibesco, professor of Red Sox at a girls' school in the Wellesley area, disclosed across our table at the Casablanca in Harvard Square, "is a black hole in the universe.

"And the problem is," he added, leaning closer, "we suffer from an absentee third baseman—with 'ostronaut' problems, as is well known. Inner ear difficulties. They knocked John Glenn out of the race, if you will recall."

True, our third baseman, Americo Petrocelli, had left the team earlier this year, citing dizzy spells as the reason for retirement at thirty-one. Rico was beaned by a fast ball late last season, badly beaned, and, like Tony Conigliaro—skulled even worse in '67, between life and death for days, nearly losing an eye in the end—never quite came back. But Rico did return, and came alive with his bat in September's stretch drive, helping our darling Red Sox to a divisional title and the American League pennant (his glove never was in dispute).

Why, I interrupted, is third base at Fenway a black hole in the universe?

"Why," answered Bibesco, "is the Bermuda Triangle a black hole in the universe? Well," he abruptly switched, "I must be getting back to the Wellesley area. My regards."

A's Manager Alvin Dark, after the humiliating 7–1 loss in Game One that day, suggested the second game is the most important in a short, three-out-of-five series. Dark was confident in the knowledge that the A's always lost Game One of the pennant series.

"If we lose," admitted Dark, "we've got to win three straight." Lose, they did. Three straight.

After that first game, Sox star Carl Yastrzemski, a hero in all three games of the truncated series, also was brought to the special press interview area, and talked about playing The Wall in left after nearly two seasons away from there (at first base).

Said Yaz (Claudell Washington, please note): "The one thing that bothers players at The Wall is the carom. You must decide, and either stay with it, or go back and play the carom. You can't turn your back on The Wall. That's the one thing you can't do. You must decide—if it's going high up The Wall, turn your back on it, and play the carom."

Someone asked Yaz how it felt to play The Wall again after so long an absence. "I can play it in my sleep."

Claudell Washington did. So jittery was the A's regular left fielder with that thirty-six-foot-high sheet metal monster at his back, that the *Globe*'s Peter Gammons was moved to write: "Claudell played left field as if he were reacting to a 4:25 A.M. phone call."

By the way, our *Chronicle* dispatched no one to Boston to cover the two games there, so you're probably getting this for the first time; whereas the *Globe*, Boston's counterpart to the *Chron* as the dominant morning daily, sent five writers and two photographers to Oakland for the third and final game. (The *Examiner* did cover the Boston games first-hand.) Even newspaper guys from Toronto, which doesn't have a major league franchise, went to Boston.

Claudell Washington did not return to left field for Game Two. Joe Rudi was sent there instead, after A's owner Charles O. Finley meddled with Manager Dark's line-up. Could you blame him, though? In that first game the A's set a new major league playoff record for most errors in an inning: three, in the first; and a new American League playoff record for most errors in a game: four.

Following the 6–3 loss in Game Two, Alvin Dark was willing to admit: "We were out-played today. They out-played us. Fellahs, these fellahs up here on the platform behind me have just out-played us, that's all. They beat the best reliever in baseball," Dark said of Rollie Fingers. "This is a great team."

Fingers was the third Oakland pitcher in Game Two, starter Vida Blue having departed after thirty-eight pitches and three-plus innings. The score was 3–3 when Fingers entered with none out in the fifth and Cecil Cooper on second with a double. He snuffed the Sox in that inning, but gave up three earned runs on five hits over the final three, and was credited with the loss, a rare occurrence. He yielded a home run to our third baseman, Americo Petrocelli, who knocked it, as we in baseball say, off a light tower above The Wall.

That was it for Fingers in postseason '75. He was not used, of course, in the hilarious Hall of Errors that was Game One; nor did he appear in the one-night stand at the coliseum here (there; is there a there, there?).

He was not the man depicted by Tony Conigliaro up in the press box. I asked Tony, who sat next to me at both Fenway games (wait'll ya hear who sat next to me in Oakland!), to rate Fingers. How good is he, Tony?

"I never hit him."

What makes him so exceptionally good a pitcher?

"He's low. And he's viciously hard."

Fast balls?

"No. Hard sliders and hard curves. He doesn't miss and he's *always* down low. When he misses, he misses by this much." (Tony brought his hands to within an inch or two of closing.) "You swing because it's a strike, and then it turns out to be a ball. His stuff tails away from right-handed batters."

Right-handed batters. Here, analyzing Fingers for me, was a man destined to be one of the all-time great right-handed hitters, perhaps the greatest. Tony Conigliaro. Sitting up in the press box at the age of thirty-one, when he might've still been in his prime down on the field, leading the Red Sox to a pennant as he did in '67 before a hack Angels pitcher names Jack Hamilton crushed his skull in mid-season with a pitch. (When Tony began to bail out of the batter's box, correctly sensing a brushback pitch, but too late, his helmet flew off, and Hamilton struck him in the temple.)

Tony C. Yeah, Tony C. A local kid, the darling of ethnic Boston, crown prince of Fenway. Tony Conig.

Before he was twenty-one, he had knocked more than a hundred career home runs. No one in the history of baseball had ever accomplished that. None likely will.

He was apace of Babe Ruth and Hank Aaron—and with all those years yet ahead. Then, on a July night, he was on the ground, dead as a ball player at age twenty-two, almost a dead man.

In 1970 he was named Comeback Player of the Year. But he faded. Gone was the pinpoint vision that told him when to swing, when to hold, when to duck.

He tried again this year as a designated hitter. He got the first Red Sox base hit of '75, a single on opening day. On the first road trip, in April, in Baltimore, he knocked the first Red Sox home run of '75. But he faded. And the Red Sox could no longer hold back Jim Ed Rice, a marvelous rookie star who might have won the RBI title (runs batted in) were it not for a broken hand late in the season in Detroit.

Conigliaro went to Pawtucket and tried to play his way back to the Red Sox, who surely would have brought him up at season's end for morale during the championships. Tony knew, however, that he was through. So, when the opportunity came, he accepted the job of sports announcer for a Providence TV station. Such opportunities do not last forever. That is how he came to see a baseball game at Fenway from the press box . . . for the first time in his life.

Was there any enjoyment for you in playing at Pawtucket this year? "No. It was a drag. I was either injured, in the dugout, or in Pawtucket."

Did you ever hear from Jack Hamilton? Conigliaro grimaced at the mention of the name.

Ah, Tony, Tony. You didn't deserve the random wickedness you were dealt. Sweet boy of summer.

Below us, on the Fenway green, our Sox were taking it to the A's. The world champions were done, everyone in America watching could sense. The king is dying; long live the king.

The A's came alive only for a moment in the three games. In the first inning of Game Two, Reggie Jackson knocked a two-run homer deep into the right field bleachers, several rows up in Section 42. It was caught, someone said, or rather stopped, by the ample and boozy belly of the notorious one-eyed sporting writer George Kimball, who has positioned himself there all seasons, being as he is, banished from the press box for a variety of just causes. (In Game One, the masterful Luis Tiant, on his way to a three-hit victory, always checked with Kimball out in Section 42 while winding up to pitch flashing his back to the batter, showing off his number twenty-three to the plate, or so the uninitiated thought. In truth, the wily Cuban was checking last moment signals with Kimball, who kept an eye on the batter for Tiant.)

"You have any idea how hard Reggie hit that?" Conigliaro asked after that mighty knocked homer. Of course I had no idea, but that is not the point. "Look," Conigliaro said, pointing to the flagpole in center field, "the wind is blowing *in*. The air is heavy today. I saw them in batting practice. They couldn't even get it out to the warning track."

That was it. Reggie's blast into Kimball's mid-riff. Perhaps Reggie thought Kimball would crumble. No longer would he be able to keep an eye on opposing batters for Sox pitchers as they wound up to throw. Instead, the A's crumbled.

The scene in Oakland two days later was ugly. Ugly! Thank God it was brief.

The best of the day was its beginning: a leisurely brunch at the Sincere Cafe on Sixteenth Street here, where we in baseball dine while in town. Afterwards, we drove to Oakland in the staff car, photographer Tim Page, a horribly gnarled and crippled British subject, half of whose body is in Vietnam, at the wheel. The Hyatt, Holiday and Hilton out near the coliseum were deserted. It had not occurred to us that the players and wives and writers would be spending the day in San Francisco. But of course!

We were hours early. The parking lot at the coliseum was yet a tar prairie. For reasons perhaps known only on high, a solitary vehicle crossed the lot, in reverse gear, toward us. There was not another car for acres, yet this car was clearly on a collision course with us as we motored slowly toward a parking space close to the press entrance. Then it happened: not with the squealing of brakes followed by silence, but with a BANG! The rear fender of the staff car crumbled like so many A's. The backward motorist turned out to be a coliseum guard.

Eventually, Kimball arrived at our seats with another bucket of beer. Was it fate that placed me in Press Box D, Seat 84, and this bulging, huffing, mustachioed monster in Seat 85? (Conspiracy buffs, please note: after all, Kimball is eighty-six at the Fenway press box. How is it that I have Tony Conigliaro as a neighbor for the Fenway games, and Kimball out here?)

(Numerologists, please note: Conigliaro and Kimball are both thirty-one years old, although one could never guess it of Kimball . . . no, not in a million years.)

In the middle of the ninth, Kimball and I left our seats and headed for the elevator down to the field, to avoid the crush of the lumpenproles at game's end, and to have clear access to what would be a champagne-soaked clubhouse, provided the Red Sox held their two-run lead, which they did, 5–3, to sweep the A's in the minimum.

A routing ground ball to second base (or sand bag, as we in baseball say) ended all hopes for the A's of winning a fourth consecutive World Series. I sprinted along the tunnel to the clubhouse, mere hoofbeats ahead of thundering, whooping Red Sox.

A security guard blocked me at the door, players piling into me from the rear. "Everywhere!" I shouted at the guard, pointing at the yellow card I clutched in some hand. And I was through!

There was no one in the clubhouse!

I had beaten them all.

(I didn't learn until sometime later that the players were to have been permitted about ten minutes of private revelry before anyone else—press included—was permitted entry.)

Here is my scoop:

I stood there furiously lapping champagne. (Why not? Spoil Sport Charlie Finley had canceled the hospitality room dinner and drinks upon his team's elimination, meaning that not only the press, but commissioner's people, executives of other clubs, old players, graphologists and the like, would go hungry. The food and the estimated two thousand dollars' worth of green and gold flowers on the tables would just have to sit there, like the waiters from the caterer. Charlie O. would eat those considerable costs rather than let the people party! That is where he is at: an eccentric individual.)

Soon, however, there were more reporters in the room. And my scoop was at the end.

These new reporters were asking questions! "Howz it

feel?" they'd inquire of players, unable, for some strange reason, to fathom what they were witnessing. "Howz it feel?" they'd ask our champagne-splotched darlings, who were all hugging at each other, patting fannies, embracing, showering with champagne, joyous in their championship. Howz it feel? (O'Connor of the *Palo Alto Times* was the worst offender.) "Great!" a player would answer when tested. Howz it feel? "Great!" (Writers perhaps don't know it, but we in baseball are taught that word for just this occasion.) I got caught in this frenzy and, being professional myself, had second thoughts about how capably I was discharging my correspondency. So, very soon, I found myself running up to players, and asking them, "Hey!"

"Great!"

("Hey" is a very special word to baseball people, and, as much as I'd like to—because you are my friends—I cannot divulge its secret meaning, for that would compromise my correspondency. I'm sorry. But, well . . . you know how it is.)

Howz it?

"Great!"

Howz it feel? "Great!"

When Finley lost, he unleashed his fascist insects to prey on the people.

An old man tried to enter the clubhouse as I peered between the cops at Page. They closed ranks and jostled the old-timer. "I'm Carl Yastrzemski's father," the old man said.

"I don't care who you are," said Zeigler, who did all the talking. "If you don't have a yellow pass you don't get in."

I entered the dispute. That's Carl's father, I affirmed. I know him.

Old Mr. Yaz acknowledged my effort with hopeful face and expected entry. But the cop spun toward me.

"And who are you!" he challenged.

Red Sox press, I said.

"Nobody gets in here without a yellow pass."

Look, you asshole, that's Carl Yastrzemski's father. I *know* who he is. Now are you going to let him in, or not?

Wait just a moment, Mr. Yastrzemski, I said, and reentered the clubhouse proper, spotted Dick O'Connell, executive vice-president and general manager of the Sox, told him the problem and watched him take action. Old Yaz entered the clubhouse and embraced his thirty-six-year-old son, his baby, the hero of the 1975 American League championships. Good! Now I had equity with O'Connell and set to work on Page's behalf. Dick, I said, these guards won't let my photographer in. They're ruining my story! (The cop heard this as I led O'Connell back to the doorway . . . and guffawed in my face.) "Nobody gets in here without a yellow pass!" the cop repeated.

O'Connell drew back, reached into his inside coat pocket, motioned me over, and handed me an everywhere pass. The cop observed. O'Connell and I and Page were like a fire brigade passing a bucket of water. I leaned through the cop and passed the yellow everywhere to Page.

"I saw him give it to you!" the cop screamed at me, referring to O'Connell's conspicuous move. I said, look you turkey! I've had all I'm taking from you. He's got an everywhere and he's coming in! And you're not stopping him! Get it?

What happened next was fairly incredible. (Too bad those cops didn't wear name tags!) The cop grabbed my arm, yanked me out the door and into the tunnel, backed me against the wall, blocked me there, out of sight, with his fat body, and rammed me two or three times in the stomach with either his elbow or his nightstick.

It was the Altamont of Baseball.

"Now *you're* out!" he triumphed.

Hell I am I'm everywhere, and I'm *in*! You know, my friend, your limited powers have gone to your head. You're an arbitrary mad dog fool!

"That's just what I called him!" shouted Page. "Arbitrary."

"Two-dollar words don't move me," confessed the cop. "Why don't you coin a new one?"

Haywood Sullivan, vice-president—the number three man in the organization, was closest. Hey, Haywood! This guy over here won't let my photographer through because he saw Dick O'Connell slip me an everywhere pass to give to him. What kind of nonsense *is* this!

Sullivan moved for the doorway. At six-four, this former U of Florida All-American quarterback (and eventual second-string Sox catcher) dwarfed the Hun.

Once inside, Page thanked Sullivan. "Help yourself to a beer, kid," said Sullivan.

Meanwhile, I was with O'Connell, thanking him.

"I dunno," shrugged O'Connell, as if to say . . . who can figure it. "They let a guy in a while ago who's trying to sell striped kicks. [Kicks is a baseball expression for shoes.] Anyway, help yourself to a beer."

Yes, the Red Sox official family was in fine spirits.

PR director Bill Crowley, one of the men responsible for banning Kimball from the Fenway press box (although he is welcome in every other American League press box—why, I'll never know), all but hugged the one-eyed writer in the warm glow of victory. "Well, George," Crowley beamed, "I guess we're gonna give you another shot at the press box during the Series." It was a time for the granting of plenary indulgence.

Grateful, Kimball tilted closer to Crowley, stopped his glass eye from falling out again, and, nose-to-nose with Crowley, said, "What am I supposed to do, thank you?!"

Later, Kimball cadged a ride with us back to San Francisco. In the parking lot he kept dropping things from his briefcase and coat: his score card, notebook, stat sheets. I picked up after him. He wobbled. He could barely walk, so lushed was he. Only an hour before, I swear, he was sober as we left the press box for the clubhouse. Somewhere near Yerba Buena Island he vomited all over the back seat of the staff car. (And denied doing it!) Down went all windows. Kimball was silent the rest of the way and did not stir when we reached his destination. I turned around. He was asleep. His right eye stared coldly back at us.

The End of the Bo Sox As We Have Known Them

> *"So the Reds tugged on champagne bottles which they personally thought were long overdue in arriving. They were not so much winners as they were survivors."*
>
> *Wells Twombly*

Cincinnati had to have it on paper. That is what comes of regimentation. When you permit yourself to be made into a machine, when you submit your constitutional rights to proscription by a whimsical fascist, you must have that championship on paper, certified. You suffer a crisis of confidence because somewhere down deep you know it is wrong to let a man tell you what kind of hair you may grow and at what length, and because you know it is wrong to play baseball on Astro-turf, and wrong for grown men to chew bubble gum.

This is what this World Series was all about: two different points of view about life, two conflicting approaches toward the same goal, two clashing political realities. For when the One Great Scorer comes to write against your name, He marks—not that you won or lost—but how you coiffed your mane.

That is why the Reds *really* lost. God sees to things like that.

The Big Red Machine came to Fenway Park on October 11, and went pff-fft, losing to the Old Man, Luis Tiant, 6–0. The Old Man threw the ball fast. Slow. Slower. Straight. Curved. Forked. Sliding. "How many strike-outs did he have?" Pete Rose of the Reds mumbled after the game. "Two? Three? What kind of shutout is it with three strike-outs?"

Game Two began the same way. Bill Lee, like Tiant the day before, retired the first ten Reds. Lee threw the ball fast. Slow. Slower. Slower than the Old Man. Straight. Curved. Screwed. Forked. Sliding. Our Red Sox led 2–1 going into the final inning. In two games, the Machine had managed but one run and nine hits in seventeen innings. But then Johnny Bench doubled to open the ninth. Darrell Johnson removed Lee. Johnson, however, would not have removed the Old Man under the same circumstances. Johnson dislikes Lee. Johnson lives in Pinole, within haunting distance of San Francisco. We can haunt him this winter for his blunder.

The Evil Dick Drago, a mustachioed flame thrower, was Johnson's choice to save Game Two, and almost did, retiring the next two batters on hard sliders and heat, and getting two strikes on the final batter . . . before he no longer was the final batter. The Reds scored twice to win, 3–2.

In the postgame interview room beneath the stands, a writer asked Lee his impression of the World Series after two games. "Tied," deadpanned Lee. Someone asked if Lee would like to meet Henry Kissinger, who had thrown out the ceremonial first ball. "Sure. I'd like to ask him where my wheat's going." A few feet away, in NBC's hospitality tent, Red Sox Fan Walter Cronkite confided to his many well-wishers that he was a bit glum. Weren't we all.

The next stop was close-cropped Cincinnati. (Cronkite would not go for fear of his mustache.)

From the airport, fifteen miles inside Kentucky, to downtown, Greater Cincinnatians tog themselves in red and white, the team colors, boasting welcome to The Baseball Capital of the World. The citizens are very serious about their technocratic dream, the Big Red Machine.

Not much else goes down in the Rhineland, one quickly senses. The dailies lead the cheering and page one is given to the Reds. It is as though the world outside is a warp, a black hole in the universe, unencountered. Cinci, just another forlorn border-south Queen City, the Gateway to something or other; just another midland metropolis that looms up with no hint as you crest rolling farmland. The breadbasket of the Silent Majority, the only major American city that never had the pleasure of voting for Franklin D. Roosevelt.

Unfortunately for the World Series, which in 1975 is a sizable traveling show, there was no room at Stauffer's Inn, the designated World Series headquarters. Cinti, as it is also locally known, booked a convention of the National Rehabilitation Association during what turned out to be World Series Week. Even though the Reds have been in three World Series in the last six years, the chamber of commerce had no faith. Stauffer's was forced to deposit the World Series in obscure function rooms. And when the National Rehabilitation Association moved out, a convention of the National Pigeon Association moved in. So much for The Baseball Capital of the World.

The Red Sox, because of the shortage of downtown accommodations, commuted from Sharonville, Ohio, a thirty-minute drive. As much as I would have liked being out there with our darling Beausox, at the intersection of two interstate highways, graced by Hilton, Holiday and Ramada, I perished the thought.

And came to rest at the Milner, three blocks from Stauffer's, and trying to upgrade its image: An advisory taped to the front desk now warns employees not to "let winos or bums use the rest rooms." (Ah, so we won't be bothered by the World Series press!)

There would be a night to kill before the Series resumed for three games at Riverfront Stadium. In Cinti, the night belongs in Newport, Kentucky, across the Ohio River. At the Pink Pussy Cat on York Street, Gina Bon-Bon did incredible things to her do-do on stage and when her act was over she said, "Can I hear a little applause, for crissakes." At the Brass Ass on Monmouth Street, a woman from Barcelona permitted me to address her in Portuguese, at $4 a drink. Later, at another place on another street, there was Phyllis, a high-cheekboned mountain gal (yum-yum), who consented to tell me about her day gig as a file clerk, first at $1.25 a drink, and then, somehow, at $2.50 a drink. I think Helen, the bartender, had problems with arithmetic. But I was sympathetic because I realize hilly-billy persons have been culturally deprived. Poor Helen also had trouble with her eyesight, for she seemed forever to be removing my full drink, pouring it down the sink, smiling at me, and inquiring whether I would care for another.

My poke was shy nearly two yards when I awoke the next afternoon (a yard is a baseball expression meaning a hundred dollars).

Then, suddenly, there was Game Three. I'll not soon forget my first moments inside Riverfront Stadium, setting rookie foot on Astro-turf, actually Tartan-turf, a second-generation sponge. Well, there I was, standing on this shit. I can't even describe it. I mean, what is it? Deep within this electric doughnut, standing in this plastic pasture, not at all knowing where I am, when it occurred to me: This is what the moon was like.

Rick Wise, a former National League pitcher who threw a no-hitter against these same Reds four years ago in this same nightmarish setting, started for our adopted team. For three and two-thirds innings Wise was hardly scathed, a replica of Tiant and Lee in Games One and Two. Wise was burned in the fifth. Carlton Fisk, our catcher, walked to the mound to calm him, dribbling the ball on the plastic . . . like a basketball! . . . a supreme putdown of the environment, a perfect squelch to the nomads and technocrats who designed Riverfront. But nothing obtained: Wise never completed the inning. The Red Sox battled back, however, tying the game in the ninth on a two-run knocked homer by Dwight (Dewey) Evans, our right fielder. The Cinti partisans choked on their bratwurst. They were amazed that the Red Sox had won even one game from the Big Red Machine.

In the bottom of the tenth there occurred the most outrageous baseball injustice of our time. The Reds had a runner on first and Sparky Anderson sent in a pinch hitter, Edison Armbrister, to bunt. Armbrister bunted, and then just stood there. Carlton Fisk couldn't get at the ball in play. Then Armbrister laid a beautiful body block on our Fisk, who finally shoved him out of the way and fielded the ball into center field, sending the runner to third and the canny Armbrister all the way to second. The home plate umpire, Larry Barnett, a resident of Prospect, Ohio, refused to call interference on Armbrister, although the rule book plainly states that a batter or runner is automatically out whenever he gets in the way of a defensive player attempting to field a ball in play. To Barnett, the interference was merely an unfortunate "collision."

The dangerous Pete Rose was intentionally walked to load the bases. The infield moved in to force a play at the plate.

Jim Willoughby, who had pitched three neat innings in relief, was yanked by Darrell Johnson, who replaced him with left-hander Rogelio Moret. It was a percentage move, as we in baseball say, for the next batter, Ken Griffey, is left-handed and left-handed batters aren't supposed to hit left-handed pitchers. The move works: Griffey strikes out.

The infield moves back slightly. If we can get a double play, we're out of the inning. But the game is over if Joe Morgan, another lefty, hits even a medium fly to the outfield, which remains shallow to cut down the potential winning run at the plate. With the speedy Cesar Geronimo at third, the outfield *must* play in. They have to cut down Geronimo at the plate if there is a fly ball. If Morgan hits the ball deep, or even medium, it'll just have to sail over the outfielder's head.

Morgan hit what would have been a routine out to medium center and Fred Lynn just watched it sail over his head, a game-winning technical single. But that's baseball.

So, the Red Sox were jobbed out of Game Three and the bubble gum–chewing Big Red Machine took the Series lead. Middle America relaxed and Nixon, Rebozo, Abplanalp and C. Arnholt Smith made another call to their bookmakers.

After the game, Darrell Johnson was his typical tight-lipped, seething self: "Well, his [Barnett's] interpretation of the interference rule is different than mine. There is no way you can appeal an umpire's judgment call."

But in the clubhouse everybody wanted a piece of Barnett, who failed to see what everyone else in America saw, even though he was closest to it.

"Bring back Emmett Ashford!" Bill Lee was yelling, hands cupped to mouth. (Ashford, the first black major league umpire, now retired, was terribly inept, though a great showman.) "Where's George Kimball when I need him!" Lee demanded. Answered Wells Twombly of the S.F. *Examiner* truthfully, "They wouldn't let him in the park." (Kimball was out in Sharonville, at the Ramada Inn, banished from yet another park, watching the game on TV.)

Everyone was going berserk: "Those yellow, gutless, cocksuckers. They can kiss our asses. Five of those six are the worst umpires in baseball! And they're in this Series! And you print it! Fuck the fines!" (It serves no good to identify the players, but that is what they said.)

Until recently, umpires were selected for World Series assignment based on achievement during the season. Now, for reasons perhaps only Commissioner Bowie Kuhn can explain, they are picked by annual rotation. Therefore, none of the six turkeys working this Series had ever worked one before! It is done this way, one could surmise, simply so they can have it in their biography. One of these turkeys, Nick Colosi, is a former headwaiter at the Copacabana, defunct; another, Dick Stello, last year married Chesty Morgan, a stripper with seventy-three-inch assets. Not only that, but Stello blew bubble gum bubbles during Game One. I mean, what is this!

Captain Carl Yastrzemski, exhausted in front of his locker and looking older than his thirty-six years, spoke wearily to a clump of reporters. "Look," Yaz said, "these are two great teams. The fans deserve the best umpiring. I don't know where they got the idea of rotating the umpires. Maybe they ought to rotate the teams. Next year, maybe we ought to have the Padres and the White Sox."

Old Luis Tiant, the soul of this team, chuckled quietly to himself in front of his locker, sitting there in his shorts, a big Cuban cigar in his mouth. "Wha good it do to protes?" he asked no one in particular. "We jes haf to sleet the mawtherfucker's throat. Yes, thas wha we do. Jez go over and keel heem. What else can we do?"

This was now more than a World Series. It was now of mythic proportion: the freedom-loving Boston (and S.F.) Red Sox vs. the martinet's Rhinelanders.

The players cooled somewhat next day and Jim Willoughby found time to play the pariah Kimball a game of chess at the Ramada, way out in Sharonville. "He was all right for a while," Willoughby declared during practice before Game Four. "But then I took it to his kitchen" (chess talk).

Shortly after Willoughby reported this, it began to rain artificially. At 8:15 P.M., however, precisely fifteen minutes before game time, Stadium Control shut off the rain. "It is designed into the system," a keeper of the Tartan-turf explained, "to heighten excitement."

That is not Riverfront's only marvel. Stadium Control also can blare an artificial bugle charge through the sound system whenever the Rhinelanders appear to have something going at bat. The speaker nearest me was situated some ten feet from my left ear. A man in a Cincinnati Red necktie, seated next to me, noticed that I winced when the high-pitched bugle call was fed into the system. Either out of embarrassment for a lost past, or to serve notice, he offered, "You're in the Heartland, you know."

El Tiante, El Conquistador, hurled Game Four. Old Luis had no fast ball, no control, and his slow stuff was being timed by the Reds. Luis this night was a mere shadow of his nonpareil Game One self. Tagged for two runs in the first inning, Luis struggled. After the game, he would say his shaky first inning occurred because the mound was too high and it took a while to make adjustments. But our Sox came back, and Luis checked the Reds to win, 5–4. He threw a total of 163 pitches to gain his second World Series triumph. He evened the Series at two games each, though he worked with only three days rest. He beat them on nothing more than courage and instinct. In the clubhouse, reserve infielder Bob Heise (of Vacaville) noted that "after the seventh, Luis was really bringing it." Fisk thought that in the fifth, Luis "looked like he lost his velocity." And reserve catcher Tim Blackwell believed that when Luis struck out slugger Johnny Bench in a crucial eighth inning situation, "I think he struck him out on a real good spitter. He throws it about once a month."

Old Luis, good Luis . . . you the bes, baby.

In Game Five, Cinti finally looked like the 108-game winners they were this regular season. Their ace pitcher, Don Gullett, from over the river in Kentucky, was, simply put, overpowering. Afterwards, in the interview area set up for the hundreds of reporters, Gullett offered thanks to "my Maker for giving me the ability to throw a baseball."

And his manager, Sparky Anderson, noted that Gullett was a future Hall-of-Famer, and that he, Anderson, would not risk a future Hall-of-Famer's arm in Game Six relief in Boston, even if it meant winning the championship. "He'll go as long as he can in Game Seven, if there is one. I won't damage his arm. No championship is that important to me."

Soon we would be out of the Rhineland, back in Boston. In my four days and nights in Cinti, I never got out to Norwood, Ohio, which, I had been told, was the entire population of Hazard, Kentucky, transplanted. If I had only gotten out there, I knew. . . . If I had only gotten out there and tried real hard, I know I could've gotten me one of those nice, high-cheekbone Loretta Lynn types. I cursed my rotten luck.

Somehow it got to be 3:00 A.M. again and I was in a neighborhood called Walnut Hills, rather high above the town. I wandered streets in search of a pay phone from which to summon Brady Cab. When all of a sudden, as if delivered from *my* Maker, there appeared in front of me, discharging a fare, an honest-to-goodness Brady Cab, which I hailed. To the Milner, please, I instructed.

"You'll never guess what I got tonight!" exclaimed the driver, beaming as he turned to face me. What'd you get?

"This!" he said, flipping a baseball into the back seat. "And it's signed by the entire Cincinnati team! Johnny gave it to me!"

Bench? "Yup. I was out at the Quality Inn, in Norwood. Been there all night watching the game on TV," he said, emphasizing the *T* rather than the *V*. Ah, so here was Norwood, more-or-less, come to me; although the cabbie didn't at all have the kind of cheekbones I was looking for.

"Johnny came in the door and looked around—this was only a couple of hours ago—and he came up to the bar and said, 'Are you Paul?' I guess he didn't recognize me because I got this green cap on."

"You know Johnny Bench?" I asked, returning the ball.

"Yup. Had him in the cab a couple of weeks ago, and he asked me was there anything he could do for me and I told him I wanted a ball with his autograph on it and he said he didn't have one with him at the time. But I guess he went out and had the whole team autograph one."

Are you telling me, Paul, that Johnny Bench, right after a World Series game, late at night, went way the hell out to Norwood and back just to give you a ball?

"Yup. Cain't figure no other reason."

Maybe he was looking for Loretta Lynn?

"I already refused an offer of a hundred dollars for it. And I got it right here where I know it's safe," Paul said as he stopped in front of the Milner. "Right with all my other balls. And there's only one that's autographed."

Rain poured in the morning as Brady Cab drove me out to the airport. The rain followed the plane to Boston and Game Six was postponed daily from Saturday. NBC finally permitted Commissioner Kuhn to announce resumption on Tuesday night.

During the lull, I stayed away from World Series headquarters, which had shifted back to Boston's Statler Hotel, and kept far from the 2:00 P.M. daily Darrell and Sparky Show, direct from Stauffer's Inn. I was already being isolated by the hard-core baseball writers because I had no leisure suit. I went underground with friends in Cambridge and laid low throughout the inclemency at the Casablanca in Harvard Square, where I met once again with H. Bibesco, professor of Red Sox at a girls' school in the Wellesley area.

"The trouble with Cincinnati," suggested Bibesco, swirling his Rémy, "is they all look like state troopers."

And then Bibesco blew my mind.

"You know, there was no . . . there is no . . . no inner ear problem. According to Malzone, Americo was cracking up and wanted to retire in August. Malzone was delegated to talk him out of it. They made up the story of Rico's 'ostronaut' problem—inner ear problem. It was purely cosmetic, for public consumption. But, you see, Rico was cracking up because of the pressure of playing third base at Fenway, which, as you know, is a black hole in the universe."

More than three inches of rain soaked Fenway Park during the postponements and out-of-town writers wondered aloud why old Tom Yawkey, the Sox owner, hadn't installed artificial turf. When the Nor'easter blew itself out, an Indian summer sun arrived. Tuesday, October 21, was warmer than predicted and NBC informed Commissioner Kuhn that Game Six would take place that night. Three helicopters hovered above the outfield grass (Bermuda bent green) all day, driving the wetness into the superior drainage system. The field that night was not merely playable, it was excellent.

Darrell Johnson, because of the three-day delay, changed his pitching rotation for Game Six and announced that the Old Man, and not Bill Lee, would be on the mound. Lee, understandably, was upset. Johnson said he was "going with my best," since there was, as we in baseball say, no tomorrow. Tiant, though he threw 163 pitches in Game Four, had rested six days. Which meant that Lee, if there were a decisive Game Seven, would work after ten days of inactivity. Sparky Anderson, for his part, refused to change plans and said he would not use his ace, Gullett, until Game Seven, despite the fact that his Big Red Machine could end things now. When Game Six took place three days late, Gullett had had his normal four days of rest. But Anderson insisted again that he would not risk ruining the arm of a future Hall-of-Famer. Instead, he would pitch the meatball, Gary Nolan.

For Tiant it would be a chance to join a rare circle: three-game World Series winners. Since 1920, it has happened only four times; and in all, only twelve times. Sparky was virtually conceding Game Six by going with the meatball, Nolan, whom he pulled after only four innings of the Infamous Game Three because of "a crick in the neck." But maybe Sparky knew something: Since 1960, nine World Series have been 3–2 after five games and, without exception, the team trailing has won the sixth. And in seven of those nine years, the team trailing after five games, lost the seventh. In the projected seventh, his ace, the Christian athlete, Don Gullett, would be there, opposite that pro-busing crackpot from San Rafael, Spaceman Bill Lee, who was busy at the moment reading a book on pyramid power and who was apt to become so engrossed that he might forget to appear, anyway.

The Old Man was riding an incredible hot streak at Fenway. He was undefeated, and barely touched, in his last five appearances there, pitching five complete games while allowing only one earned run (two in all) in forty-five innings, and an average of only four base hits a game, to compile an earned run average of amazing grace: .22 per game.

He had broken the Big Red Machine in Game One. And he had done it without the aid of Kimball out in Section 42, the right field bleachers, who kept an eye on things down on the field so Luis could probe the stars while in full wind-up motion. But could he do it again without Kimball? Of what use would Kimball be to the Old Man if seated up in the press box after two and one-half years in Section 42? Had the Red Sox official family inadvertently blundered by reinstating Kimball? What did Fidel Castro think about all this as he sat by his radio in Havana and waited for the Old Man? He thought, as he chopped the end off a fresh cigar and lighted it, that the Old Man was good, and Castro glowed from the knowledge that the only earned run off the Old Man in his last five complete games came in the ninth inning, and that the only other run (unearned) came in the eighth inning of the opening playoff game against the A's. But then a knit crossed the brow of Castro, and he was thinking back . . . back to the blindness of Horace Stoneham, who had not been impressed by the young pitcher Castro during a tryout. His failed ambition burned within, for was he not, like the Old Man, a Cuban? And what did this mean? This meant that had Stoneham signed him, had he not been forced into politics at an early age as a consequence, there would be other Cuban ball players in the Big Leagues today, not just the Old Man and his sidekick Diego Segui, and Tony Perez of the Reds; relics. This meant, as Castro pondered well, that it would be he, and not Bill Lee, hurling for the Sox in Game Seven, after his buddy, the Old Man, stopped the Big Red Machine tonight. And his old friend, the former president, John F. Kennedy, would be in a box seat and they would relive the glory over rum and Coca-Cola later at the Eliot Lounge. Yes, he mused, his eyes misting, Kennedy would have been in a box seat instead of a box had he had his good heat on his velocity, and his good location, when Stoneham looked him over. But that's baseball.

The Old Man took the mound, and looked uncertainly out at Section 42, while 35,205 persons screamed, "Loo-ie, Loo-ie, Loo-ie." The Old Man was in position to become the first World Series pitcher in history to claim a third victory in only six games. The moon was full.

The Old Man dug deep and didn't give up his first hit, a single to Pete Rose, until two were out in the third. Meanwhile, our sensational rookie center fielder, Fred Lynn, who seemed destined to be his league's Most Valuable Player (unprecedented for a rookie), knocked a first inning three-run homer off the meatball Nolan, causing Sparky Anderson to hook him after one more inning because of another crick in the neck.

In the fifth, however, the Machinists solved the Old Man and tied the game at three. With two out, Fred Lynn raced back to The Wall in deep left-center, at the 379-foot mark, and leaped. The ball sailed over his glove and Lynn hit The Wall and lay motionless. Two runs scored and the batter had a triple before right fielder Dewey Evans could come over and return the ball to the infield. Minutes passed as Lynn lay crumpled against the monster. I found myself in a most extreme eeriness as I stood silently with more than 35,000 others at Fenway, some 80 million more Americans watching, also silently, the scene on television, along with countless other persons in Canada and Latin countries. Lynn at length regained his feet and stayed in the game. "I wasn't out," he said in the clubhouse. "I was just numb. I didn't feel anything. It lasted only a minute but it seemed like an eternity." The Wall had caught him on his tail bone, we learned.

The Sox were stopped by a succession of Rhinelander relievers, stranding four men in scoring position in the third and fourth. The Old Man dug deeper.

And came up with less, and less. But he would stay in there and throw pitches at the Machine all night if he had to.

The Old Man gave up two more hits in the sixth, and was stung in the seventh by three hits, producing a 5–3 Cinti lead, after two were out. A lead-off home run to Cesar Geronimo in the eighth put him out of the game. "Luis wasn't pitching that badly," said Darrell Johnson after. "You can never tell how fast a man can lose it. Sometimes it just happens."

The Old Man had given up eleven hits in his seven-plus innings. As I stepped to a phone to book a seat on the noon plane to San Francisco, I wondered about Kimball not being out in Section 42 to keep an eye on things for Luis. I thought about the Old Man and The Machine. And whether Jack Hemingway was watching on TV from his home near the Big Wood River in Idaho.

And then, in the Sox eighth, it happened: the most dramatic homer in baseball since Bobby Thomson's "shot-heard-round-the-world" for the Giants in a then-rare play-off game to decide the National League pennant in 1951.

With two runners on and two out, Johnson told Bernardo Carbo to grab a bat and hit for the pitcher. "Maybe I should just play through June next year," Bernardo had said after knocking a pinch-hit homer in Game Three at Cinti. "I could go to the Cape for the summer and when September comes, they could say, 'oh, Bernie, the playoffs are here; come back now.' "

Bernie Carbo, the Reds' number one draft choice in 1965, chosen ahead of Johnny Bench. The National League's rookie-of-the-year in 1970, chosen ahead of Johnny Bench. But, for some reason, Sparky Anderson picked on him, and Carbo was soon a much-traded marginal player. Bernie Carbo, who keeps the many visages of Buddha in his locker for good luck; Bernie Carbo, who used to travel with a stuffed toy gorilla until his mates stole it and burned it; Bernie Carbo, who, it is said, doesn't know what day it is, let alone where he is; Bernie Carbo, who kidded former teammate Pete Rose, a scrappy banjo hitter, as he rounded third base after his Game Three homer, "don't you wish you had strength like that?"

Bernie looked awkward at the plate. He had two strikes. Rawlins J. Eastwich III, the Reds' fine young reliever, fired a fast ball that rode in on Carbo. "I had to do something, " said Carbo later, "because it was a strike, so I swung late. If the ball ever has been hit fair, it never would've made it back to the pitcher." So, Carbo took what he called "a Japanese swing," and squiggled the ball foul. Leigh Montville of the *Boston Globe* called it "the worst looking foul ball that probably ever has been hit in a World Series." How retarded was Carbo's swing? Umpire Satch Davidson called "ball" before realizing that Carbo was, indeed, swinging, however late. On the bench, Carlton Fisk witnessed the swing and moaned, "Oh, no, this guy isn't going to do anything." The Sox, Fisk believed, were dead. "Our whole dugout was dead. We were four outs away from the end of the World Series."

And on the next pitch, Bernardo Carbo became the first Basque baseball hero when he knocked a screamer to dead center, about ten rows up in the bleachers, nearly 450 feet away, a real Ted Williams shot. Three runs scored. Carbo had tied the game. The Evil Dick Drago came to the mound for the ninth inning, testing his mustache against the Huns' crew-cut coiffure, his chaw of tobacco against their Fleer's Double-Bubble addiction. The Reds failed to get the ball out of the infield and were retired in order.

The Sox loaded the bases in their ninth with none out. The game, we knew now, was over. Fred Lynn, with two base hits in three at bats, was up. He lofted a short fly to left. It barely traveled 150 feet. Suddenly Denny Doyle broke from third for the plate. It resulted in a disastrous double play.

Our third base coach, Don Zimmer (who once captained baseball and basketball teams at Cinti's Western Hills High, which also produced Pete Rose), defended himself: "It wasn't a gamble. It was suicide. I yelled at him, 'you can't go!' I saw where the ball was, and yelled at him, 'Don't go; you can't go . . . no! No!' I guess he thought I was telling him, '*Go . . . go . . . go*.' Maybe I should've tackled him." Pete Rose, who could hear the instructions from his third base position, turned to Zimmer after the play, and asked, "How many times can you tell a guy 'no'? " Doyle, asked later if he thought Zimmer was sending him home on the play, answered, "Obviously."

And then, in the eleventh, Dewey Evans thwarted a certain home run by making an improbable, leaping, one-handed grab of a fly ball deep in the right field corner, taking it on the dead run and whirling and throwing instinctively toward Yastrzemski at first base for an inning-ending double play. "It wasn't the best catch I ever made," the characteristically modest Evans said later. Yaz thought more of it: "It was one of the greatest catches I've ever seen."

On the second pitch of the twelfth, Carlton Fisk knocked a tremendous homer off the foul pole high above the net atop The Wall in left.

At four hours and one minute, it was the longest game in World Series history. In Boston, we danced all the way home. We had witnessed the limits of machinery.

Bill Lee, our pitcher in the decisive game, was twitting the writers during pregame practice. "Yeah," he told us, "after the game tonight, Gullett's going to the Hall of Fame. And I'm going to the Eliot Lounge."

Gullett was in trouble from the beginning and blew sky high in the third, walking four batters, including two with the bases loaded. Lee held the Reds scoreless for five innings on five singles. The Sox could taste the champagne that would toast their first world championship since 1918. Then, in a fateful sixth, strange things began to happen. Again.

Johnny Bench, with one out, hit what appeared to be a perfect, inning-ending, ground ball to short; hard-hit and right at Rick Burleson, who fielded it and flipped it neatly to Denny Doyle at second for the force on Pete Rose. The sliding Rose by no means wiped out Doyle on the play. He didn't even come close. But Doyle unaccountably threw the ball into the Red Sox dugout as Bench, the slowest of the Reds, chugged to first.

Up came Tony Perez, the Machine's other premier slugger. Lee, under a waning full moon, offered Perez a moon curve, his specialty. But Bench, who was awarded second base on Doyle's overthrow into the dugout, picked up the signals and flashed "moon curve" to Perez at bat. Perez stood there, timed the slow offering, gauged its arc, and knocked it over The Wall, over the net, onto Landsdowne Street, and brought the Machine within a run at 3–2.

Lee left the game with one out in the next inning, after walking a batter on four pitches, a blister on the thumb of his pitching hand. Rogelio Moret could not hold the lead and was replaced one out later by Jim Willoughby, the game tied. The Sox were practicing their own *omertà* and managed only one hit, a single by Petrocelli, after Gullett retired following four innings. Willoughby had knowledge of the Machine, though, and kept the ball in the infield in the eighth, retiring the Rhinelanders in order. With two outs in their eighth, and Willoughby due to bat, Darrell Johnson decided to send up a pinch hitter, Cecil (one-for-nineteen-in-the-Series) Cooper, who fouled out to Rose on the first pitch. It fell to rookie Jim Burton to lose the game with two outs in the ninth.

In the clubhouse, Lee was fuming over Doyle's error and his own blister. "Catch one seam the wrong way, and you've got a blister, a second-degree burn caused by friction. That's what comes from not pitching regularly." Somebody wanted to know about his moon curve to Perez. Lee, though, wanted to return to Doyle's error. "I should've been out of the inning by then. Dynasty, my ass. Ah, fuck, the pitch I live by, the slow curve, I died by. They're a third place team if they had to play on grass. They distort the value of the game."

To some, of course, this was sour grapes by Lee. But was it not true? For, after all, we still play the game with a leather ball and a wooden bat.

In the clubhouse of the new World Champions, champagne slid right off the sides of Pete Rose's bowl haircut and cascaded to the floor. Astro-turf hair!

It was a fitting finale for America: the Machine wins.

In Boston, we settled down for an Irish wake. At the Eliot Lounge, one could not buy a drink. "It's on Sparky," said the bartender. Ah, but you know, I could cry.

The Maltese Sangweech

These are a couple of pieces I did when I had a monthly column in San Francisco *magazine. They are, I contend, actual restaurant reviews while being at the same time two connected short pieces of semifiction.*

I got the idea for these so-called restaurant reviews one day while reading the San Francisco Examiner. *It seems the FBI had engineered a sting against the Mafia by posing some agents as underworld characters dealing in hot securities. On several occasions both restaurants were used as the meeting ground for the Feds' morality play.*

And both restaurants, I sensed, were actual Mafia turf. The real stuff. I thought that if I could allow my paranoia to ramble a little I could have some fun. In addition, I had wanted for some time to bow humbly in the direction of Dashiell Hammett.

Sal's Espresso Café, the subject of part one, was a daily stop on Jimmy (The Weasel) Frattiano's rounds. It is no longer there. Neither is Jimmy. He did some chirping and later went public in a book called The Last Mafioso.

The Ristorante Italiano, the subject of part two, in time became my favorite restaurant in all San Francisco, though for some reason they never framed my piece and hung it on a wall. Then one day a few years later they kicked out all the waitresses, replaced them with formally-attired waiters, gussied up the joint, jacked the prices, and overcooked the calamari.

As I have been instructed to recall, smoke from my cigarette curled and drifted through the high-rise studio, while I gazed down on the pleasant view of the city's soft southern slope. Memories of past assignments collected in the back rooms of my brain and were bubbling there when the phone rang. I knew the voice.

"We want you to put a cover on a couple of restaurants. We don't know what's up."

"Okay."

"Lunch at Sal's Espresso Café, 287 Ellis. Dinner at Ristorante Italiano, 622 Green. We want you to go eat. Take the Legman. Tomorrow. Both places. Eat. Enjoy. Got it?" There was a click. The line went dead.

Sal's Espresso Café is a dimly-lit little place near Taylor, featuring "Italian Sangweeches" and pizza in the throbbing heart of the twisted Tenderloin. There is a sticker on the front door that says, "Teamsters are Progressive." There are four booths inside, and Chianti bottles hang from the ceiling. We entered at 12:59 P.M.

The walls are papered with autographed pictures of the well known. There is a cigarette machine, an espresso machine, a jukebox. The counter has no stools and behind it is a tiny kitchen. In the kitchen was a thin, middle-aged woman wearing glasses. A languid blonde waitress sat alone in one of the booths. A clean-cut young couple shared pizza in another booth. The third booth was occupied by three apparent students, two male and one female, who discussed class action suits as they awaited pizza. The Legman and I slipped into the empty booth, nearest the counter.

The Legman is my physical affairs advisor. A one-time pro-football player, he played on a college team so bad that in his senior year they were booked to six homecoming games, serving as red meat for Army, Iowa, Houston and three conference teams. The game against Houston was in the Astrodome. "It was like playing inside a pinball machine," he once confided. "The exploding scoreboard was lighting up on every play. They beat us 72–6. We scored on the opening kickoff and missed the point after."

No one waited on us. The phone rang and the cook answered it. It was for the waitress. She went behind the counter and took the phone.

"I don't have any money," she said. "When will you be in town? . . . No, I don't have any money."

She hung up a few moments later and returned to her booth. The door opened and a man of average height and build, wearing horn-rimmed glasses, a dark blue V-neck sweater and gray trousers, entered. "Where's Sal?" he asked the cook.

"He's out," she replied. "He'll be back sometime." She noticed us in the booth. "Just a minute," she called over. "I'll be right with you."

The man in the horn-rimmed glasses was looking for an envelope. "I need something to put these W–2s in," he said to the cook.

"Upstairs," she said, rolling her eyes.

He nodded, reached up, and on a shelf above his head found an envelope. He put the reputed W–2 forms inside and placed the envelope atop the refrigerator . . . in plain sight. He, too, noticed us and began to putter around behind the counter. To avoid his curiosity, we turned our attention to the array of pictures on the walls: Vaughn Monroe. Frankie Laine. Bob Hope. Sammy Davis, Jr. Robert Blake. Muhammad Ali. Willie Pep. Rocky Marciano. Bobo Olson. Gene Tunney. Pete Herman (the old bantamweight). Harry James.

And in the middle, in the place of honor, the largest picture, the boss of all pictures . . . Frank Sinatra. My mind raced back to another assignment—to Naples and the California ristorante, decorated like this dimly-lit little place with pictures of celebrities. One picture there, showing Sinatra in conversation with someone named Lucky Luciano, was removed a few years ago. Gino Cuoma, the owner of the California, was visited one day by "some men I did not know" who requested that he remove the Sinatra picture. He did. This guy Sal, I realized, must be well-connected.

The man with the horn-rimmed glasses remained interested in us. I refused to grow nervous. "Why," I muttered indistinctly to the Legman, "do they get in touch with me for assignments like this?" The Legman stared at me for a while, then hunched forward. "Maybe," he whispered, "it's because you see things most other people don't."

The cook came over to our booth. "What'll it be?" she asked. She appeared to be nervous.

"Two coffees," the Legman said. "American blend. We'll order in a minute." She went away. (Yes, two coffees. That's good. The Legman is a pro. Isser Harel, head of the Israeli Secret Service, once taught me the value of not using liquor or drugs during an assignment.) We studied the menu board on the wall over the counter. It read:

SANGWEECHES

Meatball $2.00
Italian Sausage $2.00
Eggplant Parmigiana $1.75
Veal Cutlet Parmigiana $3.00
Roast Beef $2.50
Roast Pork & Pepper $2.50
Pepper or Melted Cheese 25¢ extra
Pizza: Cheese, Meatball, Combination.
Sicilian, 50¢ plain, 75¢ cheese.

Ah yes, Sicilian, I mused. Fifty cents plain, seventy-five cents cheese. . . . What could that mean? I wondered. The cook returned with the coffees. "Do you have any pork?" the Legman asked. "No," she said. "No pork."

"I'll have the veal cutlet parmigiana," I said. She wrote it down. "Me, too," said the Legman. The door opened and we heard steps and voices. Three pairs of expensive, highly-polished black shoes glided past.

"Hi, Sal," said the cook. "Hello, Sal," said the blonde waitress from her booth. "Sal," said the man in the horn-rimmed glasses who had been observing us. Sal looked over at him. The man motioned Sal behind the counter. The other two who came in with Sal leaned on the counter and threw glances our way. We spotted Barbara McNair, and a familiar-looking black entertainer wearing a medium Afro. His name was on the tips of our tongues. Then, my eyes fell upon a postcard tacked to the wall. It was to Sal, and it read: "Am going to New Orleans. Tony Licata fights Monday night. You pal, Champ Willie Pep." What could that mean?

Sal is the kind of guy who looks like he needs some sleep. Huge, dark rings encircled his eyes. He looked to be about fifty years old, thin, intense, with gray hair and a wisp of a goatee on his underlip. His two companions wore leisure suits. One was short, fat, balding, and had a black mustache. His suit had tiny checks of black and white. He was, like Sal, about fifty. The other man was taller, about ten years younger, and possessed the quick reflexes of an athlete. He wore a very dark, almost wine red leisure suit.

Suddenly, all four men huddled by the counter. In that moment, they took on certain characteristics of a mob, being, as they were, all mobbed-up. We could feel their eyes on us. They all began talking at once, using a lot of Italian words. The blonde waitress left her booth and said, "Excuse me," as she tried to go behind the counter.

"Hey! The worker wants to work," said one of the four men. "Give her a ring! Diamonds! A bracelet. Look at her work. Such a sweetheart. . . ." She refilled her coffee cup and returned to her booth. Then she said, "Sal," and motioned him to join her. "I've got to move my car," she told him. "It's parked in a thirty-minute spot."

"Okay, honey, you move it," Sal suggested. She got up to leave. Sal and his two companions went with her. Our veal cutlets parmigiana arrived. The man in the horn-rimmed glasses put some money in the reputed envelope. He called the cook over and showed her what he was doing. "See," he said, "here's the money. If they ask, just tell them that it's with the forms. I've got to go. I wasn't here. You didn't see me." The cook nodded.

"This is a cold sangweech," I muttered. The short, fat guy in the check suit came back in. He paced in front of the counter, staring at us. It made the Legman nervous.

"This is a great sangweech," the Legman said, loud enough for the cook to hear. She came back to our table. "Everything all right?" she asked. "Could I have a little bit more coffee?" I asked. "Sure," she said. She got the coffee pot and poured more coffee. The short, fat guy kept staring. The cook tallied our bill. She said it was her first day on the job. She hoped the sangweeches were good. The Legman complimented her. I maintained silence. First day on the job, huh? Who, then, was the previous cook? Why was the previous cook let go? Where is the previous cook now?

The bill appeared and we prepared to leave. "Tell me," I said to the cook, pointing to the picture on the wall of the black entertainer with the medium Afro, "who is that?"

"Oh," the cook said, "that's Dobie Gray. All of those people in those pictures are customers here. They all come in here. Usually late at night. Seven-thirty until two-thirty in the morning. That's the best time to see them in here." She took the money and went to the cash register. Ah yes, I mused . . . Dobie Gray, the singer. That's who it is. His big hit was "I'm In with the In Crowd." The Legman poked me in the ribs and nodded toward the picture. "Somebody ought to have a talk with that guy," he said. "He'd sing."

Yeah, maybe so. Maybe they all would, I thought, surveying the picture gallery for the last time. But we couldn't tail them all.

The Legman went outside, picking his teeth. Two doors down, in front of a drugstore, Sal talked with a man in a yellow jacket. They saw the Legman and began to walk toward him. He stood his ground, picking his teeth. They entered the café. I emerged, followed by the short, fat man in the check suit. The Legman and I strolled to Taylor and Ellis and split up. I turned left and walked south on Taylor. The Legman continued west, hurrying his pace and darted into a phone booth on the other side of Taylor. From the phone booth, the Legman could see the short fat man in the check suit standing in front of Sal's, looking both ways on Ellis. The man in the yellow jacket came out of Sal's and walked to the corner of Taylor. The Legman could see him from the phone booth walk briskly north on Taylor, clutching a rolled-up magazine in his right hand.

We had taken the precaution of parking outside the district, at Eddy and Taylor, and used separate, circuitous routes back. It was 1:59 P.M. when we rendezvoused at the car. Safely inside the Legman turned to me and said, "They could get five years for what I saw them do today."

"How's that?" I asked.

"Looking suspicious. Standing around and loitering. Talking Italian."

"Yeah," I said, and pulled out into the traffic.

The Maltese Sangweech Part II

A police car coursed slowly along Green Street and turned right on Powell as I handed my keys to the parking attendant and entered the Ristorante Italiano. The Legman was at my side. I had picked him up a half hour earlier along a little-used side street on the outskirts of the Inner Richmond, taking care that no one see us. It was 6:30 P.M. Europeans are in the habit of taking a late dinner and we wanted to appear natural.

A pleasant-looking, middle-aged brunette approached us inside the door. "Would you like to have dinner?" she asked. She carried two copies of the menu. "Yes," I answered. "But we'd like to have a drink at the bar first."

The Legman peeked around the corner of the bar and looked into the dining room. It was nearly empty. I ordered a Bombay martini, straight up, with two olives, and ice on the side, from the young mustachioed bartender. The Legman ordered an Amaretto Old-Fashioned.

There were several empty stools on either side of us along the bar. The bar itself was well-stocked. Three pictures of clowns reminiscent of Emmett Kelly hung over the front door, facing us.

"That makes sense," the Legman offered.

"What's that?" I replied.

"A lot of clowns must come through that door."

"Oh."

There was a jukebox behind us against the wall, and a hatrack. Two blonde waitresses occasionally came from the dining room to the drink station at the end of the bar to our right and conferred with the bartender. To our left, down by clown alley, was an underused pay phone and a cigarette machine.

"What's happening?" I asked the Legman.

"Well," he said softly, "there's a faded, washed-out blonde back by the cigarette machine, and she's locked in conversation with two guys. The younger guy looks like he's right out of Ratso Rizzo Midnight Cowboy. The other guy is older, slicker, wavier, better-dressed, and looks like he spends a lot of time in rented cars. The younger guy is describing a party that he's been to for a week, and is doing so in great detail. The blonde can't possibly be as interested as she appears to be."

The night bartender came in and sat at a stool to our right. A brunette joined him, drink in hand. They spoke with the day bartender. Everyone was giving us the once over, it seemed. I took out a pocket notebook and scribbled furiously. The guy who looked like he spent a lot of time in rented cars moved down the bar toward us, pretending to scan the jukebox, though I could feel his cold stare over my shoulder. He probably wanted to see if I was filling out a summons. Had word filtered up from the Tenderloin that afternoon that there were two guys in town?

Indeed, the lunch we had taken earlier that day at Sal's Espresso Café on Ellis had been more than we anticipated. We knew we were in deep now. Isser Harel, head of Israeli Secret Service, long ago taught me the value of not using liquor or drugs while on assignment, yet to survive our present circumstances I realized we must change tactics. I ordered another Bombay martini. The Legman this time called for a Godfather, being of equal parts of Amaretto and Scotch, over ice. When it was served he took his maiden sip and chuckled cryptically.

"What's up?" I asked.

The Legman scoped the bar. "The day bartender," he said, "is talking with the night bartender and his girl. A third guy has joined them. He looks to be about forty and well-fed. He looks like he's got a few drinks in him."

The new man was speaking. I strained to hear his words.

" . . . you can't smoke in any store in San Francisco," he was saying.

"You can in a shoe store," insisted the bartender waiting to go on duty.

"Well, in a department store, no . . ." said the third man. He paused slightly, then continued. "I know, because I talked with a guy." There was a longer pause. Then, the third man added carefully, "Think I'll be going home."

"Take care, Frankie," said the night bartender's woman.

"Okey-dokey," he replied.

"Ciao," the day bartender said. And then he admitted, "That means good-bye in Italian."

What the hell is this? Translations built into bar patter? Storm clouds crossed our faces as we sipped our drinks. I caught the head waitress's eye and she led us to a rear table. She placed the menus side-by-side so that we would face the front door, our backs to the wall.

"One of two things is happening, Legs," I said. "Either they are treating us with respect, or we are being set up like Joey Gallo was in Umberto's Clam House. Let's try to play it down the middle, like tourists. Let's get another drink."

We could see all who came into the bar, and most of those in the dining room. "Waitress," I called. "Another Bombay martini and another Godfather."

Over by the men's room door a stocky man stood motionlessly. His chin was tucked into his chest, waiting for a bullet. He was six feet but looked about five-ten. He had both hands in his pockets. He took one look at the Legman and tucked his chin down another inch, waiting for the shot.

They changed bartenders on us at this point, and sat a Japanese businessman across from us.

We watched the front door open. The Legman tucked his chin into his chest. A young, slim, modishly dressed man entered. He wore a mustache and a leather coat about two inches longer than it should be. He walked the length of the bar, scanning everybody. He looked in the nooks and corners and over at the pay phone, then turned and walked back towards the front. He conversed hurriedly with the new bartender, exchanged nods, and left quickly.

A busboy brought us water. As he turned away, the Legman palmed an ashtray, under cover of napkin. The ashtray said: "Ristorante Italiano. 622 Green Street. Mary, Jack and Ron." This was at odds with the menu, the Legman noted. "The menu says 'Marty and Ron,' " he whispered.

"Hush, Legs."

A blonde waitress who said she was Swedish came for our order. The words "crab cannelloni" were barely out of the Legman's mouth when the front door swung open.

The young man in the leather coat was back, this time in the vanguard of a flying wedge of five well-tailored, expensively shod men. They moved at hurricane clip through the bar and were seated immediately at a large table next to the kitchen. Three of them were young and two were old. The two older men, like us, sat with their backs to the wall. The younger men looked around the dining room constantly. One of the older men looked like a tired Jesuit who's handed out too many basketball scholarships. The other looked strangely like Lester Maddox and wore a small felt hat on his head during most of the meal. They both seemed to be named Don.

They noticed us noticing them.

Our waitress wouldn't talk. She just kept placing clam chowder and antipasto and plates of ziti macaroni in front of us. The head waitress placed three apparent gays, who said they were from Carmel, between us and the table of five men, obscuring our view. But we could still observe that as the older men bent forward to eat, the younger men looked around the dining room.

"How is your crab cannelloni?" I asked the Legman.

"*Bono,*" he said. "In fact, it is one of the best meals I have ever had in my life. They must have used four crabs to make this cannelloni. And how is your calamari?"

"In truth," I answered, "it is the finest calamari I have ever had in my life. How can they serve a meal like this for six and a quarter? It gives one pause. . . ."

With the last of his bread, the Legman sopped oil from his salad plate. He patted his ample middle and pronounced, "*bella.*"

The waitress brought lemon cake and coffee. The Legman ordered more bread. "I am stuffed," he said. "The mind of a fat man is like a brilliant gem after a good meal. Henry Miller or Nero Wolfe said that."

I looked at the table of five and caught them looking at us. "Let's get out of here, Legs," I commented.

We duked the parking lot attendant a dollar and were soon among the Friday night North Beach throng. Minutes later we debriefed over a nightcap at Joe Nobriga's Showcase, a bistro along a desolate part of Franklin Street on the outskirts of the Civic Center. Before long, I noticed the bartender noticing us. Like calamari, I gathered, their tentacles are everywhere. "Let's get out of here, Legs."

We drove quickly away, peeling rubber around corners, using low gears only. I deliberately chose a random pattern of streets. "Brooom," we went. "Erkkkk. Brooom. Erkkkk. Brooom." Around and around. I dropped the Legman off around midnight at Third and Brannan, a desolate warehouse district on the outskirts of Skid Row. I never saw him again.

Singing in the Canaries

This is a travel piece, one of a projected three-part series. It was done around the same time as the restaurant reviews and, like them, contains elements of fiction. I was striving to create a Jacques Tati sort of central character. A bumbler. An Inspector Clouseau. And I wanted to wed him to insights about nineteenth-century shipboard crime gleaned from Pinkerton's autobiography, which I was then reading, and which was greatly altering my day-to-day perceptions.

One day I walked into the offices of San Francisco *magazine to turn in my column. Terry McDonell and Umberto (Nino) Tosi were running the show. They were smiling at me. Cheshire smiles.*

"How would you like to fly to Los Angeles and then from there to Las Palmas and get on a cruise ship to Dakar and back across the Atlantic to the Caribbean?"

It made sense.

I phoned Mary Chong and invited her along. The next day we were on our way to the Canaries. I had only recently met Mary Chong and had not yet gotten around to mentioning that I once lived in Las Palmas. I feigned ignorance of the place upon arrival but unerringly steered her toward some old haunts and, well . . . as some are given to say, it was to die.

Faces dropped when we entered the café El Gallo. Old English drunkards of long acquaintance shouted "Bill!"

And the Scotch flowed. (Years earlier I had taught the bartenders there how to build the martini cocktail. They are to be served in water tumblers, I instructed, with many olives. That is the American style, I explained.)

The ship sailed at midnight. On the way to the dock Mary Chong exclaimed her surprise to find that I knew people six thousand miles from San Francisco. "I am known," I admitted in my most imperial fashion, puffing slightly, "in some places."

A few weeks later I was putting the finishing touches to part two back in Sausalito when dreadful news interrupted: A KLM 747 and a Pan Am 747 had collided on a runway in Tenerife, killing 581 people. The worst air disaster in history. The Pan Am plane had been prevented from landing at Las Palmas because of a bomb scare. (Some lunatic demanding independence for the Azores, Madeira, the Canaries and the Cape Verde Islands . . . taken as a confederation of archipelagos, a very weird confection indeed.) The neighboring island of Tenerife, about sixty miles away, received the diverted plane. The Pan Am flight originated in Los Angeles and was taking people to meet the ship. The same ship. The same cruise. A new batch of fun-seeking passengers. I withdrew part two from publication and hung it on a spike. It sits in a cardboard box somewhere along with the notes for part three.

Aye, and we be in Las Palmas again. Eighteen hours ago, San Francisco; now, this scorched jut of Atlantic soot. Exhausted by jet lag, rank-smelling and wrinkled, yet lucky to be here, seated once more where I thought I'd never sit again, in the parque Santa Catalina, sipping cerveza Tropical in the Derby Bar after an absence of five years.

The last time I sat here, a warm Sunday in June 1972, a column of men in baseball suits strolled by. Though I had grown accustomed to accept the curiosities of the island, the bizarre sight finally impacted: What were baseball men doing in the Canary Islands off the coast of Africa? I had to find out, and eventually learned that they were Cubans from a fishing fleet, on their day off. And so I began to frequent the dock area to see what else I could learn, and soon encounted hundreds of Communist seamen from all over the world. I conveyed these findings to the U.S. consul, who was a native of Arizona engaged in the heavy construction business on the island. I indicated to him that I probably knew more about the common Communist than any State Department hand, and hinted carefully that our CIA might find my information of value. A few days later the consul left word to meet him in a café outside the tourist zone.

"Look," he said, "this job is a pain in the ass. I'd like out. It's killing my business. Washington has no idea what's going on here. You know that we've got three hundred American oil workers and their families over here, and that each of them has a problem of some kind. I get a budget of five thousand dollars a year to run the goddamn office and I end up reaching into my own pocket to cover expenses. How'd you like to take over?"

Stunned at the rebuff, alarmed that I had failed to connect, I departed in haste, made my way to San Francisco, and established my own operation.

Which explains in part, actually, how I've come full cycle. Recently, an assessment I made of a Chinese restaurant, the Sincere Café, on Sixteenth Street in the Inner Mission, was leaked to the public. Among other things, this report dealt with a devastating arson fire there in 1975. Precisely as the report was being leaked, the place burned down again. Coincidence? Moreover, on the heels of that, memoranda of mine concerning the clientele and cuisine at two Italian restaurants, one in the Tenderloin and the other in North Beach, were made public. Friends in high places alerted me that the boys down at arson, and the Sicilians, would be asking around. If I didn't want to be caught in the squeeze, I'd best get out of town until matters cooled. An editor who owed me a favor arranged a travel writing assignment aboard a Greek ship called the *Golden Odyssey*, which was about to commence a repositioning cruise from the Mediterranean to the Caribbean for the winter trade. There was scarcely time to grab my secretary, credentials and suitable habiliments for an ocean voyage.

There are worse fates, as you can understand, than posing as a travel writer and sipping a Tropical in the Derby Bar and chuckling softly as a forgotten memory—an old, rouge-crazed woman who sells Doublemint gum from a basket—shuffles past in her bedroom slippers. The entire long-lost scene is suddenly kindled to actuality, the hordes of predatory Spanish men still preying upon the hordes of Scandinavian female tourists under the bright night lights of the cafés . . . all as I remembered. The waiters in many cases have familiar faces, and the same shoeshine men in blue overalls hunker on shoshine boxes near a kiosk that offers post cards. The cool beer put me right with the world, and I realized I would like another.

"Chong," I said, rising, "let's go change some money."

We walked quietly along memory lanes, my secretary silent and obedient three paces back. Only once did she hesitate: "Do you know where you're going?" she asked.

"I have an instinct for these things." The reply, though coy, had a purpose. A good operative is not inclined to divulge his reasons, lest the aura of mystery so important to command be destroyed. In this case, however, Chong was satisfied. This is the great thing about Chong: she accepts. Whatever I say is fine with her. Half Irish and half Chinese, a perfectly framed five-foot-two, with apple cheeks and almond eyes, Mary Chong is a find. I found her at eight o'clock one morning last spring in the Nightcap, a bar at O'Farrell and Hyde in the Upper Tenderloin. She's been with me since. And during this time, I've been careful never to remove my jacket in her presence, lest the aura so important to obedience be destroyed.

Without realizing, I led us toward the Half Note, a nightclub with which I had been associated. We passed a bar I knew, El Rancho, which caters to American teachers of the oil workers' children. The bar is owned by a man named George, a native who speaks English faultlessly but claims never to have left the Canaries. "Let's have a drink," I said, guiding Chong inside.

Eucalyptus leaves hung from the ceiling—perhaps the same ones. Bob, one of the school teachers, gasped at my apparition. So did George behind the bar. Chong, though surprised at their reactions, said nothing. I learned that Bob was leaving to assume a post at the American School in Malta, that George still hadn't been off the island, and that the Half Note, once the showcase for Dexter Gordon, Zoot Sims, and other jazz masters, was now a gay disco. We hurried our drinks and left for the Reina Isabel Hotel, where I knew I could exchange money at any hour. Crossing the parking lot, I could not help but scan the rows for Don Ricardo's gray Buick Riviera. The last time I was at this hotel, I left in the Buick. It was the only Buick Riviera in all the Canaries. Traffic cops saluted it. They'd jerk to attention in their white pith helmets, white gloves and jackets, drop all else, and wave Don Ricardo through like he was some kind of generalissimo.

Which may have been close to the truth, for many in this city of 250,000 believe Don Ricardo owed his charmed life to a long association with that maximum generalissimo, Francisco Franco himself. I never asked; to have done so would have been impolite. (There is much that I have learned from Chong.) Don Ricardo, with the winners in the Civil War, became the Count of Bilbao and lived opulently in an endless villa in the verdant highlands overlooking the sprawling, boomtown desert resort. It was rumored that the estate belonged to his wife, Luisa, a descendant of the island's first governor. The chapel in their home was the most magnificent private room of worship I'd ever seen, yet they were two of the all-time cutups. You could count on bumping into them most any night, dancing wee-hour rhumbas in some club.

He was sixty-five, and she sixty, by their own admission. Don Ricardo's hair was winter white, silky and full. It also hung below his shoulders, luffing gently against the velvet of his suit. At night, he always wore velvet, either black or maroon. His suits were made in New York, which gave him, he said, a chance to get there every year. Born in Basque country, he was given at odd moments to warble folk songs from that distant region, delighting in the vibrato he trilled from somewhere down deep in his gullet. Ricardo and Luisa gave dinner parties regularly, either at home, or in a private section of the rooftop dining room of the Reina Isabel. After dinner, we'd careen around the clubs. Ricardo always picked up the tab. He did this to keep Don Roberto, his rival, on guard.

Don Roberto was the Count of Salamanca and when Ricardo was not giving a dinner party, he was. He was also the Liggett & Myers representative in the Canaries, and a rich man. The Canaries, on the main shipping routes connecting the Americas with Europe and Africa, have been free ports since the last century. As many as two thousand ships tie up each month in Las Palmas or in Tenerife, the chain's other important island, to take on cheap fuel and cheap provisions . . . and that's a lot of cigarettes. During one dinner at Don Roberto's bay-front villa, he took me out to the patio to show off his new grass. "What do you think, Beel?" he asked as I looked down at the patio. "Astro-turf! The first in the Canaries!" he beamed.

Now, as the (costumed) doorman prepared our entrance into the Reina Isabel, I made one last final sweep of the parking lot but could not conjure the big, gray Buick Riviera that had once so dominated the dwarf cars of Europe. Nor was any bold successor present, for a car owned by Don Ricardo would surely be a statement. I dared not inquire of the doorman, for that would invite discovery. No, a social call on such a flamboyant as Don Ricardo would have to wait, perhaps eternally. I would live with memories. I remember in particular one course of that last dinner here, a favorite dish of our host from his native Bay of Biscay: tiny, white sea worms, sautéed live, and served writhing in agony. At a reasonable distance, it could pass for a side of spaghetti, but one had never seen spaghetti excited so. I recall Don Ricardo winking at me across the table, opening his mouth for my eyes only, and revealing a cave of serpents.

Although unsettled of stomach as we left, I willingly entered the back seat of the Buick as Don Ricardo careened across town to what he promised was a sensational night club. The featured act was a shapely Peruvian singer, who performed a striptease finale, maintaining a stream of Spanish patter as she discarded clothing. All eyes were on her voluptuous breasts as she tore away her bra, exhibiting a manly and hirsute chest. *"Soy todo chico!"* this impostor cackled triumphantly. Oh my God! I tried to stumble outside. I came to on the floor of the coatroom, a damp cloth pressed against my forehead, the singer ministering to me. Five years ago.

After the transaction in the hotel, my pockets bulged peseta notes. Across from the Reina Isabel is an old haunt, the tavern El Gallo, which caters to the English tourist. I once taught the bartender how to make the martini cocktail. He poured them in water tumblers and charged me the equivalent of about twenty cents, figuring "what the hell, it's only gin and vermouth and olives." I went there a lot. "Let's go there," I said to Chong, pointing to the El Gallo.

Inside, Peter Painter nursed a drink at a rear table. I could have predicted it. I waited for the shock of recognition, which, when it came, nearly swamped him. He broke from his drinking companions, who later identified themselves as an Australian and an Irishman, and rushed to me. Peter Painter is a diminutive, gray-haired chap from Cornwall who always wears bright red corduroy pants and a powder blue corduroy cowboy jacket. He ekes out a living by doing quick sketches of tourists along the beach front. A year ago he popped in on me in San Francisco. To celebrate the occasion, I asked him to go out and buy a bottle of Scotch. He returned with a pint, and I hit the roof. It left a deep impression on him, for he continued to apologize.

The Irishman immediately cornered Chong in a long, private conversation. The deadline to board the ship came too soon and my farewell from Peter Painter was emotional. As the taxi neared the pier, I took a last look at Las Palmas for the second time in my life. Chong broke the reverie. "I had no idea you knew so many people!" she gushed.

"I am known, my dear," I explained, "throughout the world."

Our first glimpse of the white and blue *Golden Odyssey* was shattering. White is fine, but blue is a color of the sea that, in some parts of the world, is never used to paint a ship. Bad luck would surely follow. Otherwise, the ship was a sleek and handsome creation of Denmark's Elsinore Shipyards, built at a reported cost of $19 million and launched February 7, 1974. In the old days, when the Vikings launched a ship, they lashed slaves to the skids. As the vessels rolled into the water, the slaves popped, speckling the hull. This custom is not being maintained by their descendants at Elsinore, my sources insist.

At midnight we waved good-bye to Las Palmas from the deck and went to our stateroom, passing on the way a man in a white sailor suit and hat, carrying binoculars. I recognized him as the night watchman and called out. He turned and I walked back to him, brandishing a twenty-dollar bill. I gave him the money and we shook hands. I could hear him whistling along the passageway, long after he was out of sight.

"Why did you do that?" asked an incredulous Chong. I informed her that it was standard operating procedure, outlined nearly a century ago by Allan Pinkerton, *the* Pinkerton, in his 1884 compendium, *Thirty Years a Detective,* which became the Bible for operatives.

"Pinkerton pointed out quite correctly that the shipboard thief usually finds that the wise bestowal of a twenty- or fifty-dollar bill is often productive of wonderful results from watchmen. You see, Chong, the men usually employed in such positions are, as a class, of exceedingly extravagant habits, according to Pinkerton—which is not to condemn them all, of course—and their pay is entirely inadequate to gratify their notions of luxurious living."

"But . . . you're here as a travel writer, not a private eye."

"True, my dear. But, as you know, we never sleep."

Stateroom 407, though smaller than I imagined (one is never prepared for such dimensions), was bright, and comfortable. Once secure inside, I asked Chong what the Irishman told her at such great length back there in El Gallo.

Chong tumbled out a torrent. "He said his wife of twenty years and his thirteen-year-old son are insane. His doctor told him that if he didn't think of himself, he, too, would go insane. So he came to Las Palmas and partied like crazy for two weeks. Suddenly, he got cystitis. He was on his deathbed. He prayed to God that night. At two o'clock in the morning he awoke and felt fine. But he still has to have a prostate operation. He also said he had problems with his luggage and was ripped off by two taxi drivers in Liverpool, and two more in Las Palmas. He was carrying stereo equipment and his life's possessions, he said. . . ."

"He should've rented a car," I interrupted.

"Are we sailing?"

"Yeah. For a thousand pesetas he could've rented a car for a day, a little Ford Cortina."

"Yes, but he was helpless."

"Well, whatever. . . . Chong, that was a positively brilliant summary. You never know about information like this. Anything else you remember?"

"He said I had the map of Tipperary on my face."

"Hah!" I said. "Not to mention Shanghai!"

Like any dame, Chong can be taken in by a compliment. I felt the need to instruct her. "The necessity for caution in making travel acquaintances is always imminent, my dear. Pinkerton warned of that. He said, 'the smoothest tongue, and the fairest face, may belong to the most desperate criminal, and an intimacy is sure to result in disaster.' "

She digested the words, and I continued. "Remember, also, not to fraternize with the crew. Relations with a paid crew are always formal. And remember, too, that almost any woman aboard ship looks good to men who have restricted shore leave. Amy Vanderbilt would tell you as much." And then, quite unexpectedly—though I had never done so before, nor even entertained the idea—I broke a cardinal rule, destroying the fragile, mysterious aura so necessary to command . . . "May I remove my coat?" I asked.

The Second Coming of Monti Rock, III

I first saw Monti Rock on the Carson show in 1967. He was so open, so vulnerably honest. A rare man. I wanted one day to meet him. That day came a few years later when I was working on a paper in Los Angeles. A press release came across my desk announcing that Monti would emcee some sort of Sex-Expo in a downtown rathole. You could say he was down on his luck. I have always been partial to stories about the indomitable, indefatigable loser. For is that not one of the great notions that define us? The loser's locker room, rather than the winner's. Stale liniment versus cheap champagne. The story of the loser is generally more difficult to do but sometimes there is a great story to be had. You can get your throat slit in the loser's locker room. Easy. But in the winner's clubhouse are the glad-hands and the clichés. Not for me. Take your pick.

Monti was living in a badly furnished apartment in the flats of Beverly Hills but, as he pointed out, it was Beverly Hills. This, he insisted, was important: a Beverly Hills address. He had cold, boiled potatoes in his refrigerator and he gave me one. When I got home that night and played the interview tape, nothing was on it. Strange. I had to call him and explain the mysterious situation. That's okay, he said. Come back tomorrow. We'll do it again.

We became friends. Every morning around eight o'clock, it seemed, he was pounding on the door of my Hollywood bungalow. He was having a lot of domestic trouble with Leni, his then-lover. My then-wife and I would invite him in and we'd sit and talk. I can remember him in my kitchen, scissors in hand, cutting my hair and wigging out. "I can't do it!" he would moan. "I'm finished!" A crisis of confidence, a crisis of artistry. "You're doing fine, Monti," we would sweet-talk. One of the best barbers I ever had. Wonderful memories. Long feather earrings. Lavender jumpsuits. Oh, he was outrageous!

One night we were driving west on Santa Monica Boulevard. A Corniche rolled by at high speed. (Though I raced Volvos professionally in 1964–65 I have since become a slow driver. A couple of years ago, three thousand miles from Beverly Hills, I was taking my little pal, Michelle La Freniere, to her riding lesson. We were late. "Oh, Billy, won't you please drive faster?" she begged. "I only drive my age," I answered sententiously. She thought that one over and murmured, as if to the wind, "I can't wait for you to be seventy!") The Corniche bore a vanity license plate. "Jesus, Monti, if I were Cher the last thing in the world I would have is a vanity plate! I'd grab every moment of privacy I could!" He was quick to correct. "You gotta keep your name before the public, baby. Can you dig it?" In that moment I understood show business.

A year or so later my own marriage busted up. The first person I told was Monti. "I'll be right over," he promised. And was. We went out for a few drinks and I told him I was going to Aspen and think things over. He scribbled down the phone numbers of a couple of lady friends there. Not only that, he called them and said I was coming. God bless you, Joey Montañez.

It is not unnatural for a star to become upset when people say they never heard of him, especially in the case of a world famous personality who was the once and several times darling of New York. During the '60s, it has been estimated, Monti Rock, III, earned upwards of $2 million and blew it all. He had been poorly prepared for the tax man.

When Monti Rock made his debut in October 1964, at Trude Heller's discotheque in the Village, the columnists wrote that the crush of adoring Uptown women was not to be believed. Among those who queued up that night were Sybil Burton, Huntington Hartford, Bernard Buffet and Betsy von Furstenberg. Peggy Hitchcock arrived with a party of thirty-four in a double-decker bus loaned by Sardi's. *Women's Wear Daily* began to report regularly on "El Cajones, the ballsiest hairdresser in town," and the first of several hundred television appearances began with a spot on the "Tonight Show."

When he returned from a Whiskey au Go Go engagement in Miami Beach in February 1965, he found he was no longer on the payroll at Saks Fifth Avenue, but within months he was rehired because of popular demand. His creations were in all the fashion magazines and were frequently photographed by Richard Avedon. It has been recorded in *The New Yorker*'s "Talk of the Town" that "his customers were rich and beautiful and he himself was outrageously elegant, with his shoulder-length hair, his velvet and brocade suits, his jewelry, his mauve scarf, and his feather boa." He was always invited to the right parties in East Hampton. Lee Radziwell was his client and he was the envy of all the hairdressers.

The New Yorker synthesized it: "For our part, we think of Monti as a symbol of an undefinable something that was loose in the land in the mid '60s, and as the purest living example of what Daniel Boorstin has called 'the human pseudo-event': the man who is known for his well-knownness."

Monti was all New York in those salad days. "I cannot live no place else," he told *Screw* magazine. "I lived in California, everyplace, but this is my town. This is where I live. In California, in Hollywood, you get in a car, you know, you end up smoking pot too much, you end up getting too much speed because you have nothing to do but raise muscles, go in the fucking pool and take a sunburn, and everybody's doing the same thing."

As his career lulled into the '70s, he sang a new tune: "I've decided that my future is in television. I am not a recording artist. I am famous as a television personality. I am an island unto myself and those people in their living rooms are islands unto themselves. They can dig me on the tube talking about me, myself. I am the first honest phony. They can understand that." Of his decision to shift West, he told *The New Yorker* that "New York has abused me. It has abused my stardom, my friendship and my wonderful sense of humor. So I feel it's time for me to go to California, where they're wet and tired, and bring them good tidings. California needs somebody like me . . . with my insanity and chaos. I was put on this earth to create chaos, but it's got so very chaotic for me that my chaos is not working here. All I'm taking with me to California are my portraits of myself, and my ego, which is the biggest thing I have to offer."

So he packed it all up and drove out to southern California. During dull stretches of the drive, Monti would sing "Haw-lee-wood."

Donna Lee Phillips, forty-five, lives in an efficiency unit near La Brea and Sunset in Los Angeles. She has given up smoke, drink, everything, and brews tea and reads horoscopes. She has frizzy gray hair shooting out from the top of her head, and I think she may be a witch. At midpoint in her room there is a shrine to Buddha and on each side of this shrine is a small black and white picture of Monti Rock, III in top hat and tuxedo.

Donna Lee is a hard-core Monti Rock groupie, one of only two on the West Coast. The other is a six-foot-six guy who won't give his name but shows up unfailingly wherever the gig happens to be.

Donna Lee is explaining her relationship to the star.

"I used to be, you know, very tight, very strong, with Dick Buckley, and Monti is actually, I think, funnier and maybe even hipper than he was." Dick Buckley? she is asked. "Lord Buckley, you know?" Oh.

"Meeting him only cinched it. The cat's real, man. Integrity. He's got twice as much in person. I know a lot of stars and he's the only one I was impressed with after getting to know. I was in Florida visiting my mother the first time I saw him on TV. I said, 'Is this guy for real? He's fantastic.' You may think this sounds funny but when I flew back here I had a feeling of emptiness for the first time. And this has been my home for twenty-five years. It kept coming, this feeling, heavier and heavier. Then one night I saw his name on the marquee at Filthy McNasty's. 'Is this for real?' I said. I was there every night. I was hooked. And every night it was different. Every night he got better and funnier. He changed his hair and his costumes every night. Wild things. He was fantastic. I got my money's worth. I brought along a rose, a rose that hadn't fully bloomed yet, you know, to give him one night. But at the end of the show he had me spellbound. When he walked by my table I couldn't say 'beautiful' or hand him the rose. I was mesmerized—just like a stone statue."

At length, however, Donna Lee reclaimed her tongue.

"I walked up to where he was standing and told him, handing him the rose, 'Only you could get me out tonight.' He said, 'You're beautiful, baby' and I said 'that's what I wanted to tell you.' "

Donna Lee didn't catch his opening at Filthy's. It was, by most reports, bad. "I bombed, man; I was pretty wrecked when I went out there." He had had a snoot full of Scotch, a nose full of coke and a wig full of reefers, and his lighting man was off balling and never turned up. The performer insulted his audience and told them they were no-talent, tacky faggots who were there free. Now some of these persons were important celebrities come to witness "The Unpredictable Monti Rock The Third." Only they all weren't prepared for the unpredictable after all—for the man *Women's Wear Daily* used to call lovingly "El Outrageoso." His opening night act was savaged by the critics. "Sickest act in Hollywood," one wrote. But Monti Rock played eight weeks.

Statement of *Gayboy* Magazine: "Monti is what most of us wish we were and that's CLASS. . . . With a complete new format and show to offer Los Angeles, Monti Rock opened June 14 at the Purple Lion Supper Club. And may I say he was just super FANTASTIC. . . . But for some weekly publications in Los Angeles, this was not enough. The Critics were just that. It seems as though the Critics of Los Angeles can say nothing good about anyone these days. God help our entertainers."

We are in the kitchen of the apartment on the wrong side of Beverly Hills that Monti shares with Leni Lindstrom, his close friend of two years. Leni, like Monti, is a hairdresser and he is cutting Susan's blond hair into a long shag cut, his favorite. Monti is assisting and, meanwhile, tapping his faucet of consciousness, as we ready for a cocktail party at the 1520 A.D. Club on La Cienaga. Ray Engel is staging the party in advance of his Halloween Straight and Swinger's

Ball and Erotic Products Trade Show for which Monti will serve as master of ceremonies.

Monti, because of his Cuban heels, seems taller than his accredited six-foot-one as he moves in his apartment with natural grace, sometimes like a man, sometimes like a woman. She-man, they used to call him. He has a Swiss-movement's mind and a memory to match.

Monti is carrying on now about the apartment, which he rented long distance and sight unseen from New York at $170 a month because, after all, it is a Beverly Hills address, although he didn't know at the time it carried a West Hollywood telephone number. But that's little matter to someone who is driving a secondhand Chevy these days. "They told me on the phone that this place had a dining room," he says, pointing around the kitchen. "They also said it had two bay windows, the schmucks. I can't wait to buy a house up in the hills."

He studies Leni's work. Susan looks down at the blonde locks piling up on the floor tiles and begins to get nervous. It has been many years since she had this much cut away. Leni is working out, enthralled. He is in reverie and is later to confide that "cutting hair gets me off. Nothing else does," he insists, not styling, not washing; just cutting. What the hell, there used to be an obituary writer at the *Brooklyn Eagle* who got off chewing raw newsprint.

"Hey, you know, I'm going to be the nude roommate of the month centerfold next month in *Zipper* magazine," says Monti, "and I'm not going to hide it behind my forearm." (A similar caper on stage once cost him his lucrative engagement at Caesar's Palace in Las Vegas.)

Monti passes out Hires root beer, "the best in the world," and entreats us to join him in eating some cold, boiled potatoes from the refrigerator, before retreating to the bathroom to finish applying his make-up.

Don José Moses Montañez, alias Monti Rock, III, reflections on the life of, as viewed through a Puerto Rican prism: "I'm a spick faggot bisexual gay from the East Bronx. My mother and father were Pentecostalist preachers and I quit school in the eighth grade. I married a bull dyke model who used to beat me up. We had three dogs and split up after four months. We slept in separate beds so don't talk to me about hard times, baby, because I've known them all. I've been up front all my life. I'm a star. I'm famous for not doing anything. I'm Rhinestone West, the gay caballero. I'm the first Puerto Rican god and I owned a brownstone on Sixty-fifth Street when I was nineteen years old." (To acquire that brownstone, the young Senor Montañez, last of seven children, borrowed the down payment from someone named Sokosky, who liked him, then gave a rent party, inviting people to "come twist with Mr. Monti" in 1960. He netted four hundred dollars and paid off the loan.)

Don Jose, reflections on the appearance of, as viewed through a Portuguese prism: "He is taller in person than he looks on TV. He is six-foot-one and gaining weight. He blames this on an overdose of Scotch when he was losing his touch in New York. He is thirty-two and his eyes are now too small for his rounded face. His nose is a long, pointy Spanish beak, not unlike the Manolete proboscis. Sometimes he talks unnecessarily loud. He is a symphony in suede. He has seventy-two pairs of shoes. He is, he acknowledges, a shoe fetishist."

We are driving east on Beverly Boulevard, heading for the 1520 A.D. Club. Monti can't get over the idea that he is recording at noon the next day. He has only been called hours ago by Bell Records. "I'm recording tomorrow. It's such a shock. I thought they'd forgotten about me. I said to the guy, 'What if I don't know the song?' and he said, 'You'll know it. You're such an egomaniac.' "

Marty from Brooklyn is in the back seat. As we pass an abandoned car in the middle of the road he mysteriously uses this as a pretext to throw down a challenge to Monti Rock, III. "*You* say you're well known," he challenges.

"I am well known," says Monti. "In New York, especially."

"Yeah?"

"I owned clubs, beauty shops. I'm not a collector of people. Uh, uh. I don't collect people." Leni adds, "No way."

"People have been the most disappointing thing in my life," continues Monti. "Isn't that always the case?" suggests Marty. "Not really, because if you want to be a schmuck you can accept anything." Monti goes on to try to make a case for the people here being warped worse than they are in New York but nobody in the car is buying.

Eventually we entered the valet parking line at the 1520 A.D., the old Climax Club. "What is this, by invitation?" Marty wants to know. "I'm the star," Monti matter-of-factly responds. "I'm supposed to be throwing this." Leni explains that "it's a promotion for him because he's doing the Ball Saturday night."

Inside, we meet Ray Engel and Mike O'Hara, who introduces himself as "Lance Rentzel's roommate." Our party smartly responds to an offer of champagne. We smooth quickly into champagne doubles. It takes about five minutes to realize that the party is a dud. Monti and Leni blame it on the folk musicians. "Nobody's dancing," observes the former Mr. Monti of The Twist. "Shit on this."

The place empties very quickly. Everybody has gone out to the parking lot for a front-row view of One City Block burning down across the street on La Cienaga. It is a gallery and art supply house. Lotta thinner going up over there. Ray Engel, the twenty-four-year-old promoter of the costume ball Monti will star at three nights hence, sees an opportunity. "Looter tickets here. Get yer looter's ticket."

Leni suggests a hamburger some place but we are all

more or less broke. Marty, who owns property in West Hollywood, produces a tenner. Thus flush, we drive to Ben Franks on Sunset, parking next to a tan Bentley. "I know the guy who owns that," announces Monti. "He's a queer racketeer I used to know in New York. A baby gangster." When we enter the coffee shop, he goes over to say a few words to a man wearing a wide-brim hat, the baby gangster.

Monti is still excited about the recording session. It will be the second record he ever made. He is still looking for his first album. He will eat a Reuben sandwich and go home. He has to prepare for tomorrow.

The Smothers Brothers Get Their Sh–t Together

This piece on the Smothers Brothers is sort of flat and lacks my usual zip and that is because I was at the emotional bottom of my life at the time. My marriage, which I foolishly thought was forever, had ended and I was barreling around the country on credit cards, botching one magazine assignment after another, smashing rental cars in Harvard Square, drunk, fistfighting, hopping on planes, and destroying my friendships coast-to-coast. These days of rage ended some three months later but not before I had become an accomplished nitwit and persona non grata just about everywhere.

I wound up in San Francisco, on a water couch in the dank, sunless flat shared by Tim Cahill and Susan McBride in the fog-weary Inner Richmond District. La McBride, ever the poetess, soothed me by playing a Nilsson song that went: "You're breaking my heart/ Tearing me apart/ So fuck you!" She played it for me every day. It helped me to heal. La McBride liked bourbon and I liked Scotch. Every day, while Cahill was at work, we would sit and drink and talk at the kitchen table, for the window there provided the only possibility of catching a ray of sunlight. In the entire house! They owned a vicious Bouvier bitch named Grendel. Though Cahill spent a lot of money to have her schooled, she was disobedient. This dog's heart was black! We would go over to Golden Gate Park in the late afternoon and watch Cahill try to put Grendel through her paces. What a howl. Grendel was good for only two things: furiously attacking other dogs and biting me every night while I slept on the water couch. It went on like this for weeks.

One noon I was staring at a local talk show. The Smothers Brothers were the guests. They were promoting their appearance at Harrah's Reno, their first engagement in years. Their comeback. That might make a good story, I thought. Here are these guys who got canned by CBS for being "too controversial." What a joke. In the context of the times, they were a taffy pull.

They proved to be personable, eminently approachable, friendly, candid and frank. Trouble is, Dick kept pushing on me the goodness of herbal teas and the array of kelp and nuts and beans he adored. And Tommy kept gainsaying that the sniffles I had were from a head cold . . . and pleading with me, in his patented I'm-on-to-you-leer, to cough up some of what he insisted I obviously had stashed on my person.

"What?" I would protest, palms upturned, "you want a head cold?"

It looked like the same old Smothers Brothers. But Dickie—thirty-five years old now, his hair flecked with gray and longer than one remembered—and thirty-seven-year-old Tommy—lines ceaselessly etching his taut forehead from which fine, sandy hair still recedes—were walking into the spotlight in a Reno night club, not in a CBS studio.

The vintage format was there: straight, snippy Dickie harassed by sly, sputtering Tommy, as Dickie tries to get them through a rendition of some classic—tonight it happened to be a Gilbert and Sullivan song, "Poor Wandering One." It's the same format they'd used for three years on "The Smothers Brothers Comedy Hour," until the series was canceled by CBS censors in April 1969.

Now it was November 5, 1973, almost seven months to the day since they'd won a court victory over CBS on that cancellation. Not the victory they'd wanted, a decision on the still-clouded issue of artist control versus network control of program material, but a welcome one all the same: A judgment of $776,000, the amount of money they would have made had CBS let them finish out the fourth year of their TV show.

In his opening monologue at Harrah's Club this night Tommy found himself unable to resist taking another whack at the solemn men who silenced their act during its peak years. Pausing for the full effect of his trademark leer, he declared, "We whipped their ass!"

The sold-out first night audience—a Reno crowd of rednecks, louts and middle-aged out-of-towners, scarcely a youthful face to be seen—roared with laughter. Unprotected by CBS censors, they loved it.

Buoyed by this Middle American acceptance of the once-forbidden word, Tommy started to push the limit a little more. "Anybody here from Philadelphia?" he called, in the night club comic tradition of milking hometown rapport. Some voices cheered. He ran through a few more towns, and finally called out "Ely, Nevada?" (Was it by chance he chose Pat Nixon's hometown?) When someone responded from the dark, plush depths of the club with a cheer, Tommy flatly declared, "That town sucks."

Next day, Tommy was asked by the management not to say, "That town sucks," any more. He agreed, but the incident raised the ghost of their years of fighting censorship.

"A few years ago," Tommy commented over herb tea in the penthouse Star Suite of Harrah's Club, "I would have said, 'Up your ass, man, that's the way it is; it sucks.' I'm not allowed to say fuck. I'm not allowed to say shit, or whatever words. It probably means that we're headed for a nice long comfortable career of mediocrity."

"Oh, you're just so full of shit," blurted Dickie. To the others present in the twenty-fourth-floor suite, as if seeking confirmation from those who know his brother, he added, "Tommy has a feeling that he's really getting pushed around if he can't say fuck, you know."

"I don't feel it because I accept it," countered Tommy. "I say that for me to accept it is to be one of those assholes. . . ." He paused now, lost in one of his pocked moments of doubt, and regarded the snow-topped peaks in the Nevada distance. ". . . a long happy career. . . ." he said to the window.

"No," argued Dick. "It's called compromise. If it's a valid point, integral in the premise, then it's a whole different trip than saying, 'That town sucks,' or. . . ."

"No, that's not right. My point is, it doesn't have to be an integral part. The fact is that I should be able to say what I want to say. That's the point. You give away any of those little points and you end up being very easy prey."

"Compromise, Tommy, is a way of life, see. A lack of compromise, you're dead."

"I know it. I'm doing it easier now. I'm simply saying I don't like. I don't have the energy to do it, to say it sucks, which I prefer in actual language."

"Well," said Dickie, attempting to conclude the subject, "actually I find it distasteful. I just don't like it. I think it's not as comedic."

"Well, I do."

"I know, but you're wrong in this instance. You want to say it because you want to make a point out of it."

"I didn't want to make a point out of it," insisted Tommy. "that's why I'm not saying it now . . . or else I would've ended up saying it in the midnight show."

Now a touch of anger crept into Dickie's voice. "Tommy's the kind of person that if he's happy, he questions it. He tries to snatch defeat out of the jaws of victory. 'If I'm successful, I'd better not enjoy it,' which is a pretty depressing and self-defeating attitude, I feel.

"It's like, he looks out and sees that we've got the same road to travel and then says it might be better that we don't do this. And then he becomes a hired writer at two hundred dollars a week. Because that's new ground. And I buy a little farm somewhere. That's bullshit. There's no such thing as new ground. Go and become a dirt farmer. But talk to a dirt farmer. He's traveled that road, you know, for twenty years. He's planted the same goddamn oats and corn. And to him, it's the biggest crock of shit in the world to see something grow."

So here were the Smothers Brothers, traveling again over the same ground, agonizing over it; but doing it because, they have decided, this is what they know how to do. The shows last night were the official beginning of their first organized night club tour together in over four years.

The Brothers' manager Ken Fritz acknowledged they were playing it by ear. "We don't even have a recording contract," he allowed, and Dickie had said, "As soon as you're off television, it's just a cliché but everybody thinks you're dead. We've been having a good time, but I don't know where we've been."

(But there was no dismissing the feeling that Fritz and the Brothers were merely biding time. It would really come as no surprise when three months later Fritz would exclaim, "It's coming in on all sides, we're getting it like it was before, across the board!" By which he meant not only night club engagements, but Carnegie Hall and Greek Theater concerts, and a flood of college dates: Michigan, Wisconsin, Florida State, Drake—even Central College, Iowa. And this by request of college students who were thirteen years old when the Brothers TV show left the air. But if the near-capacity audience was mostly young at Miami's Eden Roc, at the Fairmont in Dallas the SRO crowd was in its thirties or older—perhaps because of a twelve-dollar cover charge—but still gave the Smothers standing ovations at all of their last six shows.)

Dickie raised a cup of herb tea to his lips and suggested that the Brothers were faced with a challenge greater than before, the challenge to "really come back and make it bigger than it was originally. Now we see how difficult it was. Before, it was just like a bunch of idiots marching down that road of life and one thing led to another, and there we were. You know, 'Yesterday I couldn't spell it, today I are one.' "

The harbinger of their renewed activity, of course, was the favorable disposition of their suit against CBS. It was a cleansing. After marking time for four years just waiting for their day in court, they were no longer mired in the past, and the present was the penthouse at Harrah's.

"It's like the residue, the vestiges of 'The Smothers Brothers Comedy Hour,' " Tommy said. "We have to search out and put more politically and socially oriented material in our show. Which is totally opposite of what the pressure was when we were doing the 'Comedy Hour.' Now we have to live up to that kind of image."

Dickie could see what the future might have been like, if it hadn't been for CBS's canceling the show. "The summer before we were fired," he recalled, "we produced 'The Summer Brothers Smothers Show'—the Glen Campbell show, remember? We planned to have our fourth and final year and then produce another summer show. And that's how the whole production trip starts. When you're tired, you take your own show off the air. But also you've got four or five other shows going meanwhile. Like Sheldon Leonard, like—what's her name? Lucille Ball. Thank you. And Desi Arnaz. You don't want to perform any more so you pull your own show off. When comedy is really good, it's the creative thing involved in the production."

In remembering those halcyon days, Ken Fritz thought they had the makings for several strong productions. They had, after all, introduced network audiences to the Byrds, the Who, Jefferson Airplane and Buffalo Springfield, and premiered for North America the Beatles singing "Hey Jude." They'd presented talented writers and musicians like John Hartford and Mason Williams and given work to people who had no chance elsewhere.

A case in point is Murray Roman. "Here was a guy," said Dickie, "who couldn't have gotten a job anywhere. Murray to me was a totally undisciplined weirdo. The kind of comic that would bomb half the time. But he had these weird ideas. He wrote a skit that we got so much comment on—it was on 'Honey,' that nauseous Bobby Goldsboro song. Remember that? And Murray Roman did a thing where we had the Honey Amusement House, sold tickets and you walked inside and saw the dead dog, you know. And the people entering said, 'Oh, this is a real guy and he's sad.' They came out and Tommy comes up and says, 'Well, you got to do it again. Step right this way, ladies and gentlemen.' This kind of concept of Murray's just wasn't being done." (By coincidence, that afternoon Murray died in Los Angeles from injuries sustained in a car accident.)

But it was this kind of chance-taking that eventually cost them their series. At first, CBS just thought it had a pair of well-scrubbed folk musicians in red blazers—nothing to worry about. In early 1966 the network placed them opposite NBC's seemingly unchallengeable "Bonanza" on Sunday nights, a midseason move regarded as an act of desperation. Instead, the ratings climbed and Tom and Dick became network heroes. People like Dr. Frank Stanton, then president of CBS, and Board Chairman William Paley, began to visit regularly with the boys whenever business took them to Hollywood.

And then an odd thing happened. Dr. Stanton and Mr. Paley stopped coming around for coach-team chats. "If you know what you want and go after it, you get known as being difficult," Tommy remarked at the time.

Skirmish soon became full-scale war and on March 9, 1969, CBS replaced the scheduled show with a January rerun because the latest show had not been "submitted in time to be previewed." The network was no longer taking chances. Curiously, though, within the same week CBS signed the Smothers for a fourth year, committing them to twenty-six shows at a cost of $4.5 million.

At the time Tommy beamed, "Next season we'll book who we want and do what we want. We've tried to do it CBS's way, now we'll do it ours."

Almost simultaneously, Bob Wood, president of CBS's television division, advised the brothers in a yard-long telegram that they weren't free to use the show "as a device to push for new standards. If you cannot comply with our standards—whether or not you approve of them—'The Smothers Brothers Comedy Hour' cannot appear on CBS."

The show, delayed from March 9, was finally seen on March 30, 1969. It went over the air mutilated. Comedian Jackie Mason's monologue was butchered in half. Worse is what was done to Joan Baez. In introducing a song, she commented that she was dedicating it to her husband, David Harris, "who is going to prison in June for three years." She added that his crime was opposition to the draft and militarism. "Anybody who lays it in front like that," she said, "generally gets busted, especially if you organize, which he did."

Viewers only heard that her husband was going to jail. Scissored was the reason why. "It's pretty goddamn disgusting," Tommy said the next day. "It leaves the impression that maybe he's committed grand larceny or something." Tommy claimed that in the final year seventeen of the twenty shows were edited. "It's been a fight all the way. From the fourth or fifth show, I would say that in the three years, 75 percent of the material was edited in one way or another."

For instance: CBS refused to let them use two taped interviews with Dr. Benjamin Spock, who at the time was facing trial for antiwar activities. On the opening show of their third and final season, they lost seven minutes of Harry Belafonte singing a calypso song, "Lord, You Must Stop the Carnival," against a backdrop of news film showing police atrocities at the 1968 Chicago Democratic Convention.

Yet CBS was right in one area, at least. The show did irritate viewers—outdrawing all other CBS shows fifty to one in mail response, most of it adverse. Networks are notoriously sensitive about adverse mail, sometimes a degree beyond sensitive. Once at a party at Senator Vance Harke's house after the show was canceled, Tommy spoke with a group of Midwestern broadcast executives. "Am I dangerous to you?" he asked them rhetorically. "You're dangerous to me," said one of the broadcasters, "because you're incompetent to make social comment."

But in view of the inflamed political temperament of the period, it is an irony that the show at times rated among the five most popular programs of the week; that's out of eighty-five prime-time shows. And in retrospect, the material was surprisingly mild. "There's no question that they were forerunners," said Gary Pudney, vice-president of variety programs at ABC. Take, for instance, the recent furor when the protagonist of "Maude" was debating whether to have an abortion. Four years ago, one publication noted recently, she wouldn't even have been able to use the word "pregnant."

CBS finally snuffed the brothers on April 4, Good Friday, just three weeks after the contract renewals had been signed. The message, addressed to Tom, read:

"As we have advised you on several occasions, most recently in my wire of March 27, your obligations to us require you to deliver an acceptable tape to us no later than the Wednesday preceding the scheduled broadcast date of each program. . . . We hereby notify you that by reason of your failure to make such delivery yesterday (April 2) we are forced to treat this failure of delivery of an acceptable program as a substantial and material breach of your obligations to us, and as conclusive evidence that you have no intention of performing these obligations in the future.

"By reason of your breach you have not afforded our Program Practices Department an opportunity to consider the acceptability of the program. On the basis of our information about parts of the program, we believe that the program in its present form would not be acceptable under CBS's standards because, at the very least, it contains a monologue which in our opinion would be considered irreverent and offensive by a large segment of our audience and, therefore, unacceptable even if this were not the week of the Eisenhower funeral rites and even if Sunday were not Easter Sunday.

"Therefore, we hereby notify you that the agreement between you and us is terminated, subject, of course, to rights and obligations which as a matter of law survive such termination.

[signed] Robert D. Wood"

(The highlight of the later trial would come when Robert D. Wood testified that he did indeed fire the Smothers for breach of contract, only to admit he didn't know what the contract stipulated. "He'd never even seen it!" said Tommy. In fact, there never was a final contract, although several drafts made the rounds between the William Morris Agency, acting for the Smothers, and the network.)

Though the network hadn't even seen the program, the Brothers were fired "on the basis of our information about parts of the program." The controversial "parts" turned out to be a David Steinberg sermonette satirizing the religious lectures used by many stations to sign on and off the air. The horrifying passage: Steinberg compares the Jewish and Christian version of the story of Jonah. The Jews claim Jonah was swallowed by a whale; "and here is where the Christians," he says, "grab the Jews by the Old Testament"—to wit, whales have small gullets and can't swallow human beings, ergo: Jonah was swallowed by a huge guppy. The Program Practices Department also didn't like the slogan, "Put the 'Christ' back in Christmas and the 'Ch' back in Chanukah."

The counterattack began the next day. Tom flew to Toronto to watch the canceled program on Canadian television. The censorship allegation looked the more like fact once people realized that just across the border Canadian audiences had seen all previous Smothers shows without editing and without holocaust. By Monday, April 7, the New York Times editorialized that it was naive to believe CBS's claim that "breach of procedures" was the reason for the cancellation.

But CBS stood firm. The last first-run Smothers Brothers show was aired April 20, 1969, and the season was filled out with reruns. Tommy could run around Washington, D.C., as much as he liked, but the Smothers were off the air.

The muzzle was lifted briefly the following year when NBC gave them a one-shot special, "The Return of the Smothers Brothers." The best part of that show wasn't even seen by viewers. It occurred the following day; Los Angeles Police Chief Edward M. (Crazy Ed) Davis, in a letter of protest to NBC, called the special "putrid" and objected especially to a scene involving a male choir in police uniforms. "It was a very realistic costuming effect . . . sidearms, badges and cap pieces," Davis noted. As part of the dialogue the choir leader said he had smelled something wonderful in the air at Woodstock and that whatever it was, he hoped it would keep growing.

Chief Davis released the text of his protest to the press and the next day Tommy Smothers convened a press conference in Los Angeles, across the street from the NBC offices, to assure the chief that the choir was composed of actors and not real policemen, and that the flying nun doesn't really fly. Tommy's blue eyes leaped to life as he sat in the Harrah's Club penthouse three years later, savoring the almost forgotten episode. He recalled the press conference:

"And then when the media got ready for the questions they were going to hit on me, about Woodstock and dope and people smoking grass and, 'Don't you think. . . ?' and all those questions—how do you answer those kinds of questions?—then in walked this guy who played the cop leading the choir and he came up and said in a very grave voice, 'Tom, I told you not to talk about the police. Now you've got to come with me.' And he dragged me out. And as I was being pulled out the door, in came the waiters with margaritas and all these things for the press. And they clogged up the door. So I was, aha, hauled out."

It would have made a golden swan song—had the brothers retired from show business at that moment—with margaritas clogging the doorway.

Instead, they gambled with ABC on a summer fill-in in 1970, agreeing to submit tapes nine days before showtime—a longer blue-pencil period than CBS had ever sought—agreeing to submit scripts to censors two weeks in advance of broadcast and yielding a complete control of the show, including the selection of writers and guests, to the network. They gambled and lost. Nobody watched.

"I wanted a show more than anything after the CBS show went off," Tommy remembered. "Then I got a show, but I didn't know what I wanted to do on the show. I just wanted a show. I proved I could get a show. But then I didn't know what to do."

After this failure, Dickie absorbed himself in auto racing, entering fourteen races that summer. Tommy made one more try, with Westinghouse, as host of a syndicated lemon called "The Tom Smothers Prime Time Organic Space Ride," patterned after Public Broadcasting's more successful, though similarly short-lived, "The Great American Dream Machine."

With these turn-of-the-decade disasters behind him, Tommy was choking. He'd shown a film of the censored material to Nicholas Johnson, the FCC Commissioner, at a gathering of the liberal House Democratic Study Group. Johnson lamented the censorship of such innocuous material; lamentation aside, nothing came of it. Tommy's plans to direct films and create a writers' workshop never materialized. "They were all the trappings and trimmings of what you can accomplish when you have momentum," he said in Reno. "After the show, after all the things, it was much more difficult." He no longer had the position of advantage. He couldn't just pick up the phone and get whomever he wanted. He was losing.

He turned recluse in Mill Valley on San Francisco Bay, and spent his days sitting and staring and tuning his guitar. He starred (with Orson Welles, Katharine Ross and John Astin) in *Get to Know Your Rabbit*, a so-called lost Brian De Palma film—so-called because it has never been in general release. He moved to the Fairfax section of the Los Angeles flatlands, taking a modest bachelor apartment in a neighborhood in transition from Jewish to black. And in Hollywood and Beverly Hills he wandered around at parties, consumed by the past, shuffling from foot to foot, hard-pressed to conceal his gloom. When you're hot, you're hot.

Brother Dick, meanwhile, tapered off the auto-racing circuit and resumed his family man's life—he is married to a former college classmate, Linda Miller. His life revolved around skiing and sailing, buying groceries, picking up the kids at school.

For one brother, it was a time of solitude; for the other of quietude. "It did get a little tiresome, though," admitted Dickie, "because eventually there's no direction." Tommy: "It just wasn't . . . it's very hard to catch the seventh wave."

And they worked on laying the groundwork for their trial. Legal fees, after four years of depositions and interrogatories, mounted to nearly $250,000. They primed themselves by getting into shape. "We were on diets," remembered Tom. "We were doing vegetable things and fasting and keeping clean inside, getting up early, getting down to the courthouse and sitting in that room and listening to the bullshit that goes on in federal court. And there was Ellsberg and Russo fighting for their lives in the same courthouse, so, you know, how could we complain."

"Basically, we were taking a shot," Dickie observed. "I told Tommy in front, there's a chance we can't get six people to agree that CBS is guilty. So I was happy for any guilty charge, even though the issue of creative control and who owns it was never decided.

"There was a lady on the jury, a policeman's wife, who thought that we were dirty and didn't like cops. CBS had a $1-million cross-suit and she was going their way. I can't see how we could have financially or physically retried the case. I think we would have had to lay right there. Because look what would have happened if we had lost: We would still have had a quarter of a million dollars for legal fees, plus it would have wiped out any savings we did have and we would have been broke. And then CBS would probably have been the nice guys and said, 'Well, you don't have to pay us all the money in one lump; spread it out.' "

CBS agreed during the trial that Comedic Productions, the Brothers' company, did have creative control but "subject to CBS program practices and standards." In other words, it was established that the Brothers could do what they wanted, but so could the network. In other words, grok Catch-22.

The CBS counterclaim, pinned on the assertion that the Brothers failed to conform to the network's "program practices and standards," was easily undone. Testimony indicated that when the Smothers Brothers tried to obtain a copy of the standards they found them to be nonexistent. The standards had been ad hoc. They were whatever the network wanted them to be, whenever they wanted them to exist. CBS now has a list of practices and standards. This may be the only precedent set in the case.

In the event of a return to television, the Brothers recognize they would face tremendous industry pressure, especially after "whipping their ass" in court. "Oh yes, there's a whole different trip now," commented Dickie. "Before they didn't know. 'Fine, a couple of nice boys. They're popular, let's put them on.' "

Problems with network officials would be changed only in specifics, not in intensity, they feel. "We could use words we couldn't use then," Dick added. "But that's not the major thrust. They still don't want you to get into the political trip and you still can't get into any religious satire. You can't even say, 'That's a one spicey meatball.' "

"There is a difference, though," Tommy interrupted. "We had a lot of battles over trivia that are no longer important. The background was so conservative that the little political satire we did was like blown out of proportion. There were many major battles over bullshit that we wouldn't have now on any level." Such as the line, "Ronald Reagan is a known heterosexual." That was a no-no. Or perhaps the name Mary Jane Roach; the censors wouldn't allow that, though the alternative name Goldie O'Keefe (or was that o'Kief?) got through. It was never spelled out.

Standards of broadcast taste are advancing, Tommy opined, but only slightly. "The closest it gets is Archie

Bunker. They've got more police shows than ever before. Now they've got the undercover agent, the informer, like 'Mod Squad.' They're making 'Mission: Impossible' valid so that people can accept Watergate as valid. My son [by a now dissolved marriage] now told me he wants to grow up to be a policeman. It's disheartening to me."

"You know what?" said Dickie. "Some people say we paved the way for 'All in the Family.' Well, if we went back on now, maybe 'All in the Family' would have paved the way for us. Things are really getting loose when Johnny Carson does Watergate jokes. He's not exactly a spearhead of social conscience, you know. And he's doing Judge Sirica now, all cool. It's like when the war was almost over and all these people that had been afraid to say anything were coming out doing antiwar stuff."

"It's OK," Tommy countered. "It doesn't matter when anybody joins with anybody." He reflected a moment, remembering what it had actually been like. "It was pretty draining, after all, to fight all those battles over whether you could say 'sex education' on television. If it hadn't been us, it would have been somebody else. The decade was one of great consciousness. We were just reflectors. It was all a matter of time and circumstance.

"Really, there's no way around it. It's a matter of working out some kind of agreeable arrangement, through accommodation and through pushing and through saying it more cleverly and more deceptively. Because the number-one communication form in a society, whether it's television or radio, is always the most controlled and what you have to do is just be a better artist and deal with those things as best you can, get the most that's possible on."

"There's just no way," said Dick, "we could have a show with any meat or any statement in it that isn't going to offend a major segment of some society somewhere. And if we anticipated all that, which is what the networks are trying to do, you end up with nothing. So I say, screw them. You have to do what you think is right and just throw it out and see what happens."

"Jesus," someone in the penthouse roared, "you're more militant than ever."

"He's more militant after the fact than before the act," said Tommy.

"No, no, but the thing is. . . ."

"And I'm more mellow now."

Evel Is Dead

Bobby Knievel might just be the worst creep I ever met . . . although down the line he could end in a photo finish with Larry Flynt. A philanderer and a bully. None of which, of course, should be held against a man. But he blew my vote of confidence because in public he was a hungry spokesman against these evils. Whenever and wherever he could find an audience. Mister Red-White-and-Blue. What an asshole. No one, however, ought to confuse his personal behavior with his professional self. No one can fault his derring-do, his daredeviltry or his willingness to risk life-and-limb. In these matters he displayed time and again that he has The Right Stuff.

I first met Knievel a year or so before the Snake River Canyon jump. He was a highly visible presence every night at Filthy McNasty's, a night club on the Sunset Strip. He was in town to jump over some cars at the Coliseum. Had his own table in a corner. Sipped Jack Daniels from his hollow walking stick. Monti Rock was headlining at Filthy's and would always introduce Knievel from the stage. Stand to accept the round of applause, wave to the crowd, crash back down onto the plush banquette.

What a show it was at Filthy's! It opened with a female fire-eater, followed by "The Black Elvis Presley," followed by Monti who would warble "On Broadway" for a couple of minutes before switching into a half-hour-long oral history, backed by the rhythm section, of his doomed and hapless life. I urged Monti to take the whole show on the road. Book it on the college circuit. They'll lap it up;

judge it outré. I remember that Danny Kaye, around 1955, toured with a similar show. The Marquis Family of Chimps was the opener, followed by Señor Wences, followed by the José Greco Dancers, then intermission. Kaye had the second act to himself. The show sold out the Colonial Theatre in Boston for five weeks. I had the souvenir program. My commission was 50 percent. I made a small fortune. You can do the same, Monti, I championed. Alas, he would not budge. Had to stay in Hollywood, he insisted.

I have an ineradicable memory of Knievel walking toward a crouching NBC cameraman in Twin Falls, Idaho, and at the last moment changing direction and kicking the man's camera splat back into his bloody face. For no reason! Man could've lost an eye, eh? That's the way it was and that's the way Knievel was: kicking a one-eyed man when he's down. Next day, Jack Perkins and the rest of the NBC crew had protest T-shirts printed and wore them the rest of the run. To get at the truth of the story—the wide-angle disparity between Knievel the man and Knievel the showman—required construction of an entirely new form of journalism: Tonto Journalism, son of Gonzo.

It came as no surprise later to read that Knievel had ambushed Shelly Saltman, who had written a book about the Snake River Canyon Jump in which he said things Bobby Knievel did not like (about Knievel's philandering, etc.). Bobby's Montana cowboy thugs pinned Shelly's arms while Bobby whacked him with a baseball bat. Damn near killed him. Went to jail for it. And, worse, lost his lucrative contract with Ideal Toys as a result. Nice guy. Finished last.

Evel Knievel plunged into the Snake River Canyon moments after being launched by a steam-driven missile in his attempt to jump it. But the parachute that was to have lowered the cyclist to the other side slowed his descent into the 600-foot deep Idaho canyon, and he was quickly rescued.

Wall Street Journal, September 9, 1974

What do they know, that's all they wrote! I was There. Snake River Canyon or Bust. Me and maybe ten thousand others, slapping grandchildren on knees in times future, recalling the century's greatest Conceptual Art event. Memory will blunt, so let's just plunge in.

Tom Rauckhorst, twenty-one, Akron, O plunged in. He dove two hundred feet from the south side of Shoshone Falls—that's a mile down the Snake from the Official Evel Knievel Harley-Davidson Mack Truck Bucyrus-Erie Chuckles-Nabisco Patriotic Launch Ramp—on a Friday, two days before Evel popped his own dive.

Rauckhorst, with three broken vertebrae, lived. Evel, with just a few scratches, didn't. Rauckhorst the imitator; Evel the exemplar. They cheered Rauckhorst and threw beer cans at him as he disappeared in the foaming pool below. They threw beer cans at Evel, too, when he resurrected briefly.

There is no record of beer cans being hurled at Cherokee Harry when he jumped the falls. Was that because Harry dove from the north side? Or because he jumped in 1905? When that historic half-breed turned three somersaults in his well-oiled descent of 235 feet, he tore a kneecap and collected a twenty-five-dollar bet. He died nine years later in Boise, a pauper. Had there been a Top Rank, Inc., then, Cherokee Harry might have been a closed-circus TV presentation. Ideal Toy might have marketed a diving doll in his likeness. Had Harry come along now, he might have been one of the openers for Top Rank on the Evel Knievel presentation, as were the Sensational Parker, the Great Manzini, the Surviving Wallendas, Gil Eagles and Bobby Riggs. Yet again, Top Rank might have told Harry no soap, as they had told Benny (Boom Boom) Koske, the Human Bomb, who traveled 2,500 miles and pleaded for three days.

In the end, Knievel fared no better than Rauckhorst or Harry, as the *Wall Street Journal* reported. And in the end, it matters not that the most spectacular stunt of the century was an aerodynamic flop. It is of no import that the theaters of North America were empty, that the live gate came from ten thousand or so people and not the predicted five hundred thousand. That is to miss the point: The point being that it took place at all; the deeper meaning being that it established Knievel not as King of the Daredevils but as King of the Conceptual Artists; the deepest meaning being that it shoved that pussy Christo under the sheets where he belongs. It was, as Evelpersons say, outtasite. Let's go:

Jan's Lounge on Falls Avenue, two miles from the launch site, in Twin Falls (hereinafter Twin, as the Potatoes call their city of twenty-two thousand in the high desert). Thirty or so hawgs are parked in front, many of their owners (One Percenters, as they're known) pissing into the night highway.

What do you think of Evel Knievel's chances? a reporter asks the road captain of the Lost Soul Nomads.

"Fook'm in the ass."

(That became a favored expression of the press.)

In dining room of Blue Lakes Inn, Official Evel Knievel Headquarters. Steaks arrive. Would need Outlaw's shiv to cut them. Crazy man in white suit arrives at table. He chef. Arrive of own volition. Very manic, flitting table to table. Come back and say dinner is free because steak is impossible. I salute chef and buy him a martini. Turns out to be Tony Guanche, old neighbor from Las Palmas (Canary Islands). Chef moves to next table (which proves bad mistake). Wells Twombly of S.F. *Examiner* explodes in proper Knievellian wrath. "Out!" he rages. "Get back in the kitchen where you belong—and do your job! No excuses! Get me a hamburger!" I give chef high sign in Spanish, tap middle digit right hand against right temple, point forefinger left hand at Twombly. Chef understands Spanish, splits. I move across street to Holiday Inn, former Official Cocktail Lounge and Headquarters (until Officially Marketed National Folk Hero refused to pay bar tab; hence Holiday Inn refuses to acknowledge His presence; marquee says "Welcome Miss Rodeo America. . . ." whereas all other marquees in Twin wish "Good Luck Evel"). Meet N.Y. Newspaperman in defrocked cocktail lounge. Has lots of white powder for nose, says it is crystallized steam; am very impressed with his *steam* Training Table for nose. Talk is of steam rocketry and so forth. N.Y. Newspaperman also claims to have steam-driven typewriter. Very pleased with way own Training Table coming and call it a night. Have forty-five-mile drive ahead, to Ramada Inn, Official Press Corps Motel, in Burley (Potato Processing Capital of the World; site of World's First Safeway Stores). Why? Evel's idea, Top Rank says. Evel holds press to bosom like Knixon (tip of the Hatlo Hat to Herb Caen for that one). Must have plenty of Training Table, keep up strength for these trips.

ABC-TV is blasting one-hour special, "One Man, One Canyon," into motels of America. It is knawful; what blather! Unconscionable departure from journalism. Jules Bergman, you shill! Out! Get out! Out of here! ABC-TV is Official Evel Knievel House Network. Later tonight they will beam the George Hamilton movie, Official Evel Knievel Screen Biography. Himself is on tube, telling Berman:

"The highest, the longest jump in history . . . that one I will not have to look forward to doing again . . . this actor and trailer is the longest, the greatest, in the world . . . cost me over ninety-one thousand dollars to build it. It has draft beer, a love seat . . . I have made love to six hundred women. . . ."

Evel is concerned with people cashing in and making money off His name. He know market value of name. He get 50 percent every time His name used. On basis of this story alone He stand to make thousands; why, Chuckles candy give Him hundred grand just to put their silly-ass decal on His helmet. This not a rich magazine and since He get 50 percent of every mention, cost mounting rapidly. Let me try ruse: He have hard time in court proving *EK* meant Him.

" . . . Dying is a part of living and while I'm alive, I'm going to live it to the hilt . . . the canyon itself is a little over a half-mile wide . . . blah, blah. . . ." (Canyon actually quarter-mile at launch site.)

At every moment, as I watch video EK, real thing is aloft, somewhere between Twin and Butte, forty minutes apart by leased Lear Jet. Goes like this all week. EK in maniacal disarray. Not content to stay one place or other. Pilot of Official Lear Jet is Watcha McCollom, fifty-one, Danville, Illinois. Watcha and crew all wear maroon crushed velvet tuxedo jackets, white frill shirts, black tie, patent leather pumps. Is Official EK Jet Uniform. Watcha say cost $300 apiece; I say they leased. I say the $6 million EK was fronted is leased, too. Watcha say EK stands on head during flight, while Watcha makes sharp banks so EK can get practice pulling Gs. Maybe he pulls 2.5 Gs this way. No one knows. EK also doing pushups and situps. Wild Turkey rounds out His Training Table. EK rubbing off on Watcha. When Watcha touches tarmac he does wheelies all way down runway, using spoilers and half-power.

Meanwhile, back at the documentary, Bergman has collared fan. Fan says, "One thing about this Guy, you got to give Him credit because He's got guts that won't quit." (Pardon me, but who will pardon Bergman and ABC . . . Knixon? Sigma Delta Chi?)

Bergman has Truax (Robert C., fifty-two, rocket pioneer, Annapolis grad, captain U.S. Navy, ret., Polaris program, Apollo mission, first Thor rocket project officer, now designs steam rockets for drag racers, designer of Skycycle X2, Official EK Engineer). Truax says, "From zero to 300 mph in four seconds . . . 108-foot-long ramp at 56-degree incline . . . 5,000 pounds of thrust . . . if you were gonna give me $6 million to do it, I'd say nothing doing."

Good night, Jules.

Friday morning, blue and clear, with just a hint of wickedness in the air to spook the Spuds. Spy Twombly in front of Blue Lakes. He has collared townie. "Those folks aren't wanted here," the Potato tells Twombly. "The County Fair is on and that's what all the real people in town are interested in." Twin residents are keeping fingers crossed, praying to be delivered from Evel.

On the fourth of July, 1973, there was no Blue Lakes Inn.

George Kerr, twenty-two, a wiry five-foot buzz saw from Newton, Massachusetts, knows. He was there. He flew out for the jump, unaccountably missing word of the postponement. Two guys from Columbus, O and a sailor from Newport, Rhode Island, also showed, George remembers.

George Kerr is the True Believer. When he began believing six years ago, there were no EK posters. "I had to take a little picture from a magazine and have it blown into one for five dollars." Today, George's bedroom walls back home are covered with EK posters and souvenirs. He has seen the George Hamilton movie five times.

George Kerr was disappointed and out five hundred dollars a year ago, and one day he and the guys from Columbus went to Quall's pasture to take snapshots. George had himself photographed while pissing off the launch ramp (then a launch mound, actually). "It was more or less my expression for Him not showing, my vain expression. I was pissed. It was just everything at once. The picture I would like most to have now is us shaking hands and both holding the cane" (Official $22,000 Ebony Cane). When this year's jump was confirmed, George called the Holiday Inn immediately and reserved two rooms.

During his year's wait, he considered and rejected several potential vantage points from which to watch the trajectory, so familiar was he with the terrain. During the year's wait, George also made his debut.

"My first professional stunt was jumping one kid at Newton Upper Falls Lower Playground. I could have cleared twenty people. . . ."

George has a twenty-five-dollar ticket but will not use it. It has EK's autograph.

"Having had a year to think, I think the best place to see it is to sneak over early Sunday to the north rim. . . ."

North rim? Man, are you bonkers! They'll shoot you. Sure as shooting. One guy said to me yesterday, "You're not going in that road because this .38 says you're not." They're hiring all the security they can get because they know the scene is going to be trashed. It's ugly out there already. They're giving $2.50 an hour . . . hiring Outlaws, Migrant Workers, Rent-a-Spuds, anybody. They're all packing pieces and knives and tire irons. It's not the New York Jews you gotta worry about, it's the Montana Cowboys (Butte is Official Hometown of EK, and if you didn't know that, get out! Get out of the story!).

"They wouldn't shootja," George disbelieved.

Hell, they wouldn't.

"And if they do, big deal. As I'm falling down, I'll see Him make the canyon and that'll be it. To me, it's everything.

"As soon as I see Him jump the canyon, God forbid—

and I'm just saying this now—He (God, in this case) could take me and I would feel I've seen it all. I've seen a lot of things in my life. I've seen the Rolling Stones, all these big things that to other people are nothing . . . to me they're something, right? And, uh, I'll be happy to leave [this earth] tomorrow."

Parking lots of Blue Lakes Inn and Holiday Inn overflowing, geeks and daredevils of North America truly in convention assembling—probably first time ever. Hear they had a great memorial bonfire last night at Shoshone Falls, where a couple thousand Outlaws and Motorhippies encamped, for Vertebrae Rauckhorst, latter-day Cherokee Harry. Have my first brush with Gil Eagles, the cycling psychic. Wish him good luck. He says thanks. Sign on pickup truck in parking lot says, "Fearless Fariss, Nevada." Also meet for first time Benny (Boom Boom) Koske, the human bomb. Benny, thirty-four, says he's been at it seven years. Blows himself up in two-by-six coffin, takes fifteen minutes to police the area after detonation. Says he does it all himself, has a safety net and full insurance coverage. I check him out. Boom Boom appears to be in one piece. Says he's Polish, from Tampa. Also says he's negotiating with Shelly Saltman (vice-president, Invest West Sports, Bob Arum's partner in the event) to get on show. Wish him good luck. He says thanks. Bump into Shelly Saltman. Hey, Shelly, I say, put the Boom Boom on the card. No dice, says Shelly. He might shake the launch site. Kitchen staff at Blue Lakes Inn walks out on Chef Guanche again. (He also official concessionaire at site.)

Went out to site, forty-eight hours to countdown. Chief Red Cloud, an EK sidekick and corn-on-the-cob concessionaire, admits that "even though the canyon is an underdog in the betting, it's a sentimental favorite." At that moment, EK being swung out over launch ramp by Official EK Freedom Crane. He soon in the Skycycle cockpit, there to sit alone for an hour, staring up the fifty-six-degree incline at

Old Glory, flying proudly in the Official Fifteen-Knot Wind.

Could He hear the Evelpersons below? We could, being separated from them only by a six-foot-high, eleven-gauge chain link fence. "Evel," they chanted, "Ev-el, Ev-el, Ev-el, Ev-el." They loathed us, those Evelpersons in their Evelmania. "Press whores . . . Pig fuckers." Because we were inside the compound, close to their Mutant Jesus . . . and they weren't. The fence would not hold, we knew.

Wells Twombly transfixed by sight of EK up there in rocket and begins to see structural steel launch ramp as Cross of Calvary. "Golgotha," he keeps saying.

"Spill the wine, Evel," Evelpersons demand. To venture out among these boozed-up, Seconaled-down Evelpunks foolish at best. Yet, some did. One found a middle-aged woman from Kuntz, Texas, Mrs. Joy Roberts, who closed the furniture store she and her husband operate so they could be here. "We didn't come pinpointed to see Him go from one side to another. We came to associate with the type of people He attracts." Cheap thrills.

The world's biggest Fat Man shoves against the chain link. On his shoulders is the Quaalude Queen, blond and naked to the waist, with the most vacant saucer-shaped blue eyes ever witnessed. Horrible! Her teeny-bop tits bruised and scratched from Lumpen hands that rise from all around to squeeze. "I want Evel," she monodrones. "I love Him. The tribes have assembled." Repeating this line over and over. Her Fat Man scaffold shouting, "We're going cra-zy. We're from Colorado. Ev-el. Ev-el. We're going crazy." Next to them, on the shoulders of another Goonchild, is perched a youth utterly clad in caked grime, proclaiming he is the State Pig of Montana. "Ev-el, Ev-el, the tribes have assembled. I am the State Pig of Montana. Come to us." (Filthy pigs! Get out of here! Out!)

Evel up there all the while, sitting in the cockpit, looking up at the end of the red-white-and-blue ramp at Our Flag, thinking about life and death . . . wondering if he will see Linda on Monday, or the kids: Kelly, thirteen; Robbie, eleven (already billing himself as Evel Knievel, Jr.); Tracy, nine.

"Ev-el, Ev-el, Ev-el. The tribes have assembled. Spill the wine."

Roger Bennett, Salt Lake City UPI bureau, ventures outside the compound to interview the State Pig of Montana, the Quaalude Queen, the Fat Scaffold and their greasy ilk. Roger, my man, one thing you should learn: Never point a microphone at the enemy during a terror situation. They trash Roger. Knock him down, smash his face, grind out a lighted cigarette on his forehead.

EK is down from the Skycycle, surveys His shantytown and says to His cowboy cronies so promoter Arum can hear: "Look at this. Sunday is the greatest day in My life, and it's being run by a bunch of goddamn New York Jews." Replies Arum: "If there's one thing I can't stand, it's a long-haired, loud-mouth cowboy." Quik Quiz: which of the two men was joking? (1) EK. (2) Arum. (3) Neither of the above. ("I'm a New York City kid," Arum told a reporter a few weeks ago. "My values are different from His. He's a cowboy. That generally is not a particularly happy marriage.")

EK retires to trailer, World's Longest Official Trailer. Shelly Saltman promises an Official Press Conference at Trailerside. The media horde jockeys for position. Cameramen shouting at Saltman. "Have him stand," demands Jim Watt, NBC cameraman.

Himself bursts out of the trailer door. "Out!" He shouts. He turns to Saltman and orders him to "tell that man the next time he looks at Me to have a smile on his face." Then, expressing Himself directly to Watt: "I'm not an actor, Mr. Cameraman, do you understand that!" ("I am not a crook," Knixon said.)

"All right," assuaged Watt.

"I said to have a smile on your face!"

"I don't smile for anybody," Watt, manhood at stake, replies.

"All right, get him out! Get him out! Out! Go on, get him out of here! Get out of here." EK takes Official Cane and whacks at Watt, smashing the camera and knocking him down. "I'll stick it in your ear, if you're not careful. . . ."

Saltman removes Watt from compound. Peace, of sorts, returns.

EK regains composure, sort of, and sits on steps of trailer. The press presses in tight. "You can see what it's doing to me," EK says, not particularly looking for sympathy. "And you'll do one thing. I don't ask for your respect. I demand it." (Gotcha, EK.) There are "right-ons" and applause from shills in compound. (What the hell is ABC-TV doing in here? Oh, right: It's their equipment and their personnel who'll feed the closed-circus spectacular Sunday to a thousand people in the Cow Palace in San Francisco and a quarter-full house in Madison Square Garden, etc.)

"Any questions?" says EK. "Okay. The cockpit is so tight, I can't get My hand over there to pull that safety belt thing so I can get out. That's the only problem We're having. . . . It's a monster. I think you all know now by looking at Me. I wish I didn't have to do this and that I wasn't here. But I'm going to. . . . I'm not worried about anything. I'm just upset. . . . Nobody can tell Me what to do." Plants applaud. "Only God. Period. And that's it."

Someone asks about the countdown. EK says He just finished writing it out by hand that morning. Here is the Official EK Countdown:

"One, strap in with the chute. Two, put the helmet on. Three, turn the radio on. Four, T-minus four minutes to blast-off; get ready and pull the pin that holds the parachute. . . . Ten, fire the blastoff. . . . Twelve, happy landing. . . . Fourteen, return to take-off site with wife and kids. . . . Seventeen, and seventeen is a lucky number, go home. And that's just what I'm gonna do!"

EK repairs to trailer again, but the Evelpersons want Him, really want Him, and the fence is gonna come down.

"Spill the wine!" He comes out and walks along the fence, shaking hands three times with the Quaalude Queen. He want to address the beery goths on the PA system. He knows the situation is out of hand, that he has set in motion a sequence of events that contains the potential to destroy even Him, their God. Walking across the pasture, He is engulfed. A bearded biker in a body cast is trapped in the swirl and almost trampled. Mysteriously, the mob parts and EK and the cripple are face-to-face. "My frame's bent, Evel," the man pleads. EK fixes him with a warm look, as if to command. . . . Stray-ten! But the man does not. The God is man. There is no miracle in the mud and dust of Quall's pasture. The man made of Godstuff asks for a pen. He signs the body cast.

"Please make sure that the fences don't go down . . . we don't want people falling into the canyon," He says over the PA. "I'm with you and I want you to be with Me. I need all the help I can get." The Evelhorde applauds and throws a baby into the canyon.

Saturday morning, penultimate press conference: Top Rank serves up: Jim-the-Greek, who lays "three-to-one He's crazy" (haw-haw, Jim); David Frost, whom nobody asks a question; and Terry Sousa of Rock of Ages tombstone company, who planted a 6.5-foot, 2,140-pound commemorative marker at the site, and said: "Unfortunately, some people think this isn't in the best of taste, but I think it is. There aren't too many people today who will try to fulfill their wildest dreams and here's a Man who's trying to live his wildest dreams. And dammit, you've got to give Him credit." One line remains to be sandblasted on the tombstone: successfully attempted . . . or, attempted.

Later, after a glass of port, Sousa confides in Portuguese that EK demanded the word "explorer" be included and in the largest letters . . . not merely "motorcyclist & daredevil."

EK smashes champagne against X2 at 3:30 P.M., twenty-four hours to blast-off. On ground, His second cousin, the Reverend Jeremiah Sullivan (Diocesan, teacher of mid-evil and ancient history, Carroll College, Helena, Montana) is asked by N.Y. Newspaperman what his position in re Suicide Liberation Movement. "Why, I don't believe in it at all," he chuckles. "I don't think Evel has a death wish. Naturally, there's a risk. I think certain kinds of men do these things, like the men who go to the moon."

Security breaks down completely. Bikers packing knives. Migrant workers. Tremendous number of unescorted "mature" women in Blue Lakes and Holiday last night, reports N.Y. Newspaperman.

Need for last-minute press conference in re security problem. Don E. Branker, chief of security, Top Rank, admits negotiating into night with presidents of several Outlaw gangs who threaten to trash launch ramp. (They always do . . . and then they always come over to the other side, become cops.) Why all these shotguns? "To make fear," Branker says. Hah! What Branker really saying here is no one in charge. I swear I remember Branker from Altamont, but he say no.

Ultimate preflight press conference. EK trashes press: "I'd like to just direct a short thing to those . . . of the news media who are sick, like a small percentage of the rest of the world, or who have so drowned their brains in alcohol that they cannot come to grips with themselves and relay messages to the public, like they should be relayed." (Knixon's complaint) " . . . If I don't die . . . someday in some town I'll walk with them face-to-face and when they look into My eyes, all of a sudden they'll have a lump in *their* throat and a knot in *their* stomach, like I'm going to have when I look at that bastard called the Snake River Canyon tomorrow. And I'll guarantee ya, their parachutes will not open. I guarantee ya that." (Applause from shill infiltrators.)

"I've carried a monkey on My back for six years: that

canyon out there. . . . No, I haven't seen Bobby Riggs yet. . . . When I look up into the sky and I see that red-white-and-blue flag flying in front of me, I'm gonna thank the Lord that I lived in this country, that I had a chance to do this. . . . If I die, I would rather go that way and have a chance to burst and . . . and be something, a breath of fresh air, than to be taken by some senseless, ignorant accident and become nothing but a piece of dust in the air. . . . Tomorrow is going to be the greatest day of My life."

Leave pressroom, bump into Boom Boom in lobby. He say Saltman won't let him on presentation. I say, I go to bat for you, Boomer. Call Saltman in his room, plead case. Saltman still say nothing doing, "he might shake the launch ramp." Tough luck, Boom. Decide to get away from Daredevils for a while, visit launch site. Bad mistake. Total trashing going on, can hear gunfire from Shoshone Falls encampment, learn later was Memorial Shoot-out for Vertebrae Rauckhorst. Two hundred chemical toilets aflame at launch site. Evelhorde loose, trash beer concession stands and beer warehouse trucks. Ten thousand cases beer stolen. Flee to safety of EK Museum inside press compound. Man grabs me by arm, says:

"Good afternoon. Welcome to the EK Museum. My name is D. J. Nettles. I'm curator of this museum. The museum was established September 6, 1974. It is dedicated to the exploits of the world's Most Famous Motorcyclist. On your left you can see the Harley-Davidson Skycycle Number One. . . . EK got a telegram the other day from the head of the Drug Administration that said, 'Good luck.' EK doesn't need drugs to do what He does. . . ."

Curator's eyes began to red-out. Must be pulling Gs. Run from museum, bump into Bobby Riggs, just arriving from Las Vegas on Harley-Davidson 175 cc put-put. Asks me where is twenty-five-thousand-dollar check. Man bonkers. Can't you see, I say, all Hell's Angels breaking loose! Run for life! Visiting Goths! Bump into psychiatrist. He say,

"EK's crazy. He comes straight out of the cultural tradition of machismo." Who asked? Rescued by Watcha McCollom. He take me in Hughes copter to Holiday Inn copter pad. Jump out and run for Blue Lakes Inn. Word comes back firefighters being threatened at launch site. Bump into Billy Kidd, one crazy Daredevil. (First man to ski north wall of Mount Washington, New Hampshire. Crazy sonofabitch because he on U.S. Olympic Team but goes out anyway and skis places nobody ski before. Result: broken legs, no make Olympic trip. Is okay, he says.) Swap Training Table with him. He have very impressive Training Table, too. Introduce Billy Kidd to Boom Boom Koske, human bomb. Gil Eagles walk by. Wish him good luck. Billy Kidd want to spend night at launch site, dig the scene. You crazy? I ask. He smile. Notice his T-shirt say "live fast, die young."

Go to poolside press party at Blue Lakes. Bobby Riggs asks me again if I got his twenty-five-thousand-dollar check. Have long talk with Boom Boom about growing up Polish in Tampa. Make mental note to ask psychiatrist if this explains why Boom Boom blows himself up. Gil Eagles entertains party. Puts silver dollars over eyes, then leather band, finally tape. Is psychic. Asks for objects to be put on table, identifies same. Uncanny. One object a wristwatch. Gil Eagles asks anyone to rewind stem of watch, bollix the time. Someone does. Gil Eagles say, "The time on the watch is 4:22." Sho' nuff, is true. English reporter turns and says, "Do you know, the other day at the press conference, the watch also said 4:22? Do you remember?"

Sunday morning, the greatest day in the life of EK.

Learn that Blue Lakes Inn bar trashed last night, all whiskey stolen by bikers. Pick up Sunday papers. Astrologer Johnny Lister predicts death for EK. Read Wm. Barry Furlong's syndicated *Wash-Post* column. Must disagree. He say, "If this event shows anything, it is that brutality is big business and that suicide attempts can be marketed in a big way." I still say is Conceptual Art. This is the Big Top.

Even if only one person showed, would still be successful art piece. Must reorient Arum's thinking. His feathers ruffled because he knows he taking bath. Must congratulate him as patron of the arts. Whether EK live or die, no one give a shit (outside of family, friends). Is not important. The piece is what counts. Furlong column also says promoters figure they have "a real genuine fake going here" in Gil Eagles. But haven't figured out fake yet and so are concerned that Eagles go right over edge.

Proceed to launch site. Good Christ! Quaalude Queen is seated in VIP grandstand, wearing top this time. Ask her how come? She just stare at me as if I bonkers. State Pig of Montana also promoted to chief of security in compound. Hard to recognize him. He took bath. Fat Scaffold now security agent in charge of canyon rim. This turning out to be really good art piece. Bump into Olympic skier Suzy Chaffee. She say high-risk sports only known cure for heroin addiction. I remember Vertebrae Rauckhorst say his two-hundred-foot plunge over Shoshone Falls was "beautiful natural rush," tell Suzy she may have something there.

Getting ugly at chain link fence again. Chosen Ones MC Club of Denver placed in charge of fence. One turns to deputy sheriff and says, "Shoot them if they give you any trouble." PA announcer tells movie cameramen to proceed to bunker and turn in all movie cameras as per contractual agreement. Billy Kidd runs up and asks, "What about knives? Did they say anything about knives?"

Bobby Riggs is taping up Gil Eagles, putting silver dollars over his eyes. Man runs up and asks Gil Eagles something. Gil Eagles says, "I don't care. Just put something out there that'll burn." Now I realize the gaff: burning stakes are planted at canyon rim. All Gil Eagles got to do is keep away from flames. Good luck, faker! I yell. Things getting uglier at fence. Middle-aged man tries to ram gate with Cadillac (state of Washington plates). Bikers slash his tires. He stuck. Front of Caddy stuck inside compound. I run up to fence for look. Biker on other side of fence say to me, "You're in jail and we're gonna keep ya there, man." I retreat. Crowd getting uglier. Reverend Bob Harrington, chaplain of Bourbon Street, cons way onto program and prays over PA system, ". . . as He goes across a canyon may we look beyond that and see a God . . . for, as we all know, it's fun being saved." A Seconal convention going on at fence. "Let the people party!" they scream. PA announcer says, "Ladies and gentlemen, I just got word Evel will not jump if you don't quiet down." Fuck you, fuck you, they yell back. Shotguns are moved to fence, distributed to Chosen Ones MC, Denver, etc. A Montana cowboy, quart vodka bottle sticking out of rear pocket, moves along inside of fence kicking at fingers sticking through chain link.

Put-put-put-put. Gil Eagles is off! People inside compound rush to rim. But, terwillikers. EK chooses that very moment to make appearance inside compound. Press and VIPs forget Gil Eagles, chase EK. So do closed-circuit cameras. Gil Eagles labors at canyon rim in obscurity. Preempted. He gets five seconds on TV. As finale, he rides through flaming arch and crashes through paper banner that says, "Gil Eagles wishes EK good luck." Banner snags in front wheel. He falls landward, luckily, into the arms of Bobby Riggs. "You were fantastic, Gil," Bobby Riggs says, helping psychic cyclist to feet. Almost kills himself, not more than eight feet of ledge between lip and fence, saved by Bobby Riggs . . . and no one watching.

Chosen Ones road captain demands that deputy sheriff get Vodka Cowboy out of front line. Causing too much trouble. New voice on PA, Biker Security, says: "Let's get down from that fence, man." Fuck you, they yell back. "Yeah! Fuck you, too!" Hey, hey, cool it, someone says, barely audible over PA. "I didn't mean that over the speakers. . . ."

The Reverend Jeremiah Sullivan, EK's cousin, commences to pray. "Almighty God . . . its difficulties and its dangers, Robert Craig Knievel . . . his dangerous dream . . .

and the courage to . . . today, His family and His friends, here and throughout the world. . . ." The crowd outside the fence breaks toward trashed Cadillac. A biker has pulled the panties off his topless Mama and deep throats her and she's going "mmmmmm" and he yanks her up and swamp-kisses her and says, "Evil . . . Baby . . . Evil" and the Evel-mania spreads and Father Sullivan is mopping his florid, fleshy face and saying, " . . . humbly pray that You will watch over Him and guide Him to a safe and successful landing, wherever that might be. For without you. . . ." A security Potato is bloody and bowed at fence.

EK is at rampside mike: " . . . Today is the proudest day of My life. For I'm living a dream. . . ." Yeah! they're screaming. We Love You, Evel! Voice of David Frost over closed-circuit TV: "Evel is saying good-bye to His family before returning to His ship. And now the ship is ready. Prepared. The National Anthem. We're just going to hear the National Anthem." Bump into Billy Kidd. He furiously ripping sealer paper off rolls of film and jamming film into camera. "Y'think they'll give me a ticket for littering?" David Frost says: "Happy landing, Evel . . . He'll be back." This place is gonna go, a reporter observes. Aloft, EK is being swung out in Freedom Crane to Skycycle. Astronaut Jim Lovell, Frost's TV sidekick, says: " . . . Evel's helmet is on . . . visor down . . . radio check . . . countdown continues." Vodka Cowboy really juiced now, flat on keester in dust. Wind gusting to Official Fifteen Knots. N.Y. Newspaperman demands immediate conference, leads me to chemical toilet, opens door, stench awful, toilet sitting in ninety-degree sun all week, shoves Training Table up my nose. Egads! Bad mistake to have nose opened in there. They're firing it up! Can hear the steam whooshing through the boiler. 3:29 P.M. We're in speechless phase now. Aloft, Watcha McCollom hovers in Hughes copter, directly over rim. Medivac chopper also aloft. Suddenly quiet. No more hear hiss of steam. Even fence quiet. All eyes on ramp.

My God! There He goes! So concentrated on act, it startles us. Jesus Christ, fastest thing I ever saw! Like a rocket! Oh, oh! Drogue parachute deploys prematurely. Watch out! Watch out! It's coming back this way! The Son Of A Bitch is gonna trash the press in one final act of retribution!

The fence is down! Over here, quick! No, no! He's in the canyon! He's going in the canyon! He's gone down!

Jesus, He's dead. . . .

Not with a bang, but with a hiss and a whisper.

Linda Knievel rushes the rim, crying, "Where is it?" Relatives shout, "Oh, my God!"

Can't see a thing, run to press tent to watch closed-circuit monitor. Camera can't pick up Skycycle. Where is it? Jesus, He *is* dead.

Announcer feeding to Brazil: ". . . enginheiro Bob Truax . . . assalto do Rio Cobra. . . ." Here's the replay, they got it now. Skycycle shown hitting rocks at edge of Snake. Reporter on horn to London: ". . . and immediately indicated with arms aloft that He has again laughed at destiny. Knievel, the father of three, had called this jump His challenge to the monsters . . . the monster that has haunted Him. . . ." Here He comes with Watcha in the chopper! They're throwing beer cans at Watcha's copter! He's coming up to the ramp now! Applause, mixed with the first boos. He's walking. He's being assisted. He's waving to the crowd. EK to Truax; "What happened? When I saw the canyon, I pushed it. I can't understand what made it turn upside down."

"You know what happened," Suzy Chaffee says knowingly, "it was a big macho problem: premature ejaculation."

EK throws Official Cane to crowd. "Throw it back. . . . We don't want them fucking rhinestones, you pussy!"

David Frost is with Him. "How do you feel, Evel?"

EK: "I just don't know what I'm gonna do. I sat in that thing and gave it my best. I just don't know what to tell you."

Frost: "It's not your fault, Evel. These things happen."

EK: "I don't right know exactly what happened. It went sideways. It twisted and turned. It just about knocked Me out. I don't know right now exactly what happened. Mr. Truax told Me that the parachute can blow off on launch and why, we don't know. But he did tell Me a long time ago if it ever got upside down and I saw the canyon wall to blow the chute open and I thank him for that. They saved My life and I'm glad to be back in one piece. Believe Me. I don't know what to say except thank you."

Frost: "On behalf of us all, thank God You're back, Evel. Good afternoon and thank God."

Snake way back to Blue Lakes, hopping farmers' fences. Not safe at site any longer. Trashing total. Crowd moves battered Cadillac toward launch ramp, sets it afire. ABC-TV closed-circuit crew abandons site. Bump into Bob Arum hopping back fences. "The result was a draw," he says. Can see fire in distance when looking back at site. All remaining concession stands, all remaining chemical toilets aflame. Bump into EK entering Blue Lakes. He say, "The damn chute got stuck on the pad. It wasn't a Truax failure. It was a metal failure. It was a metal failure."

Either it was or it wasn't and no one will ever know. Only person could release that drogue chute. Chute was controlled by forty-pound spring-loaded lever in cockpit. EK was to keep it down by using right thigh and right hand. (Drogue chute was to slow Skycycle speed when apogee of three thousand feet reached.) Is possible G forces blew his hand right off lever, for, as I say, actual blast-off was fastest thing I ever see. Also is possible, since EK never do this before, that blast-off simply too thrilling for Him and He let go the lever. If so, He macho enough never to admit it.

Bump into Chef Guanche in lobby. He weeping the blues. He say he lose everything, all life savings, in trashing of his concessions. He say he may be out $17,000, maybe only $7,500. Doesn't know yet. EK his partner at 50 percent. I tell chef not to worry, recall that it well known that

EK a man of His word, quote from the Book of EK: "All a man has is his word and I want them to say after I'm gone, 'He kept his word.' " Bump into Shelly Saltman. He telling N.Y. *Times* man: "I hope kids admire His image. But my own feelings about the private man is that He's a voracious user of people. I don't care if I ever see EK again." Shelly in good position to speak. He with EK during fifty-six-city farewell America hype-building tour, probably know EK better than any outside Cowboy Element. Bump into Governor Cecil D. Andrus (D–Idaho). Governor say EK won't be welcome ever again because of type of crowd he attracts. EK not care. He Learing way back to Butte. Money in suitcase. Watcha McCollom up front. Cowboys riding shotgun. Bump into Benny Boom Boom Koske, human bomb. He say, "They wouldn't let me on because they afraid I shake site." I say, well, they let Gil Eagles on. . . . Boom Boom say, "Yeah, and I do same act, too." What's that? "I drive a car blindfolded." I say, tell me how Boom or get a new manager. He say, "Well, just before you have them put silver dollars over your eyes, you squint eyes real tight, see, and when they put leather band and tape over, you open your eyes real big, see, and a pocket is created and silver dollars drop down." As for leather band and tape, it standard magician's see-through stuff. Benny, you a prize. Anybody out there want Boom Boom, write P.O. Box 593, Palm Bay, Florida, 32905. He presents exciting five-minute format act, as crowd-awakening opener of finale, at price suitable to your budget.

Go to Western Union, send telegram to Governor Andrus: "You and the fine citizens of your state are to be commended for presenting world-class Conceptual Art. Best yet. Keep up fine work you are doing. Best regards, Chef Koske."

At dusk, remaining security guards pulled from launch area, leaving angry crowd shouting, "Party." Burning and shooting continued through night.

George Kerr, Newton, Massachusetts, True Believer, is

in his Holiday Inn room. Disconsolate. He telling friends from Newton he sorry he talked them into coming out here just on his word. A man's word is all a man has. He mighty sorry. Pshaw, his friends console. Is okay, George. We loved it. It was an . . . an event! That's right, I say. Look at it this way. Was great piece of art.

We stare out window at flames a mile away lighting night sky. The King is dead. Long live all the Kings in the wings.

"I saw Him go up and I saw Him come down, put it that way," George grieves. "But it left something to be wondered. . . . I don't see why He chose that way. He jerked everybody today. But he worked in obscurity for years, working up to His big day, the Super Bowl of Motorcycling. . . ."

One of George's friends, Joe Bornstein, takes me by elbow and steers me to corner near door. "It's best," he whispered, "if you leave him alone now. . . . It's like losing a friend."

Zaire

Fifty days and fifty nights in the Congo. I saw it all: Members of a High-Life band showed me a cobra in an open sewer in Zone Lemba; a taxi driver showed me the house of the Pygmy people; a man brought me the twenty-foot-long skin of a python freshly killed and was genuinely disappointed that I did not buy. They showed me things and gave me things and took me places. The people did. They brought me to their homes. The government, on the other hand, took things. A government official rudely stopped me one day as I passed his table at the Inter-continental. "You are here to write about a boxing match, not a people!" The government took my passport and never returned it. And the government took my return plane ticket, prepaid by New Times *and worth eight hundred dollars. John Daly, the copromoter, got me out the day after the fight at his expense. They detained John Daly's father at the airport. They detained George Foreman at the airport, perhaps for losing the fight. They also detained Bundini's Muhammad Ali T-shirts, which he planned to sell, because there is room in Zaire for only one leader: Mobutu, supported by the CIA. I am convinced that the CIA chief, in the guise of an AID official, slipped me a Mickey at dinner. Verily, I believe that.*

I remember Budd Schulberg frantically phoning the embassy and the political officer arriving to escort Budd and Harold Conrad from the Memling Hotel to the airport. I am standing in the hotel entrance and Budd and Harold are yelling at me to flee with them. A well-dressed European appears as if from nowhere, nudges my elbow and steers me away. Ah! I had forgotten! A Kinshasa-born

Portuguese businessman who had invited me to dinner in his home that night. I go with him. The embassy car pulls into traffic. Schulberg and Conrad are staring at me, mouths open.

Playing blackjack in the presidential villa loaned to Angelo Dundee. I am knocking over my goblet of the president's St. Émilion. A butler changes the linen. Never had I knocked over as much as one drink in my entire life. Yet, three times that night I spilled the claret. Three times the butler changed the cloth. My card partners said I was stoned on the Congo weed. No, I told them, it's the voodoo. These days, I spill drinks all the time and when I do I smile weekly and explain, "Voodoo." People seem to understand. The lasting power of the voodoo.

Then, miraculously, departure. In the nature of escape. It is a day later. Lunch in New York with Jon Larsen, the editor of New Times. *How do you want me to write it, Jon? Any way you want, Bill. Okay. At length I decided the best way to tell the story would be to tell it tired. Yes, that would be the perfect voice: tired. Tired like a downed fighter pilot at a Clark Air Force Base debriefing after having been sprung at long last from the Hanoi Hilton.*

I booked into the Chelsea Hotel and as I sat down to write a strange thing happened: A tooth fell out of my head. When I turned in the piece Larsen hailed it as gibberish. I argued but lost. Novak and his African wife fetched me. I would attempt to execute a more orthodox rewrite at their rural Connecticut home. We stopped for dinner at a steak house in Greenwich. I told them about the tooth. No, Cardooze," Victoria tried to reassure me. "No voodoo. No voodoo." She shook her head and frowned. Don't listen to her, Novak confided later. They took eight teeth from her cousin. I know because she told me.

Danny Ray, alias Big Black, a conga player from South Carolina who has spent many years in Hollywood, appeared one day in late September at the gym in N'Sele and, with Muhammad Ali's blessing, began to play for him, hoping to contribute to Ali's rhythm and timing. Big Black played every day for Ali, for more than a month. Big Black is thirty-eight and we spent many friendly hours together during this period. He liked to tell of the time he jammed with Dizzy Gillespie at the 1968 Newport Jazz Festival and broke it up. One day in late October many sportswriters from around the world gathered in the gym at N'Sele, for the fight was once again not far off. One of these writers, a chap from London, approached Big Black and said, "Pardon, citoyen, you name, please; *vous prenom*?" And Big Black, not missing a beat, turned and answered, "Big Black, man, from L.A." Stunned, the Londoner returned after an appropriate silence, and asked, "And the name of the drums you're playing?" And Big Black replied: "Congas, man—and that's with a K." Dutifully, the writer returned to Kinshasa, some fifty miles distant, and at the press center in the Hotel Memling, downtown, wrote of his marvelous encounter with an American he had mistaken for a huge Zairois. When the Londoner gave his account to the Telex operator, it was naturally intercepted by Citoyen N'golo, the sous chef de presse, or censor, of the host country. The writer had written that Big Black plays the Kongo drums, which, perhaps, says something about the state of drumming in London. Of course, N'golo found this unacceptable. "No, no, no, no," he admonished the Londoner. "This you cannot say—is Zaire drums! " And people in London the next day read about Zaire drums. In Zaire, they will have it no other way, for this is authenticité.

Authenticité is something that now you see, now you don't. It's something old, something new, something borrowed, something blue. It's whatever works . . . and don't worry about the discards. One day three years ago, President Joseph Desire Mobutu changed his name to Mobutu Sese Seko Kuku Ngbendu wa Za Banga, which, I am told, means The Cock with Fire in His Eyes Who Blah Blahs and Bloo Bloos and Leaves No Hen Intact. And Mobutu ordered all his 19.5 million (or 22.5 million) citizens to drop their Christian names, which, of course, disturbed the missionaries who have been there now for a hundred years; but they no longer count for much, thank God. In addition, Mobutu ordered the country, which has had many names in the past, to change its most recent name, the Popular Republic of the Congo, or Congo-Kinshasa, to Zaire, in the interest of *authenticité*. Some hold, however, that this was done more to end the outside world's confusion between this place and the place across the Zaire (nee Congo) River, which is called the People's Republic of the Congo, or Congo-Brazzaville, the first Maoist state in Africa, which is the archenemy of this place. George Foreman, for example, was extremely popular in Brazzaville simply because Ali was so popular in Kinshasa. I think also that George Foreman made a tactical blunder in bringing his German shepherd, Daggo, to this land, because I am sure it reminded the people of the Belgians who used to own this place and who called it the Belgian Congo, when Kinshasa was Leopoldville. The first recorded name this place had was Nsadi, which means river in Kikongo, a language not used much anymore hereabouts. That was back when the Bakongo kingdom, which included much of present-day Angola, Cabinda, Congo-Brazzaville, Zaire, Ruwanda, Burundi and Uganda, flourished. One day in 1482, Diego Cao, sea captain of Portugal (Cao means dog in Portuguese), became the first white eyes to see the river, the seventh longest in the world, which from its source near the Zambian border runs for 2,718 miles to the Atlantic, crossing the equator twice and discharging into the sea a volume of water second only to the Amazon, and which includes several unnavigated stretches because of the long and dangerous rapids, some of them up to a hundred miles long, that interrupt its journey to the sea. It has never been fully explored, this river that passes through swamp and dense jungle, and has never been navigated from source to sea. And the country that surrounds it, though mapped, remains to be wholly explored on foot and still contains secrets from man. Nor have its many natural resources been fully noted. Many indigenous diseases still cause misery and, like in Diego Cao's day, communications could be improved. When Cao first gazed upon the river, he turned to King Bakongo and said, "vass dis?" And Bakongo said, "This is the Nsadi, my friend." The sea captain took out his Bic and spiral notebook and entered not Nsadi, but Nzadi, which future Portuguese further corrupted to Zaire, and don't ask how, because, as I have told you, this place still holds secrets from man. Nonetheless, Zaire is the authentic name President Mobutu has opted for. Which, I am sure, says something about *authenticité* and bullshit.

There are, however, two manifestations of authenticité that I can wholly applaud: the outlawing by Mobutu of neckties (but is replacing the cravat with the ascot furthering authenticité?) and the admission that smoking wild hemp, a favorite pastime, is authentic . . . to the degree that it does not get in the way of creating one Zaire, one great Zaire.

Beyond this, all I can remember is that my room at the Hotel Memling was 263 and my phone number there was 601; and I am convinced that even this says something about Zaire. Also, I remember that the press corps of the world, when they returned, invariably led their pieces with references to the hyacinth pads and other flotsam floating inexorably along the Zaire toward the sea . . . almost to a man they wrote such, neglecting to inform the reader that under each hyacinth pad a crocodile smiled. This was supposed to be—begged to be—a story about the greatest "fight-of-the-century" ever, fought in the most bizarre venue ever, for the largest purse ever, an unprecedented $10 million American, double the old record. I had planned to warm you with laughing songs of my equatorial illnesses . . . my malaria, my gonorrhea, dysentery, hepatitis, food poisoning; of the world's most potent marijuana, which is called bangi in Lingala, the lingua franca of Kinshasa and the official military language of French-speaking Zaire, itself a corruption of the North African Arabic word, bhang; of Ritalin and opium purchased over-the-counter in Kinshasa pharmacies; of the strange running gang I formed during the doldrums with Cassius Clay, Sr. and how we closed bar after bar, night after night, and danced our way through the discotheques until dawn; of inadvertently eating monkey skulls with Angelo Dundee, Ali's trainer, until Gene Kilroy, Ali's white gopher ("My boy, Gene Kil-roy!") observed that the skinny chicken breasts we were bitching about gnawing on had eye sockets and teeth and were smiling at us; of awakening on my thirty-seventh birthday—September 24, the date of the original fight—in a pool of Zairehea and ending it by passing out in the Kin Casino because Tshimpumpu wa Tshimpumpu (wa means son of), the maximum chef de presse of the host country, himself a Buluba tribesman from two thousand miles away in what used to be called Katanga until it was authentically renamed Shaba province, toasted me too many times with champagne, since there wasn't too much else doing that day anyway, what with the fight postponed and all, and because between toasts I snuck too many hits on the bangi; of how a musician from Veve, the best band in the land, took me to see a spitting cobra that somehow took up residence a few days earlier in a sewer in Zone Lemba, one of the twenty-four municipal districts of Kinshasa, ten miles from downtown; of how, through the good offices of a Portuguese permanent (hah!) resident, I came to stake out the house where the Pygmy people live; of how the American fight clan saw Africa mostly from inside the Inter-continental Hotel (owned jointly by PanAm and Mobutu) in the wealthy, stately Kinshasa suburb of Gombe, and of how they very nearly never ventured into my part of town, downtown, except to visit the ivory market to buy ivory so that the bastards could go out and slaughter more elephants, babies included, in order to stock and sell more ivory to the unconcerned; of how the rest of the fight mob saw Africa from N'Sele, the retreat of President Mobutu, which was converted into a training compound for the boxers, and which had many nice air-conditioned villas and many Americans that the Americans could chum with; of how Donald King, a reformed killer from Cleveland and the first big-time black fight promoter, somehow one noon left the Inter-continental, which is some transit hotel in some airport in some Cleveland or Kuwait somewhere, and entered the Café de la Paix with his retinue of interpreters and secretaries and Zairois fight commissioners, while I sat at the bar drinking beer and eating samosas, little Indian meat pie turnovers, and waited to catch his eye so that he could say, "Cardo-zah! My man! My brother! Every place I go, there you are!" so that I could say, "Donald King . . . wachoo doin in my part of town!" so that we could share this laugh, see, because sometimes when I look into this man's big brown eyes I see a love for all mankind and not just a thug and digit operator and black racist from Ohio, not just a six-foot-four man strangely out of place with his three-story Afro and his long robes from West Africa (my God, man! this was Central Africa we were in . . . Donald King may as well have been a Martian there) and I see a vulnerable man who was reduced in stature day by day, chipped away at steadily by Mobutu's hog henchman Bula Mandungu and others, reduced as we all were, individually and collectively, stripped of human dignity by officials of a black fascist police state—and what is freedom, anyway?

freedom is what you do with it; and if, fifteen years after the Belgians have left, you come up with a black iron-fisted Hitler . . . well, don't blame me, Jack, dig?—and I see an incurable romantic, for Donald King, it is true, read Shakespeare in his four years in the joint while awaiting parole, and read what he calls "Schopenhowzer" and "Sar-tee" and only Norman Mailer had the sensitivity, one all-night dawn, to correct him and say "Sart."

I also vaguely remember Drew Bundini (pronounced Bo-dini) Brown, Ali's jester-sidekick, betting the entire Foreman camp at two-to-one and making thirty thousand dollars but not being able to collect after the fight and chasing them around the lobby of the Inter-continental and hearing Dick Sadler, Foreman's wealthy manager (and not a bad guy, really) running away from Bodini and claiming he didn't know what in hell he was talking about.

But all I remember for sure is that my room at the Memling was 263 and my telephone number was 601.

It was not one of the all-time great parties, which it should have been, because there are people in this world, like the unsmiling, cigar-smoking, Moscow-trained Bula Mandungu, and his boss, the allegedly literate and well-traveled Mobutu, who conscientiously set out to destroy the party. I have been to the mountain and the mountain is a gangster and the only color he recognizes is what we call green. They say Mobutu, in ten years, has become the seventh richest man in the world. Know what? I don't give a fuck. If I had the power, I would blow him and his ilk out of the water, kick their cynical asses out of the U.N., and let the people party. Of course, my power does not match that of Reynolds Aluminum, which is about to build a big plant in Zaire, or General Motors, which already has one. The Lingala word for money is Mbongo and the *m* is almost silent. If you want to pronounce it correctly, hum the *m* and slide quickly off onto the *b* in bongo. Mbongo is the bottom line, the top line and all the middle lines. Lingala is the language that sprang out of commercial necessity, because there are more than two hundred tribes in what is now Zaire, each with its own dialect, and the early traders knew they had to get it together. Lingala is spoken along the length of the river and in Kinshasa and nowhere else, although the word Kinshasa itself is a Kikongo word and if you ask what it means, you can find yourself in deep trouble with the security police who will want to know why you are asking so many questions and who will remind you that you are there to report on a boxing match and not on social conditions . . . and goddammit, all you are doing is asking what Kinshasa means . . . and why is this fight here in the first place, although in my notes I have five or six versions listed, none of which seems entirely plausible, and why is man inhuman, and why is man an ostrich, finally, and will not God, or Allah, or Whomever is responsible for us ever show His face and rout Evil . . . and what is this sinister force that keeps interrupting the party?

But, all I can remember with certainty is that my room was 263 and my telephone number was 601—sir. And beyond that, all I can remember is sitting in Angelo Dundee's villa at N'Sele three hours after the fight and drinking cognac because the rains came minutes after Ali stretched Foreman and we got caught and were soaked and wanted to ward off the pneumonia I knew for sure we would get because, what the hell, hadn't most of us already caught everything else? Dr. Ferdie Pacheco, Ali's physician, had his shoes off and was stretched across a sofa and we were happy because the fight went so well for the right man, and Angelo Dundee, the greatest cut man in the world, was pouring the cognac and Budd Schulberg, the boxing historian, was screaming at me because—because, my God! I was tape recording the happiness and ignorantly violating something traditional about postfight dawns, something I knew not what. No, not ever Schulberg's ethical fulminating dented the happiness. It wasn't until I told Angelo Dundee that he had succeeded, an hour earlier, in Ali's happy locker room, in doing the impossible: in making Bula Mandungu, the number three man in the government, smile. Angelo Dundee never had a chance to respond. Gene Kilroy, in a chair far across the living room, snapped, "Goddammit! There you go in politics again!" I looked at Kilroy, told him to go fuck himself, and wondered what his problem was and why, every time he saw me, he told me my girl, who was a permanent resident white woman and not really my girl, after all, since I was a mere dalliance in her life, was fucking a nigger (from New Haven!). And while I was looking at Gene Kilroy and wondering what his problem was, Angelo Dundee was giving me a fishy look . . . and I was once again the ringer, the guy out to knock the game, and not protect it, the guy who was going to write a magazine piece after the fight and, thus, not be responsible, like the *Daily News*, for putting, as they say in the game, asses in seats. It is cool, you see, to be a shill for the game. Do not ask where is Beau Jack, and where is the pension plan, and do laugh with them when they call Joe Louis "America's guest," which is really a damnable and pitiable phrase.

I'll never be able to write about the nice Zairois I met, and their warmth, generosity, hospitality and sincerity because they are little people, individuals, who don't count for much . . . when, every time I conjure them, Bula sticks his ugly and brutal face across my mindscape. Every day, when television starts—Zaire and Zanzibar are the only two African lands with color television—the viewer is fed a picture of clouds and sky. From out of these clouds comes a speck, honing toward center screen, larger and larger, until it becomes Mobutu. Mobutu! Larger than large! Which is sick; the man is everywhere. He is on the currency, on the Zaire note . . . all of them, the one, five and ten Zaire notes. Everything in Zaire is Zaire; the currency, the cigarettes, the gasoline . . . they are all marketed under the name

Zaire. What a boffo idea! Methinks Mobutu studied media manipulation and propaganda techniques at Sears & Roebuck. When you hold the Zaire note up to the light, to see the watermark that guards against counterfeiting (the money is printed by Giesecke & Devrient, Munich), the watermark, of course, is Mobutu in his leopard skin pillbox fez hat, and it's all a little unreal. I have lived three times now under the oppression of fascism, twice in Portugal, under both the Salazar and Caetano regimes, and here in the Congo under Mobutu who is everywhere. Lisbon streets, 1963. The shit-eating grin of Salazar in portraiture beaming from every shop window, every restaurant, every hotel lobby, discotheque, tavern. People afraid, acquiescent in the face of Evil. Sad, man, sad. What is this sinister force destroying the party? And I know why I spent, voluntarily, many hours in room 263 of the Memling, where my phone number was 601. Because there was no picture of Mobutu. To see him, I would have to pull a Zaire note out of my kick. Which I had no interest in doing in my private room. Rather, I would roll a massive Kinshasa joint. A Zaire is worth two dollars at the legal rate, but you can get from seventy to eighty Makuta for your dollar at the black market rate. One hundred Makuta make one Zaire. It is on the decimal system, just like our money. In Brussels, you can get 540 Zaire for $500 American. When the television goes off at night, there is a picture of the continent of Africa, which gradually transforms into a pistol. Zaire suddenly becomes the trigger and the barrel points at South Africa.

The beef and other meats that Mobutu and I eat every night come in unmarked planes from Rhodesia and South Africa. Plainclothes planes.

Rick Talley of the Chicago papers showed up fight week. He had been in Zaire briefly, during the Ice Age of the story, back in mid-September. Rick Talley won the press pool, picking Ali by a knockout in the eighth round, which says something about prognostication, because Rick

Talley also picked the Dodgers over the A's in five games in the 1974 World Series, which is exactly the opposite of the way it turned out. Rick Talley also wrote in one of his columns, after fleeing Zaire the first time, that the fight would never happen in Zaire. It would happen in the Astrodome, he said. And he had only stayed two days, and yet he knew that this was the most untogether place on the planet. It is not actually necessary to spend fifty days and fifty nights in Zaire. Hunter Thompson knew it instinctively. When Rick Talley returned, he pulled me aside and inquired about the health of Jack Griffin of the Chicago papers. Chicago is the last competitive newspaper city and I can't get the names of the papers straight anymore; there are three or four of them, I think. Jack Griffin of the Chicago papers was the codean (codeine) of the press corps with me; we gritted it out. Jack Griffin stayed mostly in the villa of Murray and Bobby Goodman, father and son fight publicists. Theirs was Villa Number One in a string of five overlooking the hyacinth pads floating inexorably toward the sea along the Congo or Zaire and there goes Bogart and Hepburn chugging in the *African Queen* and isn't that Henry Morton Stanley in yon gleaming on his way to present-day Burundi, rafting and portaging to rendezvous with a certain physician, one presumes, but first trying to find, in 1874, one of the 350 native bearers who set out with him on his 999-day trek, one of the 235 who met extraordinary fates, for only 115 reached Boma, at the mouth of the Zaire, or Congo, River . . . the one who is listed in the annals as having disappeared after smoking wild hemp, not to be confused with the one lost in the jungle, the one caught by a crocodile, the 13 missing, the 14 drowned, the 8 starvation (if only they had known about unmarked planes), the 58 battle and murder, or the 69 smallpox, dysentery and fever victims. Was the smoker of wild hemp me? For I am lost now, too, and beyond recovery. In addition, all three of Stanley's white comrades died, two of fever, the other drowned in rapids. I can't remember who was in Villa Number Two, next to Jack Griffin of the Chicago papers and Goodman & Son. Villa Number Three was Bodini and wife. Villa Number Four was Angelo Dundee and Villa Number Five was Muhammad, the right man for the right time, but basically as full of shit as me and Mobutu. Jack Griffin early on went into an eighteen-hour sleep day. Every time I visited N'Sele, which wasn't all that often during the doldrums, because it's fifty miles from Kin town and there's no guarantee of a ride back, he was curled up on his cot.

Jack Griffin began to wear a three-day stubble all the time. And his yellow Capt. Griff shirt, bestowed by sponsors of some deep-sea fishing tournament he once covered, became grimy and wine splotched with the red stains of the 382 bottles of Chateauneuf-du-Pape he and Bobby Goodman consumed because they had to, if they were to stay sane or insane. Jack Griffin, when not sleeping, wrote weird shit with beautiful datelines, like Bukavu, which is in Kivu province, in the east, next to Burundi, Ruwanda, Uganda, along Lake Kivu, not far from Lake Albert . . . excuse, please, pardon, I meant to say Lac Mobutu . . . which is where Man began, according to *African Genesis,* a book written by a man named Robert Ardrey, I think, if memory serves. And Jack Griffin of the Chicago papers would write about elephants grazing in the grass in front of him as he ate breakfast, and of gorillas in their natural habitat and wonderful tales like that as he, bless you, Jack, peered out the window of Villa Number One and gazed at the inexorable hyacinth pads. Did someone say Jake LaMotta?

Speak, memory!

When the new press came, those sportswriters from the West world, Jack Griffin and I found we had much deep knowledge of the dark continent in common. We would often wink at each other when the new guys tipped their ignorance. One day, one of them ran into the Goodmans's villa and rousted Jack Griffin from his sleep. "The ambassador's coming, the ambassador's coming!" the new man enthused. Startled from some dark dream, Griffin puzzled, "What ambassador?" The American ambassador, replied the beginner. "Aaarrgghh!" answered Jack, and dismissed the man with a wave, and pulled up the covers, and went back to the dream. Jack knew about such things.

Rick Talley of the Chicago papers pulled me aside, remember, and inquired about Jack Griffin's health. "Have you seen the stuff he's been writing?" he asked. No. "People in Chicago," said Rick, "are wondering . . . is he having some sort of nervous breakdown, do you think? You should read his stuff. I mean, one sentence follows the next and all but there's no connection, know what I mean?" I nodded, because my room is 263, and my phone is 601, and I know about such things.

At the fight, Rick Talley pulled a terrific heist because he had no seat in the working press section. He stole the first row seat assigned to *Il Tempo* of Rome. This is because the government decided at the last minute to change the credentials and delegated Bazunga N'Zinga, the number two man of the host nation's Commission Foreman-Ali presse subcommission, to distribute same. But Bazunga was drunk again and wouldn't pass them out. For four hours writers from the West world waited in a steamy room, until ten o'clock at night . . . with the fight only six hours off and the writers having traveled an average of twenty-four straight hours to get to Zaire to cover the fight-of-the-century. The White Hole of Kinshasa, an English reporter called the scene. Bazunga would call a name from his list and if the man was not present, Bazunga would stolidly await the man's arrival, and would not move on to the next name. I got mine early because I knew the ropes by then. I remember having dinner in the Memling dining room with Bud Collins of the *Boston Globe* and his three friends from the Swedish radio. They were talking about Bjorn Borg and about Jimmy Connors and Chrissy Evert breaking up. I asked who won the World Series but no one would say. Suddenly, a new writer burst into the restaurant to say that a race riot was going on in the press building, that the Zairois presse were hollering because the "American press"—and most of the mundele men in that sinkhole of a press center (mundele is the Lingala word for white folks; once, trying to be helpful, I told Hunter Thompson that if he really wanted to cut through the ice, tear away the formalities, because he was so newly arrived and time was of the essence for people like him, whereas Jack Griffin of the Chicago papers could sleep, because he knew . . . I told Thompson that instead of calling a Zairois *citoyen* [citizen] as Mobutu has decreed that everyone, including himself, be called, he should aim for informality by calling a Zairois mundele and that this would be rewarding)—anyway, most of the mundele men in that sinkhole, for God's sake, were Germans and stuff like that, Estonians, you know; not Americans at all . . . and this guy comes running into the Memling restaurant and talking about the Zairois presse going into a fit because the American press was being given credentials while they waited and waited and Bazunga rocked back and forth on his heels and smiled through gold teeth and wondered if he ever would get another beer. I left my grilled Nile perch and all the talk about Bjorn Borg and ran back to the presse center. There was no race riot. The Zairois presse, once again, was asleep. But the mundele press was now standing on chairs and looming grizzly over Bazunga and even Murray Goodman, the chief fight publicist and the dad of Bobby Goodman, who drank all that wine with Jack Griffin, could not budge Bazunga, who rocked back and forward on his heels and gleamed a smile through gold teeth and looked around for a bottle of beer, refusing to call another name until somebody named Jake LaMotta came forward for his credentials. I ran back to the Memling and my Nile perch. Within a minute, Bazunga burst through the door, chased by at least fifty enraged mundele new press, ran through the dining room, ran through the lobby followed by this irate conga line, out onto Avenue du Tchad and across Place Downtown, in front of the Memling (Kinshasa has either 1.2 million or 1.5 million inhabitants, including 28,000 or 40,000 mundele people, mostly Belgian; the Memling is named after Johann Memling, Flemish painter), out Rue Prisonniers, all the way to the safety of the brightly-lit Café Pergola, where his boss, Tshimpumpu wa Tshimpumpu, chief of all presse, a publicity hound and himself frequently a drunkard, was sumptuous on Capitan Zairois, which is Nile perch baked and smothered in hot pili-pili sauce (I preferred grilled Capitan, although I suggested to Thompson that he try pili-pili on everything). In ran Bazunga, wobbly pinned. In ran the mundeles, maddened. Sit down, have dinner, said Tshimpumpu wa Tshimpumpu. "No pro-bleme!"

Tshimp was given to say this, but whenever he said "no pro-bleme!" you could bet your iron rusty there was. You see, there always was a problem. But, of course, if you refuse to acknowledge a problem, then, well . . . there is no problem. I think this is what he had in mind. Tshimpumpu has a kid brother named Tshimpumpu Kanyinda, who smokes cigars and can be seen frequently in the company of Bula Mandungu, and who, like Bula, never smiles, unless he is on camera. Kid Tshimpumpu, though younger, actually is a high-ranking counselor to the president, Mobutu Sese Seko, far higher-ranking in fact than his older brother, who is something of a joy-boy, always chasing skirts and avoiding responsibility and taking a powder on commitments. Murray Goodman, chief publicist for the promotion (The Promotion), used to follow Tshimpumpu wa Tshimpumpu around like a puppy dog, expecting the man to for Christ's sakes take care of business; but Bobby Goodman, Dad Goodman's son and the second in command publicist, finally told Tshimpumpu to fuck off, bless him. In embassy circles, to avoid confusion, they call Tshimpumpu Kanyinda "single chimp" and Tshimpumpu wa Tshimpumpu "double chimp."

Double Tshimp was always smiling, though his younger and more important brother seldom smiled; rather he smoked long, thin cigars with madura wrappers, like pal Bula. Double Tshimp affected large and funny hats, very definitely not *authenticité,* but nonetheless hats purchased in Chicago and Los Angeles, he told me, when he toured the United States last spring with Bula in early fight promotion drum-beating. It plagued all the Americans who knew Double and Bula then, that they had received our typical, swell hospitality when they visited our land . . . and why was this not reciprocal when we went below the equator to their place? Why did they put us all in prison? But, as someone, I can't remember who, remarked: At least they let us have visitors. Why did they slip us a Mickey, and how? Oh, you may see me someday on an American street, or observe Ali in Louisville, but we won't really be there, you see. They took something out of our hide. I don't think we'll ever get out.

We all got to the fight, you know, even the historian Schulberg, who said this was the most fucked-up fight promotion since the third Mendoza-Humphries in 1797, and who never did get his new credentials, tiring as he did, of chasing Bazunga around town. (I can find no reference in the annals to a third Mendoza-Humphries. However, Daniel Mendoza, Mendoza the Jew, of Portuguese blood, residing in Whitechapel, in truth a middleweight, standing only five-feet-seven, who later became a bill collector, bloodied Richard Humphries, champion of the Anglos, of England, because he maneuvered in their first fight and, two centuries before Ali, floated like a butterfly, refusing to stand still at the line of scratch and trade punches, choosing instead to side-step, to retreat, violating the spirit, if not the letter, of Marquis of Queensberry rules . . . a very tricky man, those Portuguese. In the rematch, it is said, Mendoza the

Jew again carried the colors. Yet, I cannot find any remark concerning the rubber match, to which the Schulberg referred. Nor can I find Stillman's Gym.)

Schulberg, with whom I spent many long hours, in and out of Kinshasa taverns, including the dawn we went out to the Jumbo discotheque for a nightcap beer that cost us twenty Zaires, which was then forty dollars American because we didn't know the ins and outs of black market currency trading, insists that the first Mendoza-Humphries was the first fight-of-the-century and further pledges that there will be a new fight-of-the-century every five years or so for as long as I live; although I am disinclined to believe him since he just grins at me whenever I extend another opportunity for him to confirm or to deny that he spent the night of September 23 on the lawn at N'Sele, in front of Angelo Dundee's villa, which was Villa Number Four, sandwiched between Ali and Bodini villas, sleeping amid iguanas and kraits. I cannot remember who had Villa Number Two but maybe Jack Griffin of the Chicago papers does. I will ask him if he ever comes to Kin again. It is further alleged that the stumblebum Schulberg, whom I iced in ten seconds in our own personal rematch (he had scored a quick one-round knockout in our first fight at the moth-eaten Kin Casino, where the cards do funny things, by landing solid shots to both my kidneys and my la bonza and then going upstairs and clipping me right on the button, simply because I had not heard the bell for round one) much like Walter Cartier iced Joe Rindone in ten seconds of the first, or was it the other way around . . . or was Sugar Ray involved in that one? Was it Cartier-Rindone, Cartier-Robinson or Robinson-Rindone? I cannot remember and I beg your considerable indulgence because I know not what and since you weren't there, you cannot know, either. All I know for sure is that I have been to the mountain and the mountain is a gangster. And all I remember, sir, in accordance with Geneva parleys since time immemorial, is that my room is 263 and my phone is 601. It being further alleged that Schulberg, the stumblebum, tried at one point that night to bang down the door of the condominium (not to be confused with the five Villas in a row on the banks of the hyacinth pads floating inexorably) assigned to Howard Bingham, who has for many years, since the virtual get-go, been Ali's personal photographer, and who wears a beard . . . that Schulberg, late of Whitechapel, a man seldom up to scratch, pounded on Bingham's door, desperately whispered, "Angelo, Angelo?" so anxious was he to cop a crib and flee the iguanas and other ganglia of the night. Now, everyone knows that Angelo Dundee does not wear a beard! Budd Schulberg, although he has knocked the game in his time, should be retired for his own safety, even though there is no retirement plan for the game, because he is punch-drunk, on queer street, and can get badly hurt and become America's Guest. And will Uncle Sam wipe his back taxes slate clean . . . or seek remittance? Schulberg, I fear, if his license is not suspended, will become the greeter at the Brown Palace Hotel in Denver, or worse, the Memling.

I know this allegation to be true, about pounding on Bingham's door, because Gene Kilroy told me and Gene Kilroy does not lie about stuff.

It is also true that Schulberg based *The Harder They Fall* on the life of Harold Conrad, one of the decent men in boxing, the man who popularized Cochise and who contributed in the early days to the comic strip *Joe Palooka*, beginning himself as a boxing writer for the old *Brooklyn Eagle*, low man on the totem pole, a mere jog step above the palooka from the *Bronx Home News*. You should see the way the Goodmans, father and son, sycophantically treat the Big Guys in the pecking order, like Dick Young and Red Smith—and even Larry Merchant has to take a back seat to them, though he, like they, puts asses in seats, as the boxing parlance would have it, by thumping promotional tubs with prefight blather. Now for all the world, the Big Guys somehow never did realize the fight was in Kinshasa, Zaire, below the equator, where there is no North Star and, hence, no Vikings, and finally, no White Hope. I mean, goddammit, they might as well have been in some goddamn Felt Forum in Glicksville, or at the ABC-TV studios.

Bill Brannigan, the permanently posted Africa correspondent for ABC-TV (and it came as a surprise to learn that the two larger networks do not post correspondents permanently in Africa) who lives in Nairobi, Kenya, on the other side of the mountain from Zaire (Zye-ear), thinks that sportswriters ought to be locked up after five o'clock. And he is right. Look, in Kinshasa they got a thing going called night sentinels, men who sleep in front of shops to guard them from burglars. They are all over downtown Kin, these night sentinels. They begin at 6:00 P.M. when the shops shut, and they get good money, too—one Zaire a day, which shoots them over the national per capita income level (ninety-two dollars American per year) in less than two months. And these asshole writers come over and look at these family men sleeping in front of shops and they say, "Jesus Christ! It's fucking Calcutta! People sleeping in the streets! Gawdamn!"

Snow fell November 10 in Big Fork, Montana, according to Anthony Lewis, and in all these words we have shared, I am yet to mention the equatorial heat, for which I am sorry. I have burned through three air conditioners so far at the Memling, although I think they exchanged them merely to insert new bugging devices. I have to take fifty milligrams of Ritalin a day just to make it through the noonday sun. I also take all this Ritalin to cut through the wild hemp, which is the best in the monde, far better than those expensive Thai Sticks that were going around last winter. I mean, this shit really stones you out. The night sentinels build fires out of kindling as soon as the sun goes down, which is always at 6:00 P.M. here five degrees below the equator, give or take a few minutes due to seasonal variation. The sun always comes up at 6:00 A.M., too, again taking into account the shift of the two seasons. But it is a natural way to live, you know? Six o'clock to six o'clock. It makes sense; the Natural Life. It is hot here because of the humidity. It does, however, get cool at night in winter—which is when we have our summer in the States—and you have to wear a jacket or sweater outdoors. So the night sentinels build these fires, see, although the temperature is about seventy-five or eighty degrees. The sportswriters from the new press, knowing I have unlocked some secrets of the dark continent, ask me why they have these fires. It took me a month to find out! They must think I'm some kind of smuck. Why should I tell them? What did they ever do for me? Did they get me out, or did they abandon me? Even though this magazine up-fronted a cashier's checque for $1263 American, which entitled me to a round-trip, both ways, plane ticket . . . just like they got! . . . I never got one. So, fuck 'em. And fuck Hank Schwartz, too. Hank Schwartz (the baddest pun I ever heard), one of the too many promoters involved in this thing, who runs an outfit on West Fifty-fifth Street called Video Techniques, and who may have, I hope, promoted his last fight, and who also entered into a gaff with Mobutu called Festival-in-Zaire, which acronyms as FIZ, as in fizzle, and who burned everybody . . . and why do you just smile at me in the Inter-continental lobby, you Orwellian schwartz bastard, when I ask you where my plane ticket home is? Motherfucker, if I ever get out of here, I'll lead you by the ear to Times Square and make you shit, because you know I handed you that cashier's checque for $1263 American, up-fronted by this magazine, entitling me to round-trip air fare, and you glommed it right there and then, at 39 West Fifty-fifth Street, New York City, at 11:07 A.M. on September 16, 1974. You turkey!

Well, I would never tell those buzzards why the night sentinels really had those fires. I would red-herring them, tell them it was to ward off the mosquitoes, malaria, you know.

The real, true, reason for those fires was to keep Ndokes at bay.

Bodini Brown is an Ndoke, or thinks he is. Bill McMurray, the sparring partner who put his elbow through George Foreman's eye and caused the fight to be postponed, knows what an Ndoke is, having had one in his room at the Inter-continental all night long, one night, waking poor Bill up from a sound sleep and pacing back and forth, moving from the door to the window, interminably. I, too, know about Ndokes. They are fearsome things. They visit you at night and you must stay awake to survive. If you are asleep, an Ndoke will hit you over the head with a club and haul you away and forever you will do his bidding.

Harold Conrad, who was portrayed by Humphrey Bogart in Schulberg's movie, *The Harder They Fall,* was once being wined and dined, the toast of Hollywood, after the movie was made. One day, in a restaurant there, he chanced upon Bogart and Lauren Bacall sitting in a corner booth, and after ten quick drinks to build up some Mexican courage, went over to Bogart to thank Bogart for his marvelous characterization of him. Bogart listened briefly to this awkwardness, looked Conrad in the eye, and said, "Why don't you go and fuck yourself." Harold Conrad still enjoys telling that story, although it happened many years ago, as evidenced by the fact that Bogart don't come around much anymore. Harold Conrad also says he doesn't care if I mention smoking and bangi-bangi with him all the time over there, even though I warn him repeatedly that boxing is his livelihood and that the game is filled with lamesters who dim view that sort of stuff. I don't think Angelo Dundee gives a shit, though, he's cool. "What's gonna be, gonna be," Angelo says. And here's Budd Schulberg banging in the night on the door of a bearded black man and speaking Italian. "Angelo? Angelo?" he's saying . . . just to take a kip without lizards. But when I warn Harold Conrad that it might not be a good idea to fink on him smoking the reefer all he says is "It's okay, I'm telling ya. Ali's back on top. I'm in." Yet, Harold asks me not to mention his true age, even though, as Howard Cosell says in his book, he looks to be in his forties but is actually in his sixties. You're weird, Harold . . . but you're my main man.

This is Lucian K. Truscott IV at the keys. I just returned to the loft with a bag of groceries and a new Water-Pic pulsing Shower Massage and found Cardoso frozen at the typewriter back in the study, mumbling incoherently about Ndokes, Ndokes on the desk, on his shoulders, frozen with fear. A call just came from editor at NT, and I know I must take over now. Among the Cardosoian effects I found the garbled transcript of a tape made many moons ago in Zaire, with Cam Morton for Radio Nairobi. If memory serves, Cardoso told me Morton was the guy with the Congo-weed brownies at the fight, so thanks a lot, Cam, baby, if William were here at the keys, I know, I just know he'd bless you. Here's a Harold Conrad tape to pass the time until I can bring Cardoso around.

"I came back to New York just around the time they were doing the second Johansson/Patterson fight. Roy Cohn, the famous lawyer, was the promoter and backer of the fight. Knew nothing about boxing. They knew I had been around the boxing beat, and asked me to give them a hand, and I stepped in as publicity director. It was a gigantic smash. The fight did $900,000 live gate and $3 million closed circuit, which in those days, when a dollar was a dollar, was a lot of money."

(The Zaire fight did between $8 and $10 million worldwide, everything thrown in, all ancillaries; Mobutu laid out as much as $20 million, including capital improvements to Kinshasa for such things as streetlights and pedestrian crosswalks; so he took a beating, which is okay with Cardoso; original projections ran as high as $75 million gross revenue.)

Conrad: "Then we did the third Johansson/Patterson

fight, in which Patterson retained his title. And now the big fight—the Ali/Frazier fight of its day—was Patterson/Liston. Liston was kind of a strange character in those days, very difficult to handle, so they sent me out to Chicago to meet him. What they said is, 'You can go out and paint the prison stripes off him.' And I went out to Chicago and met Sonny. He scared the hell out of me the first time, told me off, and I just took a walk, hung around the next day or two. I went down and bought a couple of magic tricks in the lobby of the hotel . . . an electric bulb you hold in your hand . . . it lights up. I went up and nonchalantly whipped it out. Liston got very interested, and that kind of broke the ice. And of course he knocked Patterson out in Chi, a great promotion. At the time, it was a record, $6.8 million. That was a lot of money in those days. I got all the long-haired writers involved . . . Norman Mailer, Schulberg, James Baldwin, Ben Hecht . . . they were all there. And we wound up with a tremendous victory party at Hugh Hefner's mansion.

"The morning after the fight, there was a big postfight press conference; five hundred guys, they're all on edition time, waiting to hear what the champ has to say. All of a sudden I see Norman Mailer sitting in Liston's chair. Norman was in his cups for several days, and he kept telling me, 'I got an idea—I want to talk to the newspaper men right after the fight.' All the press is saying, 'Get out, ya bum.' So I ran over. I see Liston is waiting in the wings to go on. Who's that son of a bitch sitting up there in my chair? He's got six burly cops with him, and they're Chi cops, they'll bust anybody's head. So I went back and said, 'Norman, you better get outa there. Please do me a favor.' He said, 'Screw you, I'm not moving.' So I got the cops, I said, 'Please fellas, don't touch him, just go over and pick up the chair!' So they go over and carry Mailer off like some maharaja, with a silly look on his face. Everybody in the press booing him. So we get the press conference started. All of a sudden from the back of the room, a voice: 'I wanna talk to you, Sonny.' It's Mailer again. Sonny says, 'Hey, you're drunk, ya bum.' It broke up the whole conference. And Sonny kind of has a feeling for drunks, because he was a heavy boozer himself.

"There are many similarities between Liston and George Foreman. In Sonny's later days, I used to go out and see him. Foreman would be hanging around, idolized him, even to the point where Sonny was scared to death of needles. He hated to get stitched up. Foreman, here, refused to have his eye stitched up. Which is the normal procedure when you've got a bad cut like that. And he tried to imitate Sonny's smart-ass retorts. Sonny had a very good sense of humor. The kid here is really trying to imitate him.

"I think Ali's got a much better shot now than he had before. You put a guy in front of Ali with that jab, who's got a vulnerable eye. He's in trouble, because he's got a great jab. He used to cut all these guys. Frazier's face looked like it got hit by a steam roller after his two fights with Ali. Ernie Terrell, he had his eye almost hanging out. Chuvalo, he closed both eyes by the sixth round. He gets that jab working, he'll open that eye up. That's what makes the fight biz. Who knows? He's certainly the best fighter Foreman ever fought. Ali is a strange man. Ali rises to the occasion. There's some mysticism about him. He reaches down there, if he gets mad he's a tough guy. If he gets mad, he's got a terrible temper. But he rises to the occasion somehow. Ali is a master of the psyche. He did it to Liston. But you gotta know how to do it. It's not passed down or taught. Muhammad's got it.

"I got to know Muhammad. The next title fight is the big fight in Miami with Liston and Muhammad, who was Cassius Clay. He had just become Muhammad Ali, during the fight down there. Which scared the hell out of the promoters. Jesus, what am I gonna do in the South with a Muslim? They wanted to call the fight off, because Malcolm X was indoctrinating Clay. So I immediately denied that he was a Muslim. 'Are you kidding?' You know. And they're saying, 'What are you doing, kidding me? What's he doing with Malcolm X every day?' I say, 'If I get Malcolm X out of town will you feel better about it?' So the promoter says, yeah. So I went and laid it out to Malcolm, said, 'Look Malcolm, if you don't get out of town, you boy is going to lose the title shot and the money and everything, so I think it's a good idea if you take a walk.' He said you're right, no problem, and he left. We got the fight on. Sonny was like a ten-to-one shot to win. Only two guys out of five hundred pick Muhammad. And Muhammad upset him and won the title.

"Now we had a rematch for that one, too, in Boston. Liston worked like hell. He was in the best shape of his life. He really wanted the title back. And Muhammad was at his peak. The fight was sold out, big business, on the closed circuit. The fight was on a Monday. On Friday, I have five hundred newspaper men at a cocktail party. Somebody comes running in and says, Muhammad is in the hospital. Which I never believed. You hear these stories ten times a day, they shot him, or he's dead. I checked, and there he was, under a hernia. The fight's off. We had to postpone that for six months. We got back to Boston. We're going through all the stuff again, and Liston's a very tired guy now. He's left his fight in training the last time. But he's going through the motions. And every day, the DA of Boston, who is a big fight fan, who never said a word the first time, starts to harass us, brings us into court, and fines, popping us with this kind of stuff . . . I got tipped that Bobby Kennedy thought that Roy Cohn, his archrival from the old McCarthy days, was backing the fight, which he wasn't. And Kennedy told the DA, 'Get the fight out of Boston, bother these guys, harass them.' This kept going on until finally I decided these guys are liable to wait until the last day and knock us out of the box. I don't care about the live gate. We've got this thing going all over the country. It's got to go on that date. So I moved it up to a little town called Lewiston, Maine. No, I had to go up and get an okay from the governor. So I flew up and saw the governor, Reed, and I said, 'It's a great thing for the state of Maine.' He said, 'Just tell me one thing, is it going to be a good fight?' And I said, 'your honor, one of the great fights of all time.' It lasted a minute and fourteen seconds. And then of course, Muhammad was firmly established.

"And then I promoted the fight in Dublin with Blue Lewis, which was a fantastic promotion for Dublin. Then came the Army thing, and he was in big trouble. I tried for three years to get him a license and couldn't. He finally got it back in Atlanta. We were trying to get him a license to fight Frazier. And Yank Durham, who was Frazier's manager, said, 'No, every time you've been telling me, every time you call me, you've got the license in this state, and this state, and you keep embarrassing us. Let him fight somebody else to prove he can fight.' So I went back and told Muhammad, there's no Frazier fight. And he says what's the matter. And I flashed Jerry Quarry, then the number two contender, a white guy, a white Irishman. Perfect. So I call Muhammad and say, 'You and Quarry in Atlanta, instead of Frazier.' He says, 'That's great. Nigger draft-dodger fights white Irishman, that'll sell a lot of tickets.' It was a helluva promotion. It was a great promotion. And then we had a progression of fights. One Ali/Frazier fight. It was a ball going along with Ali . . . a marvelous guy.

"Listen, lemme tell you something. People think that every fight that was ever done was in the tank, that Liston went in the tank for Ali. Lemme tell ya about world heavyweight champs. After the first Liston/Clay fight, a lot of people said Liston went into the tank. I went over to Sonny's house after the fight. He got the first cut of his life. He was boozing. He was a little stiff, and I said, 'Sonny, they're saying you went in the tank.' He said, 'I know, those dirty mothers. . . .' And he stopped a minute and everything, and then he started to cry. Picture a guy like Liston with tears in his eyes. He said, 'I'll tell ya something. I've been in jail half of my life. You don't know what it means to me to walk down the street and have a guy say, hello champ.' I believed him. You see, a very strange thing about the public and boxing is that most people in America have seen a fight on closed circuit or on television. I was weaned on fights through the movies, the old Warner Brothers pictures. All those Humphrey Bogarts, all those terrible pictures with Jimmy Cagney. There was never one picture made where the fighter didn't go in the tank, or the manager or the promoter wasn't a thief. This is the general impression of the fight business. You know, it's the culture. That's where they get their impression of the fight business."

Cardoso still out; here's another tape:

It's now 2:15 A.M., October 2; Conrad and Schulberg got out of town tonight, I presume. They were going completely berserk, for four days now they have been packing and unpacking. Every night they're supposed to be on the flight to Paris, but nobody ever tells them they're not, until say, 8:00 P.M., and the flight leaves at 10:00. Tshimpumpu's secretary returned to the Memling this afternoon with the tickets, and nothing had been done to them for four days. They had been marked forfeit by the government. You can blame Hank Schwartz for this, because we all gave him the money in New York. He told us we had a press charter to Zaire, but what he gave us was a cut-rate regularly scheduled Icelandic Airlines flight to Luxembourg. Hippies and backpacks and everything!! I was sandwiched between Donald King's kid brother, who's six-foot-four, but a little light on his feet, I think, and King's lawyer, Clarence Rogers. Some press charter. The rest of the press flew to Luxembourg the day before, and were stranded in Trier, Germany, in a hotel that Mozart stayed in. Positively Mid-evil, they tell me. They were on an Icelandic, too. Where's the press charter? Now Hank Schwartz collected $1263 from about, oh, I guess there were maybe a hundred of us, so that's all front money, in his pocket, well over a hundred and twenty thousand dollars. And with backpacks and hippies, I was outraged. Closed circuit exhibitors had to put up a lot of front money, too. So somebody made money here, besides Ali and Foreman. And there ought to be an investigation. Like, where's my ticket back? Why did John Daly have to get me out of town, save my life, at his personal expense, for which he paid dearly later, when I had already paid up on September 16 for the flight out.

Okay, so Schulberg and Conrad are absolutely amok, and Murray Goodman is running around the Memling lobby, too, and so is his son, Bobby, who just returned from the States, against his better judgment. They're chasing Tshimpumpu's secretary around, telling her the tickets are worthless. Budd's wife, Gerry, unbeknownst to us at the time, has already called Javits to get Budd out. Tshimpumpu's secretary runs off with the Goodmans to fix the tickets, and this time the Goodmans mean business. "We'll get you out, Harold and Budd," they cry.

Schulberg wants an immediate conference in Suite 603 of the Memling. So we're up there, and Conrad and I are deep into the bangi-bangi (I don't know about Schulberg; I couldn't see that far), and they're worrying, what-to-do, what-to-do, wakadoo, wakadoo. Budd is calling his man at the Embassy! Conrad is telling me to get out, get out of Zaire with them. The Embassy guy comes over. Can you imagine, if the story got out, that Budd Schulberg, author of *On the Waterfront, What Makes Sammy Run?* and the aforementioned *The Harder They Fall* and Harold Conrad had to be rescued by the Embassy, what it would do to the promotion? It would positively sink it. *Daily News* headline: "Famous Author, Fight Promoter/Both Well-Known Friends of the Nigger/Trapped, Rescued by U.S. Embassy Marine Guards in Zaire."

The Embassy guy is sitting there, Conrad is shrieking at me to get out with them, I'm in a cloud of smoke, Schulberg is trying to call wife in Long Island, which is foolish since there is no record of anyone having ever made a successful call out of the Memling. You can't even get room service. I mean, my room was 263, my phone was 601. Schulberg is stammering at me, Billy goat gruff, gray hair, ruddy face twitching. "I realize there are sound journalistic reasons for you wanting to stay here and see this story through. But think a minute. How many promises have they made, and how many have they delivered on?" Conrad is saying, "These guys play for keeps." All I remember after that is Schulberg saying, "If you stay, you stay at your own peril."

We went down in the elevator, I was laughing and giggling, scared, too, because maybe they were right, and I knew they were. You see, it's not really necessary to spend fifty days and fifty nights there to know that they're speaking to some unspeakable future, Communism and Capitalism and Fascism and Racism all wrapped up in one ugly third-world package. Murray and Bobby Goodman hadn't returned, and we were all out in front of the Memling. I didn't know whether to try to get out with them or not. Somebody had to stay and cover the story, and somebody had to stay and smoke this pot, and I thought I was falling in love, too, with a mundele moisse (white woman). I thought I was going to cry. I was in despair. A car pulled up, and two mundele men, strangely familiar, approached me. They were smiling. Who were they? Jesus, the two Portuguese guys I had met a few dawns earlier in the Jumbo Discotheque, and had made a dinner date with for this very night. I had forgotten. And here's Conrad and Schulberg, completely crazy, in front of the Memling, and I had to make a choice. "Good luck fellas," I said to them, and jumped into the car. Soon, I was enjoying a nice Portuguese dinner, tramocos and everything. I mean, who would have believed it? A private house and all. I left complete fucking insanity, and within minutes was in a quiet home surrounded by my kind of people. They were stuck there (in Zaire) too.

Look, it was so bad that it cost George Plimpton $120 to get out. There's the plane warming up on the runway, leaving in twenty minutes, and there's this customs asshole practicing *mato bicho* (a Portuguese word that hangs on, meaning exacted tribute or bribe, a common, everyday word in Lingala) on Plimpton, hauling out this ten-foot-long form, and very carefully, very measuredly filling in the top line. Plimpton got the picture, and asked how much. After he paid, he wanted a receipt, damn Yankee! The customs guy asked him if he was coming back, which he was, since he was one of those leaving now, returning later. Well, said the customs, drawing his hand down his face, "*Regards mon visage.*" That's all the receipt you'll need. I don't know if Plimpton got out the second time. He was a fool for coming back. Have you heard any news? Did anyone get out? Is Donald King a night sentinel? Why have the papers dropped the story? George Foreman's gang tried a half-million-dollar heist of John Daly at the last minute.

Please tell the black guys that Mobutu's not their savior, that's the important thing. They can believe either me or Stokely Carmichael. It's up to them. Anybody think I'm dramatizing this, check out Zaire for yourself. They wouldn't even let Larry Merchant (*New York Post,* who puts asses in seats) back in, and he wrote some of the kindest, most understanding stuff about the country in the United States. All he did was interview some poor woman fight tourist who got ripped off for $2600 by FIZ.

One day I'm sitting in the pizza shack, a thatched roof affair next to the pool at the Inter-continental with Big Black and this fugitive from the Brotherhood of Eternal-

Love, the multimillion dollar Tim Leary controlled corporate structure behind LSD, who has been on the lam in Jo'burg for the last two years, but naturally couldn't miss this fight-of-the-century. Who could? James Earl Carpenter, chief of security for Foreman, goes walking by with his luggage and a raincoat over his arm. "Hey, where you going, James?" He sat at our table and smiled, "London." Asked when he'd return, he said Tuesday or Wednesday. The fight's on Tuesday night, I said. If you come back Wednesday, you'll miss it. He just smiled. Obviously, more important things were on his mind. He was going to London, he thought, with Leroy Jackson, Foreman's sometime business manager, to pick up a satchel full of cash, five hundred thousand dollars American. They were putting the squeeze on John Daly, knowing they could get nothing out of Henry Schwartz, or Don King, his front man, or from Risnelia, the Swiss front for Mobutu run by Fred Weymar, Harvard-educated native of West Germany who carries a Swiss passport and lives in Nice. The rip-off was in progress, but I didn't know it at the time. I thought Foreman was sneaking out to get some weird medicine, since the fight was only a few days away. But this was extortion, blackmail. Daly was supposed to be the fall guy, but is a self-made millionaire, and no fool. Here was the deal: Foreman said he was strapped for cash, heavy divorce costs, lawsuits, and his $5-million purse was already eaten up. I need a half million, or I will not appear at the weigh-in. The weigh-in was supposed to be at midnight, Saturday, so that it could be beamed live to Wide World of Sports, ABC-TV, at 5:00 P.M. Eastern time. Now if Foreman doesn't show for the weigh-in, people in the States throw up their hands in despair and say, ah, fuck, I'm not gonna plunk thirty dollars down for a fight that ain't gonna be. It would sink the closed circuit gate, where all the money is.

Okay, said Daly, go to London and my men at Hemdale Leisure will take care of you. So they, James Earl and

Leroy, left. Meanwhile, Daly calls his men in London and tells them to vamp on these two guys for twenty-four hours, waltz them around town, show them a good time, and we're home free. Which is what happened. Foreman's scheme failed, even though he enlisted Bula Mandungu's aid after James Earl and Leroy called back from London to report the shaft.

This is what John Daly was getting at in Chez Nicola when he said, "The fight might be off." This was the night John Vinocur, of the AP Paris bureau told Thompson, Ralph Steadman and me he was taking us to dinner on Wes Gallagher. The bill wound up $180 for four, and Vinocur found he had no juice with the owner, couldn't sign, nor could he cover the tab. We had to chip in, and it cost me my last six Zs. Daly was at a nearby table, and stopped off after dinner to give us the word. Daly, more than any of the other promoters, was inclined to tell the truth, because he, like many of us, was seduced by the historic nature of the event. He wanted to see it accurately reported, and he kept me informed.

John Daly got me out of Zaire. I owe him my life, if it's still mine and not an Ndoke's or Bula's. These recurring nightmares, you see. For the ten days prior to the fight, I chased Murray Goodman around Kinshasa and N'Sele, fifty miles apart, trying to track down my goddamn ticket out, which this magazine had paid for in cash. Murray would roll his eyes, stick another cigar in his mouth, and look at me like I was from New Bedford or someplace. See my son Bobby, he would say. Bobby would tell me to see his dad, and I would say I have, and he would tell me to see Booker Griffin, an aide to Donald King, and Booker Griffin would tell me to see John Daly, and John Daly would tell me not to worry, that he wouldn't leave me behind. I would get him at poolside, disturbing his afternoon interludes at the Inter-continental, an awful thing to have to do to a guy in Zaire.

So the fight comes and goes, and there's still no ticket for me. But all the sportswriters got theirs! And they only paid the same money, or less! I know it's curtains, because it's total dispersal after any fight anywhere, and no one gives a shit. What hurt me the most, see, is that I had to spend all this time hunting the ticket and bugging John Daly the night after the fight, telling him John, this is it! Get me outa here. Those cocksuckers, Goodman, Schwartz . . . get me outa here! We're in the lobby of the Inter-continental. Bula is berating Donald King, five feet away. It was a sinister scene. I knew the hammer had come down on the promotion. The government took a bath. Someone was going to pay, dearly. John Daly knew I wasn't kidding. Now here's the weird thing. An Air Zaire official with a walkie-talkie just happens to walk by, and Daly grabs him. He says, Give my man a ticket out of here. The guy wants written authorization from Daly. We're in front of the reception desk. Daly tells the room clerk to give him a piece of paper, and writes out the authorization, and the Air Zaire guy is asking him how do I know we'll be paid? Daly looks at him incredulously and says, "Look, my friend, next Monday I have to sign a check for $16 million. If I do not sign that check 'John Daly,' no one will get *any* money. So I'm not going to cheat you out of three hundred dollars or five hundred dollars or whatever this ticket is. It will be charged to press promotion."

I had fifteen minutes to get back to the Memling, five miles away, and pack. The plane was leaving in two hours. Most of the press would be on that plane, and it was important for me to blend in. If they had taken advantage of me departing alone, they would have gone through my things and found my notes. I grabbed a taxi just as another one was pulling up to the Inter. Out stepped Jann __________, the only Belgian journalist with the balls to go to Zaire, whose passport and money was confiscated upon arrival, and Donald Atayo, an Australian who wrote the Bruce Lee book that you see everywhere. So they say to me, hey, Bill. . . . I gotta go, I said. And they understood. I never looked back. This is what really hurts the most. Not being able to say good-bye. In fifty days and fifty nights you have no idea how many friends I made, Zairois cats and Europeans and even some press, and to leave them, fleeing with my life. I'm still sore, I wanted to say good-bye, I couldn't even buy cheap gifts, which I'd planned to do, when I could borrow money from the new press during fight week. But I had to chase that ticket instead.

Fifteen minutes to pack. I had a pound of Congo flowering tops, buds, in a drawer in my room, which was 263. I took the drawer, kicked open my balcony door, and threw the whole fucking thing into the backyard of the Memling, scaring the bejesus out of a night sentinel. It went crashing down through a jacaranda tree. The poor fucker was sleeping on a bench. I had no time to say pardon, nothing. I had to throw out five hundred ten-milligram Ritalins, too. And the opium. Everything. Drugs mean nothing when your life is at stake.

They even hassled George Foreman when he tried to get out, pulled him aside, security police, and leaned on him for an hour. He didn't know it was illegal to lose in Zaire. The Leopards, the national soccer team, by a fluke made the final sixteen World Cup teams, which played in Germany this summer. They got beat by Scotland 2–0, and played Yugoslavia next. When the score was 5–0, Mobutu pulled the plug, and TV sets went out all over Zaire. The final score was 9–0, but the Zairois never saw the rest of the game. Bula, in a hotel somewhere with Fred Weymar, demanded that Weymar, being a German, and Germany being the host country, get on the horn with his government and have the match halted. The Leopards lost their third and last game 3–0 to Brazil, and it is said in Kinshasa that Mobutu rescinded his planned gift of Volkswagens for the players. Listen, this club team from Ghana, Asante KO-

TOKO F.C., was playing this club from Kinshasa, Vita F.C., for the African club championship, and the first leg was in Accra, and the Ghanaians won 3–0, which means they would have to lose 4–0 at Kinshasa to lose the title. You understand soccer scoring? This was for all the marbles, the African club championship. So they came, and they are put up at the Memling. So what happens is someone puts the word on the waiters not to let the guest players have any bottled water sent to their rooms. And the bus that's supposed to take them out to the stadium for practice sessions shows up three hours late. They're in a tizzy, of course. At night, they're all getting weird phone calls in their rooms, but you already know about the phones at the Memling. So they're keeping these guys up all night, and they've got to play tomorrow. Naturally they take the hint and lose 4–0. Okay, so it causes an international incident, goes way beyond sports, and Ghana is at the point of breaking off diplomatic relations. They went so far as to call upon the African Federation of Sports to have member nations boycott the joint, but it was cooled out.

John Daly is thirty-five, and he hangs loose on the fringes, he doesn't care to be center stage. His father, who is sixty-seven, was one of the best lightweight fighters England ever produced, with something like three hundred fights. His uncle was a fighter, too. He's the guy who got me out, but when he tried to leave two days later, the security police pulled him aside and stuck him in a little room, but let his father go. Now John Daly put up $1.5 million, which floated the early going. So why hassle him, huh? He should have gotten a medal, instead he can't get his own mundele ass out. Without his signature, nobody gets paid, remember? So the security police tell him Mobutu wants to see him tomorrow and they demand his U.K. passport and confiscate it. Daly tells them thanks but no thanks, all he really wants is to get on the plane with his father and get the hell back to sanity, back to the North Star. But they say no, it isn't customary to decline an audience with Mobutu. Well, of course, Mobutu doesn't want to see Daly. They just want to fuck him over a bit, see. They fuck everyone over. I'm trying to tell you I've been to the mountain and the mountain is a gangster whose name is Intergreed. And there isn't any pot in the world that makes living under such conditions worthwhile. So John Daly never gets out that night, but his father does. Next day, Daly screamed on Bula, telling him that this was precisely the sort of stuff that would not reassure foreign businessmen thinking of investing in Zaire and helping Mobutu yank out all that copper, cobalt, tungsten, etc., and mine all those industrial diamonds. The real gem diamonds, of course, are in Angola, which Mobutu covets, so expect him to make a move on Angola, now that Portugal has given independence. Four black Angolan groups are fighting it out for control and Mobutu will just sit back, watch them fall, and pick up the chips.

Daly got out the next day, Saturday. Mobutu never saw him. There was no audience.

Foreman had a sparring partner named Elmo Henderson, about forty, from Reno, who was the former champ of Texas, whatever that counts for, but doesn't remember it. That Foreman camp was totally whacked out, so uptight compared with Ali, who runs a loose-goose operation . . . and, man, let me tell ya, Ali is pulling a mighty big train, building Muslim hospitals and schools for Elijah with his purses and carrying this huge retinue but the difference is that the Ali camp has the real winning spirit. Angelo picked a kayo in nine. I'm on videotape at Voice of Zaire television predicting a TKO in seven or eight because of Foreman's eye, but in the press pool I chicken out and bet Ali by a TKO in twelve. We all knew—no we didn't—that Ali couldn't lose. He went in at 208, just two pounds over what he weighed ten years ago when he creamed Liston. It was his greatest fight. Manolete jerking a bull. When Foreman was a kid hood in Houston his gang mates called him

Monkey. They say he could take out three guys by himself and that if Monkey was around they knew they'd be all right. In Zaire, if you call a Zairois monkey (or macaco, the Portuguese word that also is Lingala) you will for sure be out on the next plane or in jail, and if you go to jail you starve unless a friend or relative brings in food for you. I mean, it's Salazar's Portugal all over again. But we each found ourselves using the word . . . even people like Henry Clark, the number six (or eight) heavyweight in the world (depending on whose listings you refer to). One night even Big Black, a peaceful cat with no room in his heart for hate, said he was gonna hit one of these sonsofbitches before he left and all I could dumbfoundedly say was, you mean you ain't hit one yet?

The big chant all around Zaire was *"Ali Boma Ye,"* which means Ali kill him, rhetorically, in Lingala. And Ali has the whole country screaming this. So what to do, wonders Elmo Henderson, the Foreman sparring partner. He starts chanting "Oye, Foreman, Oye Champion, Oye George Foreman," which means Hail, hark, listen, stuff like that. Somehow Elmo gets hold of a bull horn, a real crowd control thing, metal, chrome, very businesslike. And he's running around Kinshasa with this thing, screaming. Even before he had it, it was a mistake to say Oye in front of Elmo; it would set him off for ten minutes at least. He used to swim at dawn in the Inter pool, and everybody in rooms facing the pool, their sleep was finished when Elmo hit the gray dawn Oye. One day he's coming back from N'Sele in a Mercedes, and Donald Atayo, the Australian Bruce Lee writer, is with him. They're almost back to town, there's this big industrial strip on the outskirts, and there's a crowd gathered at the roadside. Elmo sees an audience and yanks out the bull horn. "Oye, Foreman, Oye Champion." As the Mercedes passes, Donald Atayo sees that the crowd surrounds a dying man, blood gushing from his ears, a hit-and-run victim. All accidents are hit and run there. It's even in the U.S. Embassy handbook. Split, or you'll be torn limb from limb. The car will be demolished, because these people aren't used to cars yet. They're just in from the bush, two weeks. The first guy to tell me this was an Air Zaire pilot. He told me to get out of there if I ever hit anybody. Well, what happened is somebody hit me one day. I was on my way to Tarzan's house to smoke some dope and this car came from nowhere and clipped me and took off. Then this guy comes running up to me. I thought he was the driver, seeing whether I was okay. But it was some nut. He's yapping at me that he's from customs, that it's his day off, that he remembers me from the airport . . . this is all in English . . . and he insists that I have a drink with him. I protest that I've got an important rendezvous, an appointment, and thanks but some other time. Okay? Finally he gets the message and as I turn to go, he says, give me fifty Makuta. I say go fuck yourself. Can you imagine? I just get whacked by a car and this guy hits me for a half a Zaire note!

Harold Conrad calls me regularly and assures me that I'm in New York and that I'm safe. But I'm not. A tooth fell out of my mouth today. First time in thirty years this happened. I got out just before my other parts rotted. My body may be out but my mind isn't. When I try to recall the beautiful people, all I get is that brute Bula skipping across my mind's eyes. I don't think any of us gets our minds out of there. Call up Schulberg right now. I'll bet he's frozen in front of his typewriter. He knows. He slept on a lawn. He spent a few nights in the Memling and was the houseguest up in Binza, a wealthy suburb, of his pal from the Embassy, which must be the last great Prussian Embassy we're running over there. They never mix. All they're doing is running a closed cocktail circuit for Caucasians. It's the largest embassy over there. It costs us seventy-seven thousand dollars a year for each embassy employee, when you figure in all the costs. Incredible! It's some weird psychological terror: Look what they did to the soccer team from Ghana.

When the Zambians came to play, they ran the same game on them. And the Moroccans, too. It's got something to do with tension and release, tension and release. They're always tensing you up . . . and then giving you release. Right up until the last minute they've got you bananas and then it's okay, you can go. One of the guys from the Libyan embassy told me in Kin Casino one night that he doesn't trust them. Look, when an Arab tells you he doesn't trust somebody, listen. Call Schulberg, he'll tell you. Mailer and Plimpton probably couldn't, though, because they stayed only a few days at each end of the trip, and they were at the Inter, seeing Africa from the Inter! Plimpton went off on a safari, though, cost him eight hundred dollars American. But I think *Audubon* magazine paid for it. Mailer, they say, was seen at the zoo observing lions and gazelles, probably looking for some weird metaphor about how the lion always whips the gazelle but sometimes the gazelle whips the lion, even though they've both got mice and bacteria running around inside their guts. I don't think Mailer or Plimpton can tell you about this tension-and-release, though. Maybe Plimpton can because it cost him $120 to get out the first time. They're both great guys, very helpful. Mailer kept telling me I'd never have this experience again, that the first heavyweight championship fight I covered . . . that there'd never be anything like it again, no matter how many more I go to. Christ, the man's prescient!

But call up Schulberg. He knows. He slept with the iguanas on the lawn. I'll bet he's frozen stiff right now on Long Island, hunkering over his keyboard, grinning at God knows what. You fucking think I'm kidding. Like, Larry Merchant the other night in the bar saying he gave Ali four rounds, Foreman three. What the hell fight did he see at the Garden? What kind of a satellite transmission did they beam back here? Even one of the judges, the one from the Ivory Coast, gave it four rounds even, three Ali. That's not what happened. It was Ali's greatest fight ever. He pitched a shutout. It was like throwing a no-hit perfect World Series game. I was ten feet away. Murray Goodman sat with me. I taped the whole fight, blow-by-blow, like Don Dunphy. Murray was my Bill Corum. At the end of the first, Dick Saddler and Sandy Saddler and Archie Moore jumped through the ring ropes with silly grins on their faces. Foreman looked at them as if to say, well, I got through round one—he didn't take me out (when it was supposed to be the other way around, Ali was the one who wasn't supposed to survive). Already in the first round Foreman was swelling on his right cheek. Ali kept talking to him the whole fight, shoving and tugging and moving big Foreman (220 pounds) around like he was a sack of sugar in the hold of a ship on the dock of a bay, calling him a sissy and telling Foreman that Foreman was the champ and let's see your stuff; hit me, you're the champ; let's see what you got, you sissy. Ali just draped over those ropes and picked off Foreman's shots. Foreman got off about five or six clean blows the whole fight. Ali was absorbing everything with his arms. Ali was doing some strange kind of psychic counter-punching all night, popping Foreman just a moment before Foreman got set. He made Foreman an amateur. He was beaten after four. Zack Clayton, the referee, even said so, to Ferdie Pachéco, Ali's doctor. I got it in my tape recorder that he was dead after the third. Murray Goodman even put it on my tape: "He's a defeated man." And the crowd—there was between fifteen and eighteen thousand people there live; and, by the way, the stadium only holds about fifty thousand, anyway; just a little bigger than Fenway Park; in no way does it hold a hundred thousand; but you got to get used to the lies over there; everything with them has got to be the biggest and the best, when really it's the most untogether place; you should have seen the ring ropes; like clotheslines, that loose; and they didn't even have vertical supports for the ropes; they wound up with baling twine, the kind of stuff you secure packages with; and this is the biggest fight of all time, $10 million purse!—and the crowd is yelling, "*Ali, boma ye.*" After five, Foreman stood in his corner and lurched a little bit along the ropes toward the neutral corner where I was seated, just sort of blankly looking at the press, nothing registering on his swollen face, and the crowd is frenzied with "*boma ye, Ali boma ye.*" A very sad moment. He was completely out of gas. In the sixth, he was pushing at the air, punching like a woman, really. His legs were gone after four. Had nothing left. Knew it was over. When Ali creamed him in the eighth, Foreman pirouetted, spiraled downward, using the whole ring for his fall, just going around in a dizzy circle ever downward, a dream world carousel, and the look on his face as he caught Ali's eye said, thank ya, man, thank ya for ending it. That's the way it was. Now, he's bellyaching in Paris and L.A. and Honolulu about the ropes and the canvas and a short count. Actually, he did beat the count. Barely. Supine on his feet at nine. But Zack Taylor, a wise man, a humanitarian, waved it off, made believe he had reached ten. Because, look, one more shot and Foreman might have got really hurt. You should have seen the ugly purple knot on his forehead in the dressing room. The strangest sort of third eye. So Foreman's got no grief. Believe me. He got whupped by The Greatest.

You couldn't get into the dressing rooms after. Paratroopers with batons blocking the way. When Norman Mailer put his glasses in his pocket, I knew it was serious. Norman's been in a lot of dressing rooms . . . I took my cue from him. The paratroopers were beating on everybody. They wouldn't even let Howard Bingham, Ali's photographer, through. See, there was this communications problem. . . .

On September 16, at 3:00 P.M., local time, George Foreman sustained a 2.5-centimeter laceration to his face, located along the inferior margin of the lateral one-half of his right eyebrow. The laceration was deep, through the fascia layer and penetrated partially the underlying muscle bundle. The hyacinth pads floated inexorably two hundred yards away.

Just a moment before Bill McMurray, thirty-eight, a truck driver from Sacramento, who laid down in one in his last fight three years ago (against Earnie Shavers) put his elbow through Foreman's fascia layer, Bodini Brown of Ali fame was yelling up at him, "You're fighting the son of God! Get ready!"

When the blood trickled, Foreman muttered, "Damn, shit . . . goddamn." McMurray said he was sorry and Bodini ran to Ali's villa shouting, "I did it! I did it!" He thought he was an Ndoke, you know. But Ali muttered, "Jesus, now we're stuck here." And Bodini replied, "I didn't do it; I didn't do it."

Within minutes, armed paratroopers surrounded Ali's villa and Foreman's villa. Foreman soon moved into Kinshasa, fifty miles away, and took up residence on the eighth floor of the Inter, even though the government had installed a huge chain link fence so his dog, Daggo, could romp in security and not get gobbled by a crocodile or stung by a krait or cobra, or ingested by a python. Did I tell you about the python skin some guy unrolled for me one night at a house in Zone Lemba? Parchment, the longest Magna Charta, it just kept unraveling. I touched it! Eighteen feet. The guy said he skinned the bugger two weeks ago not twenty miles from town and did I want to buy it.

Ali kept spouting about "there's gonna be a rumble in the jungle and if Cosell comes over he's gonna get boiled in a pot." Which pissed off the government because they want to show you all the Danish modern furniture and how progressive they are.

We were stuck in Luxembourg. It took the government twenty-four hours to figure out what to say. I mean, they tried to make believe there was no cut, you know? They had some Air Zaire shill at the airport in Lux selling us wolf tickets to come on down anyway, that the fight was still on schedule. What's a cut, right? His arms are all right, aren't they? What kind of a chief is Foreman, anyway, that he let a cut eye stop the fight? Murray Goodman got a call through to his son Bobby in N'Sele and Bobby said, "Go back, you're still free. Go back." But a few of us went on. They gave me a room at the Memling, room 263 and a telephone, number 601.

Look: Laundering of three shirts, drip-dry stuff, a pair of Levi's and five pairs of socks costs five Zaires at the Memling. That's ten bucks! I smelled badly, naturally. Equatorial heat. But I smelled as nothing compared with Zairois masses. Cultural differences. Don't be an asshole and read anything into this. When you live among them, as I do, it makes no difference. All God's children. But, Bula, I'll rip your guts out if you don't get out of my mind.

After I made that crack to Dundee in his villa after the fight about his accomplishing the impossible—making Bula laugh in Ali's happy championship locker room—and Kilroy dumped on me for getting into politics again, I went to sleep, advising Schulberg to wake me if anything happened . . . like if Ali should arise and decide to have a fireside press conference. Which he did but, of course, Schulberg never fetched me. Which turned out all right because later, when I woke up alone, the door to Angelo's villa wide open, air conditioners going full bore, the place empty, Angelo and Ferdie Pacheco and Luis Serria, Ali's silent Cuban masseur, on a plane for Miami, a mere five hours after the fight, the villa nothing now but debris and discard, I knew then, staring into that silence, that I must go, if I could, if I could get that plane ticket owed me by Hank Schwartz, the one this magazine paid for, through John Daly, my main hope, my White Hope. I walked out of the villa and passed Ali's place next door. At that moment he stepped out into the sunshine that followed the rain—and the rains we dreaded had come, two hours after the fight; the shantytowns ringing Kinshasa were awash; the very ring itself at the stadium under water—he stepped out into the sunshine and asked me if I wanted to come in and talk for a while. We talked for two hours, me and Ali and two English journalists who joined us. Ali was no bombast but was all quiet and thoughtful and talked about a long, long rest. Somewhere I have a tape of that conversation.

My birthday, September 24, original fight day, no fight, instead John Daly: "I would rather keep all the bullshit out. This whole promotion was founded on bullshit, and it will founder on bullshit, unless somebody talks in a very realistic way, and cuts out all the cackle about how good he is with the boxers, and how they'll only work for him, cuts out all the other rubbish and concentrates on getting this promotion under way in a very professional way and making this government realize that they're going to have to work twice as hard if they want to keep any influence whatsoever in the outside world. . . ."

That's the key. There is no outside world. Mobutu doesn't care about influence outside; he only cares about spreading Mobutism by implanting Zaire permanently in everyone's mind, everyone who's been here.

". . . At the moment it doesn't stack up. At this moment, sitting here in Africa, the promotion doesn't stack up. But it's a promoter's dream. However it is also a very dangerous move. I don't think this postponement is the last incident that is going to occur in voodoo Africa. There will be many incidents before this fight takes place. Many, many incidents. They're all smiling, they're all friends, you know . . . I think they're a pretty ruthless bunch, outside of the smiles and the drinks. Had George Foreman not cut his eye, it would have been the greatest promotion ever. With him cutting his eye, it is as though powers that we are not aware of, or cannot know, delivered a blow. . . . I think they can play very rough. In my own way I've been very quietly talking with residents here, who have told me some very frightening things, I think they've got a laid-down plan that required Bula to be away for two weeks while the nasties move in and put up a certain stonewall defense . . . so that Bula made certain decisions, encouraged certain of us, gave certain pledges, and has conveniently gone to Brussels for two weeks, so that we are left saying, 'Well, you know, we have an agreement with you . . . you've told us this . . . you've told us that,' and they say, 'Who?' and you say Bula. 'Ah, Bula's not here.'

"I mean I've experienced this in a very small way by having an agreement with Bula, by bringing in a film crew, to see that film crew not given certain permissions, not given certain help, waved good-bye to, and having their equipment confiscated at the airport. But, you see, this is the ugly side to the promotion . . . But certainly this has been the most bizarre collection of people getting together to put on a world title fight. The most bizarre collection ever. You have an English outfit, a New York Jewish outfit, a Negro from Cleveland, and you have an African semi-communist, semi-fascist country . . . They have little respect for their own journalists, little respect for financial journalists, and unfortunately they don't know the difference between sports and finance. Hence, when we sat down at a sports luncheon the other day, we were given a two-hour lecture by the minister of orientation, a Goebbels, on how wonderful Mobutu, his cabinet and his policies are. Which may be true, but is in very bad taste."

Hard time sleeping that night. Am convinced an Ndoke was in the room. I told Tarzan that today when I came down to meet him for a Coca-moko (moko means one in Lingala, thus one coke). Only two kilos of cocaine came into this country in a year, and it's very tightly controlled, my pharmacist says. Today Tarzan screaming at me in my room. "I'm a connoisseur of smoke," he's saying, "I won't smoke that!" I'm telling him, for crissakes, man, this is working dope; it's what I've been trying to find for weeks!

Now I'm really straight. I am straight, by the way, taking fifty milligrams of Ritalin a day, a lot of cough medicine along with vitamin C stuff called Antigrippine Midy, also Mebucaine lozenges. I took a Valium last night, I got so . . . couldn't sleep without the Valium. I got a lot of painkillers. I got Dolviran. And I got Indocid for my gonorrhea. And I've still got Chloroquine, my malaria pills . . . still got two Prostaphlin (250 mg) caps for the gonorrhea, the most virulent strain in the world. I also started to hit the Scotch last night in my room for the first time in weeks, am feeling well enough recovered to do so.

Now I'm looking at the massing clouds from my little Memling balcony, head full of bangi clouds, and I note the clouds don't move in the equatorial calm. It's storm gray clouds, and they just hang there at 6:00 P.M. as if glued to the sky . . . and starlings swirl . . . and there goes a vulture flapping way off . . . or are those starlings bats? Yes, they are bats. Hundreds of them I can see now coming out, a little patch of blue behind the hanging clouds. Below, in the back of the Memling, they're unloading a Regla beer truck, rattling bottles of dark beer . . . urine getting dark again, hepatitis. Still pretty weak but strong enough to hit the Scotch. Beer bottles rattling below, Regla beer, not to be confused with Skol, Simba (lion in Swahili) or Tembo, which means elephant. Just a few months ago, no one even knew where Zaire was. First you had to learn where it was. So far from that now, in Kin now. It's come successively down from Zaire, Africa, to Kinshasa, Zaire, to la ville (where mundeles live) and la cité (where Zairois live), to the silence of the night streets, the bats winging overhead. Who knew what to expect? After all this had been the Belgian Congo. I remember the day Kilroy kept saying to the soldier at N'Sele that I was "Portuguese, Portuguese" (he kept pointing at me) and the guard kept saying "out, out." I was doing my best to smile and go along with the gag, but I can't remember whether the soldier was smiling. Was he or wasn't he? I don't know. I was so loaded on the bangi, who knows—it really gets in your way sometimes. But maybe bangi is the best way to . . . just get loaded up . . . because this is such a goddamn improbable story, anyway. The biggest fight ever. Thinking now about how I drop out of the boxing world and go into my own private Kin world, walking the streets, the always quiet streets. Kin, a strange combination of dirty and clean. Mucky and garbage in the streets. Yet dirt sidewalks that are raked every morning. Why, the air is cleaner than San Francisco's, which we regard as clean. The test is my eyeglasses. I only clean them once a day, and it's not because there's dirt on them, it's just the sweat marks and drops off my forehead from this heat. It's very calm now, all the time. Equatorial calms; very, very calm. Soon will be the deluge, the press returning . . . and means the end of this peaceful time among the Kinois. Makes my heart sad. A little lizard on the corridor wall tonight. A squashed rat on Boulevard 30 Juin. I have not seen a rat in the Memling since my first night, so long ago. This Congo water is good for my hair. Tap water. My scalp is good, and my hair is starting to get shiny and lustrous. The sun is giving it that nice auburn color, like when I was a kid out in the sun. Eating alone is a drag three nights in a row. My own private Kin world. They never come down here, the fight crowd, so I drop out of their world, too. Walk the streets. Safer here than in Philadelphia on a Sunday afternoon. Safer here on a Saturday night, even in La Cité. How many nights have I passed the dusty broken pane of store window glass that remains propped up in the arcade that is the shortcut to the Jumbo Discotheque; the beggars, the night sentinels, the cripples, the thirty-story banks, the two guys who sleep in the same box in the arcade . . . are they lovers or sentinels or perhaps just brothers? And the prices of shirts in the arcade—fifty bucks—the escalator up to the Jumbo, and Cassius Clay, Sr., Cass, telling me there that we're both white here and have to stick together, Americans, and we may have to fight our way out of this place. The long corridors of the Memling and the lobby, where Belgians once had coffee and said they must do something about those nuns raped in Stanleyville (now Kisangani) and put down that rebellion . . . my own special elevator, so few guests here now, it responds for me. And the room boys in their white skirts, padding around in their rubber bath slippers or barefoot calling me papa. N'golo, sous chef de presse, martineting his way across the lobby every morning, the bastard. And leaving Ali's villa with him, long hours after Angelo Dundee was on his way to Miami, after the fight, Ali the victor, the greatest in the world, crossing his lawn, teak staff with ivory inlay in hand, spotting a lizard, a little lizard, and stomping it with his staff, stomping, stomping, silent, and the lizard's tail separated from his body and flopped electrically, spasmodically, in the sun. Ah, Muhammad, if you will not respect the rights of lizards, who, then, will free boxing. . . .

WILLIAM J. CARDOSO was born in Cambridge, Massachusetts and received a conventional education there and in Boston. He is a veteran and prize-winning newspaperman and magazine writer. A hometown boy in a lot of places, he currently lives in the low desert of California.